A QUEEN FOR ALL SEASONS

A QUEEN FOR
ALL SEASONS

*A Celebration of Queen Elizabeth II
on Her Platinum Jubilee*

Introduced and compiled by

Joanna Lumley

HODDER &
STOUGHTON

First published in Great Britain in 2021 by Hodder & Stoughton
An Hachette UK company

6

Copyright © Joanna Lumley 2021

The acknowledgements on pp. 297-309 constitute an extension of this copyright page.

Picture research by Jane Smith Media.

A CIP catalogue record for this title is available from the British Library

Hardback 978 1 529 37592 3
eBook 978 1 529 37595 4
Trade Paperback 978 1 529 37593 0

Typeset in Simoncini Garamond and Optima by
Palimpsest Book Production Ltd, Falkirk, Stirlingshire

Printed and bound in Great Britain by Clays Ltd, Elcograf S.p.A.

Hodder & Stoughton policy is to use papers that are natural, renewable and recyclable products and made from wood grown in sustainable forests. The logging and manufacturing processes are expected to conform to the environmental regulations of the country of origin.

Hodder & Stoughton Ltd
Carmelite House
50 Victoria Embankment
London EC4Y 0DZ

www.hodder.co.uk

The front cover picture is one of four prints, all slightly different, that Andy Warhol did of our Queen in 1985. This one is my favourite.

Contents

Introduction

The Queen and I

Right from the very start let me lay my cards on the table: I think the world of the Queen.

Of course, I am not alone: there are millions, literally millions, of people who think as I do, but my steady devotion goes right back to a double-decker wooden pencil box with a sliding top, a stencil of Her Majesty on it and my name inked on the reverse, dating back to Coronation Day 1953. The Queen looks back over her shoulder with a calm and friendly smile, and I knew then, as I know now, that she would never let me down.

I still have it. It is kept with my tiny lead model of Her Majesty taking the salute at Trooping the Colour. Her right arm is hinged to enable her to swing it up to her tip-tilted bonnet with its plume. She sits side-saddle, easily holding the reins in her confident left hand. The mare she rides is called Burmese. This little model has pride of place on my shelf and in my heart, because I had seen the movie *The Coronation* three times, twice in black-and-white and once in glorious colour, in the huge hall in the Army School in Kuala Lumpur, ceiling fans turning lazily above the packed audience of us, the army brats. I had a Coronation medal on a ribbon, which I pinned to my chest (lost now, or I would still be wearing it) and a tiny, dazzling State Coach with horses made of lead but gilded and heavy. At seven years old I was too young to have heard and understood the Queen's vow to serve the country and the Commonwealth, whether her life be long or short, made when she was twenty-one (and I can still hardly write the words without my eyes brimming. Such a vow! Would any of us ever have promised that when our lives were just beginning?), but she moved easily to the front of the pantheon of Marvellous Ones I kept in my heart.

I know as you read this you may share my emotions: she became my Queen and I watched her every move like a fanatic. No, I didn't buy royal magazines or books, but I inspected her clothes in photographs with the beady eye a child keeps for its mother in public. She always looked immaculate . . . but was that skirt really above the knee? Did she truly wear groovy boots? How was that allowed to happen? I should have liked her to wear a crown far more often, every day in fact, and the best images were when she appeared in full regalia with diamonds and sashes and tiaras and long evening gloves.

Later, I read that her clothes were chosen to make her stand out in a crowd, therefore strong colours were favoured, head to toe: she might have to stand for hours on end, so shoes would have low heels, and the bag would always be hooked over her left arm. This was the 'day look'. The 'country look' was much more like my mother's clothes, sensible tweed coat and skirt, pearls, a scarf, laced-up brogues, a brooch. Her Majesty's hair would be pretty much the same all her life, neatly set off her face, well above her shoulders, the Queen of our coins and banknotes. (The best profile is the one where her hair has a sort of garland around it, like a laurel wreath or daisy chain, tied with a ribbon, her neck and bare shoulders emerging from a stole or dress just out of sight.) The formal classical robes a queen should wear are always my favourite, as they are unchanging, and hint at the long line of former royal figures, a constant touchstone and a comforting reminder of heritage and history.

As I write, it is beginning to dawn on me that I see the Queen as a sort of mother figure for the nation, someone we turn towards when the going gets rough to see her reactions. Her kindly and measured response to calamities settles us: to know she has sent a message of condolence or congratulation fills us with satisfaction, as though we ourselves had written it. She knows how to entertain the most famous and powerful people in the world with the same calm compassion she shows at every public ceremony. We scan the pictures of her with the assembled heads of state from the Commonwealth and marvel at how, although others tower over her, she is always the first person we focus on. We are so proud of her!

I wonder what it is in the human make-up that requires a leader or figurehead. It must be because we are pack animals: when we're organised in the armed services there is a strict pecking order, as there is in governments. Sports teams have captains, orchestras have leaders, and the many faiths have their archbishops, imams and pujaris; there are the Dalai Lama, and the Pope, the Archdruid and the Chief Rabbi. Communist regimes, in which everyone is supposed to be equal and call each other 'comrade', have the most unassailable heads of state. We have presidents and head teachers, chairpersons and master chefs; we like a structure with someone identifiable at the top. We have emperors; we have kings and queens.

Throughout history, it is easy to trace why many of these characters have gained their ascendancy, through war, or annexing land, simply by being a favourite of the ruler of the time, or being born into a dynasty. Without such a person, our tribe (and we are tribal, we humans) loses its identity. No matter what form of social or political arrangement we favour, it is generally agreed that there must be someone at the top representing us to the world. Whether that person should be elected or born or drawn in a lottery is debated hotly: should it be by the people's choice, or the general acceptance that the blacksmith's son will inherit the anvil, the chieftain's son the spear of office?

We have a hereditary monarchy. Our country finds, on the whole, it would rather have people who are accustomed to high office and are trained to bear the responsibility to be our representatives. Some say our head of state should be elected regularly, others are easy-going with the status quo, a few believe passionately in the Divine Right of Kings. But until everything changes, we have a monarchy: most people are very proud that we do, and I am one of them.

Princess Elizabeth was not born to be queen. Her uncle David was due to be king, and she and her little sister were royal princesses, born not in a palace but in a house, their father a royal duke. The happy and carefree young life the two girls had was, of course, privileged in a way we can only read about and never know ourselves, but it was touching to hear of their tight and loving family group, which their father called 'us four'. The girls loved horses and dogs, dressing-up and country life. The house where Princess Elizabeth was born, 17 Bruton Street, in London's Mayfair, was bombed during the Second World War, but by then the great rolling tide of Fate had changed the family's lives completely and utterly, and moved them from their pleasant town house to a palace. The girls' uncle David, now King Edward VIII, had abdicated, and the spotlight swung round to focus on the next in line: their father, the Duke of York, now King George VI.

Princess Elizabeth was only ten, but from that time onwards she knew that one day she would be Queen.

Can you remember being ten years old? I can easily.

Having thoughts about the future: nil.

Ideas of how the country was governed: nil.

Behaving gracefully in public: about six out of ten, as we had been brought up to be polite.

Cleanliness: nil.

Diligent studying during the holidays: nil.

The thought of having to slog away at something that wasn't about damming streams, or going to the cinema, or dodging the grown-ups, just skated past my ears. Being ten meant laughing uncontrollably into your skirt in class, playing jacks, mucking about with friends.

The huge unwanted, unexpected burden that had fallen on her father's shoulders brought with it the outline of the future for Princess Elizabeth. From that moment on, she would be treated differently from all the friends she and Princess Margaret Rose had made – differently even from her own sister.

Now, what I am trying to say here, in a hugely roundabout way, is this: do you think you would have been able to take on such a massive and unending responsibility at such a tender age?

Excuses and explanations are constantly rolled out: they had so much money, such privilege, servants . . . Some may go on to say that she had special training, didn't have to queue in the post office, never had to go to school, had her own ponies. They may add, 'Look at her pretty dresses and kind parents, and she had her own little Welsh Wendy house to play in . . .' but despite all of that I don't think I could ever have done what the Queen has for seventy years, and I bet there are millions like me.

Because of my job, I have had access to a lot of these privileges. As an actress, when you're working your clothes are prepared, and you have your own dresser to help you into them. Someone does your hair and holds up your long skirt as you leave your private trailer to be driven to the muddy location. Someone brings you tea and anything you want for lunch. Someone writes the words you speak. You are driven home, your flights are arranged, your hotels are booked and you don't pay for them. You are photographed and interviewed in rooms where visiting journalists are given strict instructions as to how long they will have in your presence – your fascinating, esteemed, adorable presence. Sometimes fans weep when they meet you, or are overfamiliar out of nervousness, or step over the line, or are too shy to hold out a pen and autograph book. Your face may be so well known that, no matter where you go, you will be recognised: people feel entitled to say how brilliant or untalented you are, how ugly your dress was, how staggering your beauty is. People not only feel they know you, they feel they own you too. (In New York, when we were filming *Absolutely Fabulous*, an overwrought admirer seized Jennifer Saunders's arm and screamed, 'You have healed me!')

Strangely, far from being a luxurious way of living, it is all a bit of a slog (how ungrateful!). When the final 'Cut!' has been called on the film set, we trundle back into our easy, normal lives, with old jerseys and gardener's hands. Then the follow-spot swings away from you onto the new kid on the block, and all the trappings and trimmings vanish, like Cinderella running away as midnight strikes, recalled only in press cuttings and on dog-eared posters, until the next time.

But through all this there was a parallel and ordinary life. Of course, I worked hard to be as good as I could be, but friends still called me by my own name – even those actresses who are dames are called their own names by their friends. Like everyone in our game, I still hoped another job would come along, but I was as free as a bird. I could go where I wanted when I wanted: I could stay up until dawn or take off my shoes and paddle in fountains, or walk very slowly round Ikea all afternoon. Reading this, I know that, no matter how different your life is from mine, you too have that freedom – considerably shaped and restricted by circumstances, of course, but you are at liberty to be your own person.

Selecting material for this book was both extremely easy and rather hard. So much has been written about the Queen already, and being neither a biographer nor a historian, I wanted this to be a discovery of her through the eyes of other people.

You will find very little about the rest of the Royal Family, almost nothing about how monarchy works, only a smattering of how things are done at that exalted level. Some of the contributors knew the Queen very well. Others stood and watched as a carriage went by, or attended a royal function. All formed opinions of her; and when you piece together these fragments a remarkable person begins to emerge, quite unlike any other.

For a moment, imagine a first-time visitor to Earth, coming across the human race. Apart from looking slightly different, we would resemble a flock of sheep, indistinguishable one from another except to the trained eye. Move closer, and you would see that people are roughly divided between men and women. From these billions of similar creatures, a few stand out, but I would defy any alien to recognise a pianist by his stature or a scientist by her weight. Dancers and athletes look like ideal versions of humans, so they can be recognised, but they trained hard to be that way: they weren't born in tutus, or leaping hurdles. Most of us are less sprightly, you might say, and completely average.

How could you ever determine which of these humans would have the stamina to be at the top of the tree for decades, never failing, never complaining, always doing their best? You couldn't, and I have a theory (which I hope will not offend you) that the abdication of King Edward VIII was like a lightning bolt that struck the young Princess Elizabeth. It ought to have burned her up, but instead, like lightning striking sand and turning it to glass, it transformed her into a fabulous new and different being. She vowed to be this new person for the rest of her life, and set about becoming all that she had promised, faithful to her word, a servant of many nations but wearing a crown. A queen for all seasons. You have only to read these testaments to her determination and sincerity, her courage and good humour, her modesty and kindness, to know that she is the one and only. By her own willpower and sense of obligation to the country and the Commonwealth, she changed from being an ordinary woman into someone extraordinary.

This is not going to be in intimate portrait of the Queen, an in-depth character assessment, a 'warts and all' analysis, following every moment of her life. Well-known episodes and familiar stories may have been left out: this book is as if I had been let loose with my microphone and wandered about among people I met at random, asking, 'What do you remember of the Queen?'

We cannot know what the Queen is thinking or feeling, as we can with other people. Who she is has made her different from us. We see her and hear her, and draw our own conclusions from occasional close encounters. This is a portrait, a celebration of her working life, her duty and faith, her unswerving dedication to being the Queen of an immense human family.

What a joy it has been reading all the contributions! This book belongs to all those whose recollections are included, and just as a jury, twelve people picked at random, can be relied on to deliver a verdict that is accepted by a court of law, so the judgement of these contributors must be taken as the broader truth. Such admiration and gratitude flow from them, such awe and sometimes compassion, affection and love. By squinting though different windows as the Queen walks by, we begin to understand more about her. But beware: just as it is said you should never meet your favourite author, I believe in the mystery of monarchy, and it is best that we don't scrabble to get too close. It is best to stand back slightly and just watch.

In theatres, a front gauze is sometimes used, a scrim, which is there when the big curtains are drawn back (the 'tabs' in show-speak), with a scene or picture projected onto it, so that it looks as flat and dense as canvas. Then the front projection begins to fade as the lights behind are brought up, and for a moment we can see through the gauze, and refocus on what is happening on the stage. Then the scrim is flown up and away out of sight. I want this book to do that: I want us to look beyond the familiar image into the drama of the character discovered. And as the scrutiny of a whole audience closes in, like a magnifying glass held over a piece of paper to catch the rays of the sun, the very intensity of this attention causes the subject to catch fire, become alive. The Queen, accustomed as she is to this most public gaze, rewards us by giving back a depth of commitment, which I think is unmatched in the world. And a separate light illumines her: that of her faith and belief. That is her follow-spot, always shining on her, operated in theatres by a chap high up on a gantry, but for the Queen . . . maybe it's the cherubim.

Six years after the Coronation, Dorothy Laird wrote a book called *How the Queen Reigns*. In it, she sums up neatly what the Queen does, and what she sacrifices in order to do her duty.

The Queen has a longer lineage than we have, she has greater means than we have, she has more resources and more opportunities. But she has precisely the same number of hours in a day and days in a year as we have. All the alternatives to duty are there: husband, children, lovely places to live in, horses to ride, hills to climb. And what does the Queen do? She spends hours each day reading worrying, dull, difficult papers about the unsolved, and it must often seem insoluble, problems of the world. She spends more hours talking gravely about these same problems to men at least a generation her senior. When she puts on her lovely hat and goes out in her fine Rolls-Royce it is more often than not to sit on a draughty platform listening with serene courtesy to well-meant but lengthy platitudes. When she travels, she has to pass by the coral beaches for the local hospital, the glorious loneliness of veld or forest for an overcrowded reception.

Why? Because the Queen is filled with a sense of duty so deep that it is a feeling of vocation. Because for her the Commonwealth is her life. She knows that if she works incessantly, cheerfully, resolutely and entirely without taking offence, she will do incalculable good.

So now the curtain rises: a familiar picture of the Queen is on the front gauze, the lights in the house go down and the stage lights come up. Settle back and enjoy this, for we rehearsed and prepared it especially for you: it is a story of a queen for all seasons, starring the Queen.

1. The Vow of a Princess

The story starts on the twenty-first birthday of Princess Elizabeth. In those days this was the age when you reached your majority and became a grown-up. Unlike millions of her future subjects who might celebrate by throwing a mad party, possibly drinking too much, dancing until dawn, the Princess made a speech on the radio from Cape Town where she and her sister were on a royal tour with the King and Queen, their devoted parents.

It is an awesome vow to make: when I listen to it again I feel my eyes prickling as her clear, high voice outlines her hopes for the future. It's not like a New Year's resolution, soon to be abandoned and forgotten: it is a promise made to the Commonwealth with the world as her witness.

If we all go forward together with an unwavering faith, a high courage, and a quiet heart, we shall be able to make of this ancient commonwealth, which we all love so dearly, an even grander thing – more free, more prosperous, more happy and a more powerful influence for good in the world – than it has been in the greatest days of our forefathers.

To accomplish that we must give nothing less than the whole of ourselves. There is a motto which has been borne by many of my ancestors – a noble motto, 'I serve'. Those words were an inspiration to many bygone heirs to the

Throne when they made their knightly dedication as they came to manhood. I cannot do quite as they did.

But through the inventions of science I can do what was not possible for any of them. I can make my solemn act of dedication with a whole Empire listening. I should like to make that dedication now. It is very simple.

I declare before you all that my whole life whether it be long or short shall be devoted to your service and the service of our great imperial family to which we all belong.

How young she was to have such a firm conviction! She knew she would one day be Queen, and she had been brought up in the ways of monarchy by her father, but even so . . . The deep faith, which has been her guide and support throughout her reign, was present even then. It reminds me of the holy vow that the nuns took at my convent school, not to be taken lightly or without absolute commitment.

Eleanor Roosevelt, wife of the American President Franklin D. Roosevelt, was impressed by her single-minded determination to fulfil all her duties without complaint. She wrote:

I have seen Princess Elizabeth on several occasions since she became queen. Her loveliness does not change but she seems to me still more serious, as one might expect her to be under the burden of her duties.

On one occasion when I had been invited to the Palace for a chat with her, a young secretary escorted me to my automobile.

'It must be terribly hard,' I said, 'for anyone so young to have so many official responsibilities and also carry on as a wife and mother.'

He looked at me with what I thought was a surprised expression and said briskly, 'Oh, no. Not at all. The Queen is very well departmentalized.' How does one departmentalize one's heart? I thought.

And how do you departmentalise your whole life as Queen? Apart from being a mother, wife and friend, you are a working woman with immense responsibilities, people everywhere expecting you to be fully knowledgeable about their occupations. There are talks with prime ministers and world leaders, red boxes, trips abroad and tours at home, always looking the part and knowing the score, never being ill, and if you're feeling a bit ropy just dissembling and carrying on so as not to disappoint . . . Most of us would fall at the first fence. She always does her best, has done since she was young, learning practical skills, like life-saving and fire-laying, mending lorries (my favourite picture of the Princess: in ATS overalls, leaning against a truck), writing, painting, riding, before buckling down to the next thing on the list.

There is a fairy-tale quality of immense importance to add to this story: the arrival of the young Prince Philip of Greece in Princess Elizabeth's life. Was it love at first sight? We want it to have been, and in fact that may have been the truth, for the young Princess at least.

Alathea Fitzalan Howard, a contemporary of hers, was staying at Windsor, in Cumberland Lodge, while the young Princesses Elizabeth and Margaret were at Windsor Castle (mostly) during the war. She spent time with them, drawing, playing, having lessons, watching films and riding. She kept a diary. On Thursday, 3 April 1941, she wrote:

I biked to drawing and we finished modelling our clay horses. It was the last lesson for this term. Afterwards, we played a French tableau game with Monty and then cards till tea. They said something about Philip, so I said, 'Who's Philip?' Lilibet [Princess Elizabeth's nickname] said, 'He's called Prince Philip of Greece,' and then they both burst out laughing. I asked why, knowing quite well! Margaret said, 'We can't tell you,' but L said, 'Yes, we can. Can you keep a secret?' Then she said that P was her 'boy'. Monty [the Princesses' French governess, Mrs Montaudon-Smith] asked me if I had one, and in the end, I told them it was Robert Cecil, which amused L. M said she was so glad I had a 'beau'! We all laughed terribly. L says she cuts photos out of the paper! I must say she is far more grown-up than I was two years ago. When I left, Lilibet said, 'We part today the wiser for two secrets,' and I biked home feeling very happy and also proud at being let into such a great secret, which I shall never betray.

The presence of this dashing young Prince Charming was the beginning of a love that was to last a lifetime. On 15 February 1945 Alathea notes, 'PM [Princess Margaret] told me Prince Philip sent PE [Princess Elizabeth] a photograph and she danced round the room with it for joy.'

They were married in 1947 on 20 November: she was twenty-one and the Prince five years her senior. From then on, he was the constant in her life, always beside her, although a pace behind, always supporting her; they became a template of how a marriage can and should work, despite some fairly complex protocols and their very different characters. His name was added to the prayer book, and we bowed our heads and asked for God's blessings on Philip, Duke of Edinburgh. His death, in 2021, the year in which I am writing this, came as a terrible blow to everyone who thought of him so highly. How much more devastating for the Queen.

But I am racing ahead. We shall start at the beginning.

Twenty-one seems very young today to become a wife, but in 1947 it was quite normal.

The Queen is from my mother's generation, and those lives were lived with much more of a sense of duty. Most women learned to cook and sew, how to run a house or make ends meet. Today's girls are in many ways both older and younger than the women who had lived through the war and were trying to put a life together again. The next generation, my generation, would enjoy a kind of freedom that was unheard of in those challenging post-war days.

At the age of twenty-one I was sharing a flat with three other girls in Earl's Court, living in Swinging London, mini-skirted and Tube-travelling, and there it was that I heard, but never saw, one of the enduring influences on the young Queen's life. The American evangelist Billy Graham held a series of rallies in the vast Earl's Court building, which has since been demolished, and we could hear the amplified boom of his voice as it floated up to our fourth-floor windows. Many people were 'saved' when they went up to the stage for the great man to admit them to the faith, but we thought it was all a bit ho-hum. Anyway, we had been christened and only really went to church on high days and holidays. Later, when I discovered that the Queen liked and trusted him, I began to think differently about his ministry. I didn't want him to be a snake-oil salesman from Medicine Hat: he had to be a good guy to have impressed the Queen. He returned to Britain several times, and I think he always met the Queen on these trips.

On one occasion when I was in Great Britain [he wrote], the Queen was preparing her annual Christmas address to be broadcast on television around the world. To illustrate a point, she wanted to toss a stone into a pond to show how the ripples went out farther and farther. She asked me to come and listen to her practice the speech by the pond and give my impressions, which I did.

I always found her very interested in the Bible and its message. After preaching at Windsor one Sunday, I was sitting next to the Queen at lunch. I told her I had been undecided until the last minute about my choice of sermon and had almost preached on the healing of the crippled man in John 5. Her eyes sparkled and she bubbled over with enthusiasm, as she could do on occasion. 'I wish you had!' she exclaimed. 'That is my favourite story.'

In my big old family Bible, the story Her Majesty loved reveals itself on crackling thin India paper, in old-fashioned type. In Jerusalem there was a well called Bethesda, where the waters were reputed to be sanctified by an angel who at certain times would visit the well and ripple the surface of the water. People would queue to take their place to dip into the holy water soon after it was 'troubled' or stirred, hoping to be healed. There was a man who was very crippled and could never get to the front without being pushed back by others, and who didn't have anyone to carry him to the well as he was too weak to walk. He had been afflicted for thirty-eight years and was desperate and ready to give up. Jesus said, 'Take up your bed and walk . . .' He did and was cured.

Wanting to make things better, wanting to heal wounds and

give hope, always looking for good in people. All of the Queen's Christmas speeches have something of redemption in them.

But first, we must hear of the adventure in Africa during which her life suddenly changed for ever.

2. Becoming Queen

In 1952 King George VI was frail: he was not strong enough to undertake a long, gruelling tour of the Commonwealth. His doctors said he mustn't go: his health had been under assault for years through the strain of the war, of succeeding to the throne so dramatically, and through anxiety and heavy smoking. Princess Elizabeth and Prince Philip would go instead of the King and Queen Elizabeth.

It must have been exciting preparing for such a far-reaching and thrilling journey, which was to start in Kenya. Anyone who has packed for a trip abroad knows how much thought goes into taking everything you might need: passport, money, tickets, the right clothes, maybe a torch and some presents, something to read, shampoo, a camera . . . but if you are a princess carrying out official duties it would be completely different. The wardrobe would be carefully selected for each occasion. A passport is not needed if you are royal; someone else takes care of all the travel arrangements. You don't carry money. Your reading matter will be largely about the country you are going to visit, the people you will meet, their customs and the speeches you will be required to make. But it is always exciting to set out on an adventure, and going by plane in those days carried an air of immense glamour and luxury. That's quite hard to accept if you're not old enough to remember it.

I love travelling, and planning where you're going to stay is the starting point. Major Eric Sherbrooke Walker was a hotelier and founder of the famous Treetops Hotel in Kenya. He had the honour of hosting Princess Elizabeth and Prince Philip on the first leg of their journey.

Of course, there was an entourage, chosen from those close to the royal couple.

Lady Pamela Mountbatten was Princess Elizabeth's lady-in-waiting at this time; she was the daughter of Lord Mountbatten of Burma, who was Prince Philip's uncle and a cousin of the future Queen. Prince Philip's private secretary and close friend, Commander Michael 'Mike' Parker, travelled with them. Major Eric's account captures the sense of jeopardy that accompanies any encounter with wild animals in their natural habitat.

In January, 1952, about the time that the forest round Treetops was taken over by the Royal National Parks, of which Colonel Mervyn Cowie was the director, my wife and I heard that Their Royal Highnesses Princess Elizabeth and Prince Philip were coming to Kenya the following month on their world tour. Knowing how interested they were in game we invited them to spend a night with us at Treetops.

On 3 February Princess Elizabeth and Prince Philip reached the Royal Lodge, Sagana, twenty miles from Nyeri; this was a wooden cottage in the forest which the people of Kenya had given them as a wedding present. The situation in our country at that time was becoming tense. The Mau Mau troubles were about to burst into the open. A state of emergency had not yet been declared, but there had been several cases of arson.

The Kenya authorities took such security measures as were allowed by the Colonial Office. Our old friend Colonel Jim

Corbett took some of his own on 4 February when the Prince played in a polo match at a ground eight miles from Nyeri and the Princess was watching. The ground had high grass and forest on three sides and a deep ravine led up to it on the fourth side and would have given easy cover to any mischief-makers. So while the rest of the local population was enjoying the match, Jim Corbett and his sister sat in their car keeping a faithful watch on the ravine on the far side of the polo ground from the pavilion.

It was about three o'clock when the cars reached the spot at the forest edge, which was as far as a car could go. We then set off on foot: Their Royal Highnesses, Lady Pamela Mountbatten, Commander Michael Parker, Mr Edward Windley (the provincial commissioner) and myself. Prince Philip, Edward Windley and I carried rifles. We made cautious progress along the forest path, which was only a few feet wide with the bush pressing in closely on each side and visibility of not much more than a yard or two. It was worrying to hear the noise of elephant carrying clearly through the forest. At any moment it might have been necessary to call to everyone to climb the safety ladders.

As we got nearer to the tree the squealing and trumpeting grew louder, and on approaching the clearing, where the big mgumu tree towered above the others, there was a white pillowcase fluttering in the breeze.

Should we go on or turn back? The question had to be decided in seconds. I put it to Prince Philip.

'Go ahead!' he whispered.

To reduce the size of the group, Lady Pamela Mountbatten and Commander Parker were then left standing on two of the safety ladders, prepared to climb right up them if the elephant came too close for safety. The rest of us continued along the path, warily and silently. When within fifty yards of the tree we had a full view of the clearing and saw the whole herd milling about. There was a fifty-yard gauntlet of comparatively open ground to cross before reaching the ladder that led up into the tree. Quite apart from the elephants' restlessness, a herd which has mothers with their young is always a risk. A cow looking after her calf does not hesitate to charge. One big cow in particular was facing us, standing right underneath Treetops, flapping her ears. Fortunately there was a cross-wind and she did not scent us. With rifles pointed at her, and watching her intently, we went forward step by step. The Princess and Prince seemed to have an excellent knowledge of woodcraft, for they moved silently without once treading on a dry twig. I had sometimes taken people along the path when elephant were about, but never at such close quarters as this.

Princess Elizabeth did not falter. She walked straight towards the elephant and smiled a greeting at my wife who was awaiting her halfway down the ladder. Then unhurriedly she handed my wife her handbag and camera, and climbed the steep ladder.

I heaved an immense sigh of relief when she and Prince Philip were twenty feet high, out of reach of the huge animals. We went back for Lady Pamela and Commander Parker, and eventually all of us were safely in the tree. As soon as she had climbed the ladder, the Princess went out onto the balcony and calmly started filming the milling herd below.

Almost as if they knew what was expected of them, the elephants put up a tremendous performance. The old bull again chased the younger ones to the accompaniment of trumpeting and screaming. Then the Prince was greatly amused when one of the elephants carefully filled its trunk with dust. Mischievously it moved up to some doves that had settled on the ground nearby and squirted the dust at them in a powerful jet, making them flutter off indignantly. The elephant 'laughed' at this teasing by flicking its trunk up and down and flapping its ears.

The Princess used her cine-camera once more when a cow suckled her little calf. This domestic scene over, the mother walked with her young one on to a small peninsula that jutted into the lake. There she quenched her thirst by drawing water into her trunk and squirting it down her throat. After this she waded into the lake for a few yards and stood, enjoying the coolness and calm. The baby did not want to be left behind. It started to squeal with anxiety. But Mother, deliberately no doubt, in the belief that youngsters must learn independence, ignored it. With much hesitation, the calf eventually plucked up the courage to follow her into the water. When it was within reach, she drew it towards her very tenderly and, supporting it with her trunk, propelled it to the far bank.

Kraa the baboon, who looked very sinister on account of perpetually revealing his fangs, having lost part of his upper lip in a fight, was the next animal to appear. He led his large family of eleven down a forest track to the border of the salt lick, striding along on his knuckles. Elephant do not like baboon; they usually chase them back into the trees. Kraa therefore began to edge round the lick most carefully. One of his wives, bolder than the rest, broke from the troop. She climbed one of the wooden supports under Treetops, reached our balcony, nimbly skipped over the cameras and field-glasses laid on top of the narrow railing and took refuge on a nearby branch. There she was given a large sweet potato, which she peeled with her teeth and ate with complete unconcern while she was photographed at a range of a few feet.

The time passed so quickly that when my wife called out that tea was ready in the dining-room, the Princess whispered: 'Oh, please may I have it here? I don't want to miss a moment of this!'

Nothing beats the thrill of filming and photographing wildlife, in this case in the fabulous surroundings of the Kenyan countryside. The Queen is a keen film-maker, and seeing elephant and baboon close enough to capture them on film must have been wonderfully satisfying. Lady Pamela Mountbatten later described it vividly, and told how the happy paradise of a demi-Eden was broken so abruptly and so tragically.

It had been decided that the Princess should undertake the Commonwealth tour in place of her parents, as the King was not strong enough for such a long, arduous journey so soon after his recent lung operation.

When we arrived in Kenya, I was immediately struck by the smell of earth baked by the sun and the brilliant colours of the birds and flowers that at once reminded me of India. After a few days in Nairobi – a whirlwind introduction to a life of cheering children, regimental inspections, hospital and church visits, lunches, dinners and receptions – we travelled north on bumpy roads, engulfed by clouds of red dust, to Sagana Lodge on the slopes of Mount Kenya in the Aberdare Mountains.

On the third evening we set off in an open jeep – the Princess and I wearing khaki shirts and slacks, drawing a few comments from Mike, who was unused to seeing us in anything other than silk or cotton dresses. We were heading for Treetops, the tree-house-turned-miniature-hotel built in the fork of a huge 300-year-old fig tree.

It was a remote spot on the elephant migration path to Mount Kenya, and promised spectacular views of the elephants and many other splendid wild animals.

The Prince and Princess safely climbed the ladder into the tree house, despite the presence of a cow elephant standing guard over her herd, anxiously flapping her ears just eleven feet away behind the thinnest of hedges. African elephants are far larger than Indian ones and cannot be tamed, and these mountain elephants had a particularly fero-cious reputation. Luckily the wind was blowing across the clearing towards us so no scent was being carried to her. The Princess was already busy filming, excited by the pres-ence of such a wide variety of magnificent creatures.

While we were standing in awed silence, watching the comings and goings before us, King George VI, aged just fifty-six and in the sixteenth year of his reign, died in his sleep. Earlier in the day he had been watching his guests shoot at Sandringham. He then retired to bed and suffered a coronary thrombosis. So the Princess who had climbed up the ladder at Treetops came down the next day as Queen.

The King had been found dead by his valet when he went in to call him. At 8.45 a.m. the King's principal private secretary had called his assistant in London, using the code word 'Hyde Park', telling him to inform the Prime Minister and Queen Mary. At 10.45 a.m. the British news agencies were permitted to announce the King's death. The news did not begin to percolate into Kenya, which was ahead of Britain by three hours, until after 1.45 p.m. local time, the time that we, none the wiser, were finishing lunch.

After lunch, Prince Philip read the newspapers and dozed on his bed, while the Princess wrote to her father, telling him about all the wonderful sights she had seen, emphasising how much he would enjoy it here and saying she hoped he could come out in the future to see it for himself.

There was a portable wireless in the sitting room where Princess Elizabeth was writing and Mike crept in, managing to get it without her noticing. After a few minutes of static and frantic tuning we finally made out the faint sound of solemn music with which the BBC had replaced all its programmes. After the tolling of Big Ben, the news at last reached us from far away, the gravity of the newsreader's tone unmistakable. Mike confirmed the news to Martin and went straight in to tell Prince Philip, who lifted up his newspaper to cover his face in a gesture of despair, saying, 'This will be such a blow.' He then walked into his sitting room and asked his wife to come with him into the garden. Mike and I watched them on the lawn as they walked together slowly, up and down, up and down.

Far away in Kuala Lumpur in the Malay Peninsula, my sister and I had just returned from school, plaits dripping with sweat after the walk from the Army School over a road of crystal quartz, past banana palms and lalang grass to our bungalow, 16 HQ Malaya. We usually had lunch and then rested under our mosquito nets during the intense heat until the air became cooler and we could take the dog for a walk to the tin mines. That day was different: my father, serving with his Gurkha regiment, came home unexpectedly with a very stern and sorrowful face and said, 'The King is dead.'

We scuttled away as he changed his uniform and went back

to Headquarters. Being six years old and far from Great Britain
I didn't know who the King was, but we could guess how
shattering the news must be.

The shock waves sped around the world. In London, Winston
Churchill addressed the nation.

When the death of the King was announced to us yesterday
morning there struck a deep and solemn note in our lives
which, as it resounded far and wide, stilled the clatter and
traffic of twentieth-century life in many lands, and made
countless millions of human beings pause and look around
them. A new sense of values took, for the time being, possession of human minds, and mortal existence presented itself
to so many at the same moment in its serenity and in its
sorrow, in its splendour and in its pain, in its fortitude and
in its suffering.

The King was greatly loved by all his peoples. He was
respected as a man and as a prince far beyond the many
realms over which he reigned. The simple dignity of his
life, his manly virtues, his sense of duty – alike as a ruler
and a servant of the vast spheres and communities for which
he bore responsibility – his gay charm and happy nature,
his example as a husband and a father in his own family
circle, his courage in peace or war: all these were aspects
of his character which won the glint of admiration, now
here, now there, from the innumerable eyes whose gaze
falls upon the Throne.

There is no doubt that of all the institutions which have
grown up among us over the centuries, or sprung into being
in our lifetime, the constitutional monarchy is the most deeply
founded and dearly cherished by the whole association of
our peoples. In the present generation it has acquired a

meaning incomparably more powerful than anyone had dreamed possible in former times. The Crown has become the mysterious link, indeed I may say the magic link, which unites our loosely bound, but strongly interwoven Commonwealth of nations, states, and races.

Famous have been the reigns of our queens. Some of the greatest periods in our history have unfolded under their sceptre. Now that we have the second Queen Elizabeth, also ascending the throne in her twenty-sixth year, our thoughts are carried back nearly four hundred years to the magnificent figure who presided over and, in many ways, embodied and inspired the grandeur and genius of the Elizabethan age.

Queen Elizabeth II, like her predecessor, did not pass her childhood in any certain expectation of the Crown. But already we know her well, and we understand why her gifts, and those of her husband, the Duke of Edinburgh, have stirred the only part of the Commonwealth she has yet been able to visit. She has already been acclaimed as Queen of Canada.

We make our claim too, and others will come forward also, and tomorrow the proclamation of her sovereignty will command the loyalty of her native land and of all other parts of the British Commonwealth and Empire. I, whose youth was passed in the august, unchallenged and tranquil glories of the Victorian era, may well feel a thrill in invoking once more the prayer and the anthem, 'God save the Queen!'

Three queens now mourned the King: his mother, Queen Mary, his widow, Queen Elizabeth, and the new young queen, Elizabeth II. It must have been agonising for them all, losing someone so dear who died so young (he was only fifty-six) and then having to share the grief with millions of people who felt extraordinarily close to this good, brave man whom they had never met, but for whom they felt a deep affection and admiration.

I wonder if it is made easier knowing that the world sympathises? Or would you prefer to cry your eyes out in private and only be with those you love best at such a time of loss? If you are royal, there is no choice. The new Queen not only grieved for her father, she had to face up to the future, which suddenly rushed up to her out of the shadows. From now on nothing would ever be the same.

Always thinking of others, the Queen Mother (as she would soon be known) wrote at once from Sandringham to the King's mother, Queen Mary.

My Darling Mama,

What can I say to you – I know that you loved Bertie dearly, and he was my whole life, and one can only be deeply thankful for the utterly happy years we had together. He was so wonderfully thoughtful and loving, & I don't believe he ever thought of himself at all. He was so devoted to you, & admired and loved you. It is impossible for me to grasp what has happened, last night he was in wonderful form and looking so well, and this morning, only a few hours ago, I was sent a message that his servant couldn't waken him. I flew to his room, & thought that he was in a deep sleep, he looked so peaceful – and then I realised what had happened. It is hard to grasp, he was such an angel to the children & me, and I cannot bear to think of Lilibet, so young to bear such a burden. I do feel for you so darling Mama – to lose two dear sons, and Bertie so young still, & so precious – it is almost more than one can bear –

Your very loving

Elizabeth

Meanwhile the Commonwealth tour had, of course, been cut short, and the royal couple flew back to England. It's hard to imagine the feelings of the new Queen as she descended the steps of the aeroplane. That moment is the one it is hardest to picture. She had been brought up to know that one day she would be a monarch, but what can it have been like, stepping down onto the tarmac where, only days ago, your beloved father had waved goodbye? Onto her small shoulders, slowly and inexorably, the weight of endless duty, separation from normality, and being treated differently for ever came to rest. The tectonic plates had shifted.

In his wonderful official biography of Queen Mary, James Pope-Hennessy described how the old Queen went to Clarence House to be the first to kiss the hand of the new Queen. From now on, everyone would make an obeisance to her whenever she appeared – everyone, including her own family.

King George VI was the fourth English Monarch to die during Queen Mary's lifetime; and now, as in her childhood and youth, Great Britain was once more ruled by a Queen. The new Monarch, who succeeded to the throne with the style and title of Queen Elizabeth II, reached London from Nairobi the next day, at four o'clock in the afternoon. At 4.30 Queen Mary drove out of the gates of Marlborough House to do homage to her Sovereign: 'Her old Grannie and subject,' she said, 'must be the first to kiss Her hand.' At Clarence House Queen Mary was received by her eldest granddaughter, who at the early age of twenty-five was thus suddenly invested with the mystic aura of the British Crown.

The coffin of King George VI, like that of his father before him, was brought from Sandringham to London, where it lay in state in Westminster Hall. This was a day of relentless rain. In the downpour Queen Mary, heavily veiled, with the new Queen, her mother, and the rest of her family, followed the late King's coffin to its place of rest upon a catafalque in the centre of the Hall. On 15 February she watched the funeral procession from her window, as it wound slowly into the Mall. She then followed its further progress, as well as the interment in the vault at Windsor Castle, on her television set.

The grand machinery of state whirrs into action when a royal funeral takes place. All would have been rehearsed and planned to the last detail, as the King's death had been widely expected. The lying-in-state, the streets cordoned off, horses groomed to shining splendour, uniforms immaculate, timings checked and rechecked, as the day of the funeral in Windsor drew near. Across the Commonwealth the funeral was broadcast. The *Canberra Times* bore the headline 'Grief and Pageantry at the Funeral of King George VI. Two million see solemn procession in London'.

> Flanked by sombre pageantry, surrounded by silent multitudes, the body of King George VI today moved from the ancient Westminster Hall to the burial vaults in Windsor Chapel [St George's Chapel].
>
> A vast assembly, estimated at two million persons, in the heart of the Commonwealth gathered in wintry sunshine to pay the last tribute to the well-loved Monarch. Great and humble joined in the ancient ceremonial.
>
> The red and gold Royal Standard was draped over the coffin on which was placed the glittering Imperial Crown, Sceptre and the Orb – symbols of kingship.

In the vanguard of the sad parade were the soldiers of Canada, Rhodesia, West Africa, Ceylon, Pakistan, India, South Africa, New Zealand and Australia, followed by Britain's own famous regiments, and finally six massed bands.

They moved at the rate of sixty-five slow paces a minute.

The crowds for the most part stood silently with bared heads as the cortège passed. But one woman gave a faint shriek and several others fainted as the procession moved along Whitehall.

The cortège moved off slowly and solemnly.

Simultaneously Big Ben began tolling minute by minute for the fifty-six years of the King's life.

The mile-long procession had begun, crunching through the sanded streets. The thud of guns firing the artillery salute sounded a thunderous background.

The proudest units of Britain's armed services led the procession.

Then came the coffin, small and lonely amid the mighty cavalcade.

Officers of the Household Cavalry carrying the Standard of Queen Elizabeth II walked behind the coffin.

The young Queen, her face pale beneath a heavy black veil, followed in a glassed-in carriage.

The Queen Mother, Princess Margaret and the Princess Royal [Princess Mary, the King's only sister] travelled in the same carriage.

The waiting citizens saw in slow motion the great panoply of British ceremonial, which has grown from the tradition of centuries.

The crowds strained to catch a glimpse of the pale profile of their twenty-five-year-old Queen.

The gilt work of the State Carriage in which the Queen travelled gleamed in the misty sunshine.

Few could tell which was Queen Elizabeth of the four heavily veiled women in the carriage, pulled by bay horses with glittering bridles and attended by footmen in scarlet coats and gold-fringed black top hats.

Audrey Russell was the BBC's first female correspondent. Writing in her memoir, *A Certain Voice*, she recalls a rare moment of privilege at the end of the emotionally exhausting day. She manages to capture the peace that comes when a body has been laid to rest.

I shall never forget the arrival of that closed landau with half-seen, veiled figures within. Quickly the door was opened and we saw the young Queen, taking precedence over her mother for the first time. She was swiftly followed by three figures in deep mourning, all heavily veiled: the King's widow, his younger daughter Princess Margaret, and his only sister, the Princess Royal. They and the four Royal Dukes (Kent, Windsor, Gloucester and Edinburgh, who had walked behind the Queen's carriage the whole way in the procession, both morning and afternoon) then followed the coffin up the long flight of steps, to vanish into the shadowy interior of St George's Chapel for the service.

As the simple, twenty-minute funeral service began, those of us outside were aware of a sudden serenity and peace. The maximum use of sounds, as counselled by Lobby [Seymour Joly de Lotbiniere. He later masterminded the televising of the Coronation and was the BBC's outdoor broadcasting expert] with his flair for such things, had been very telling, but it had meant too a deep emotional strain . . . the perpetual slow marching tramp of feet, the clatter of horses' hooves (slightly muted by sanded roadways), the bands, the bells, the gun salutes, and above all the full naval honours accorded by the bos'n's pipes plaintively piping the Admiral alongside and ashore, as the bearers of the coffin slowly climbed the steps to the resting place of the King.

Now the listeners (and ourselves on headphones) came to the climax of the splendours of all those moving sounds: the choirs and the organ music of the service itself.

The Queen reverently placed the neatly folded King's Colour of the King's Company, Grenadier Guards, on the coffin. Known as the Royal Standard of the Regiment, by tradition this is eventually taken to hang in Windsor Castle among the standards of other sovereigns. As the coffin was lowered to the vault, the Queen scattered earth from a gilded bowl, while the Archbishop of Canterbury, Dr Fisher, committed the body to the ground.

It is often said that funerals can give the impression of ending abruptly; and this indeed can with some truth be said of military funerals, where ceremonial drill rather sharply goes into reverse. As the troops disperse, solemn music gives way to a brisk march. The message seems to be: 'The living must carry on.' At all events, so it seemed to me at Windsor on that momentous day. With a minimum of ceremony or delay the Royal Family left in motor cars, while the congregation dispersed and walked to the car parks.

We were not quite so speedy. After a broadcast of that magnitude there were many people to be thanked for kind and expert help. At the same time congratulations reaching us from Broadcasting House were cheering and pleasing.

Quite unexpectedly, an official who all along had been

particularly helpful, approached me and asked quietly, 'Would you like to go into the chapel?' We entered by a side door, where I met a verger. Already a few workmen were dismantling the specially built stands, and I heard the unceremonious sound of planks being shifted and stacked. Then I was led to the dark oblong hole in the floor below the high altar. And there, down in the vault, now bereft of crown and regalia and no longer guarded by anyone, the coffin lay wrapped in the Royal Standard, with the Queen Mother's spray of white flowers at its head. In silence the three of us walked past and away, aware that quite possibly we chanced to be the very last of a good king's subjects to pay our personal respect to him.

3. 'Vivat Regina Elizabetha!'

The date had been set for the Coronation: 2 June 1953. At once the makers of commemorative mugs and plates, bowls and badges, teapots, handkerchiefs, soap-dishes and anything that could be printed with the face of the new monarch whirled into action.

This time the Coronation, like that of her late father, King George VI, would be accomplished: no Edward VIII dramas here, when coins and plates bearing the not-to-be King's image had to be scrapped (or hoarded by collectors: what a rarity!). After seven long years of rationing, the country was stumbling back to a kind of normality after the war. There were still shortages and bomb-sites, still shell-shocked ex-servicemen wondering if they could ever be employed, still widows struggling to get by on tiny pensions . . . but here at last was a real chance to celebrate. It would take place, of course, at Westminster Abbey where for a thousand years the kings and queens of this country have been crowned. There would naturally be masses of pageantry and splendour, coaches and crowds, visiting dignitaries and royalty from across the globe, but to many the first thought was: who will make The Dress? What will the Queen wear on the great day? Norman Hartnell was the simple answer. Hartnell was the most fashionable dress designer of the time, the go-to man for Hollywood stars, aristocracy and royalty. His clothes were glamorous beyond words.

One October afternoon in 1952, Her Majesty the Queen desired me to make for her the dress to be worn at her Coronation.

I can scarcely remember what I murmured in reply. In simple conversational tones the Queen went on to express her wishes. Her Majesty required that the dress should conform in line to that of her wedding dress and that the material should be white satin. It was almost exactly five years earlier that I had put the final touches to the dress which, as Princess Elizabeth, she had worn on the day of her wedding to the Duke of Edinburgh.

Altogether, I created nine differing designs, which began in almost severe simplicity and proceeded towards elaboration. I liked the last one best, but naturally did not express my opinion when I submitted these paintings to Her Majesty.

The eighth sketch, which automatically suggested itself to me from the previous sketches with the emblem of the Tudor Rose, was composed of all the emblems of Great Britain. Therefore it included the Thistle of Scotland, the Shamrock of Ireland and the daffodil, which, at that time, I thought to be the authentic national emblem of Wales. All these floral emblems, placed in proper positions of precedence on the skirt, were to be expressed in varying tones of white and silver, using small diamonds and crystals for pinpoint coruscation.

Her Majesty approved of this emblematic impression but considered that the use of all white and silver might too closely resemble her wedding gown. She liked the theme of the fifth design and suggested that I might employ the aid of colour in representing the four emblems.

Later, at another audience, the Queen made a wise and sovereign observation. It was, in effect, that she was unwilling to wear a gown bearing the emblems of Great Britain without the emblems of all the Dominions of which she was now Queen.

I then drew and painted the ninth design, which proved more complicated than I had expected. A new design had to be provided and I found it necessary to raise up the three emblems of Scotland, Ireland and Wales to the upper portion of the skirt, thus contracting the space they occupied upon the satin background, to allow for more space below, where all combined flowers of the Commonwealth countries could be assembled in a floral garland, each flower or leaf nestling closely around the motherly English Tudor Rose, placed in the centre.

An appointment was made for some members of my staff and myself to visit Sandringham House. So, on a very cold Saturday morning, we motored up to Norfolk with two car loads of people and dresses.

Apart from the now completed ninth sketch and the precious emblems, we took with us a generous collection of dresses newly prepared for the spring, from which Her Majesty might be able to select dresses for her tour of Australia in the early part of the following year.

The atmosphere of Sandringham is about as different from that of Buckingham Palace and Windsor Castle as could possibly be imagined, and I can well understand why successive generations of the Royal Family have such a great affection for this rambling Victorian country home and its encircling pine woods.

After luncheon we staged the most informal dress show I have ever presented, for it took place in a large bedroom of old-fashioned charm. The mannequins entered through a door that led out of a capacious white bathroom. From this quaint display some dresses were chosen as the basis of the wardrobe for Australia.

It was then my duty to present to the Queen the final sketch together with the coloured emblems. Each of them had been mounted in a circular gilded wooden frame and I laid out the following emblems:

England. The Tudor Rose, embroidered in palest pink silk, pearls, gold and silver bullion and rose diamonds.

Scotland. The Thistle, embroidered in pale mauve silk and amethysts. The calyx was embroidered in reseda green silk, silver thread and diamond dewdrops.

Ireland. The Shamrock, embroidered in soft green silk, silver thread bullion and diamonds.

Wales. The Leek, embroidered in white silk and diamonds with the leaves in palest green silk.

Canada. The Maple Leaf, in green silk embroideries, bordered with gold bullion thread and veined in crystal.

Australia. The Wattle flower, in mimosa yellow blossom with the foliage in green and gold thread.

New Zealand. The Fern, in soft green silk veined with silver and crystal.

South Africa. The Protea, in shaded pink silk, each petal bordered with silver thread. The leaves of shaded green silk and embellished with rose diamonds.

India. The Lotus flower, in mother-of-pearl embroidered petals, seed pearls and diamonds.

Pakistan. Wheat, cotton and jute. The wheat was in oat-shaped diamonds and fronds of golden crystal, the jute in a spray of leaves of green silk and golden thread, and the cotton blossom with stalks of silver and leaves of green silk.

Ceylon. The Lotus flower, in opals, mother-of-pearl, diamonds and soft green silk.

Apart from the Irish Shamrock, which was judged a little too verdant in tone, the Queen was pleased to agree to the *ensemble* as my design for her Coronation Gown.

The Coronation was to be opened to the world for the very first time: there would be cameras in the Abbey, and the procession would be filmed. That didn't mean there weren't hundreds of correspondents, artists and photographers all planning their pieces and positions. Luckiest of all was the great designer, artist and photographer Cecil Beaton, who would take the official portraits and group pictures back at Buckingham Palace after the Coronation was over. This lively and fascinating extract from his diary shows his powers of observation and turn of phrase.

The birds had started to sing and the sky was pale grey; already a few electric lights were on in the bedrooms of the houses opposite. An angry wind blew the branches of the cherry tree in the next door garden, and despite the heavy sheets of rain people were already going off cheerfully and hurriedly to take their places in the crowds. I watched a genteel woman, with her husband and small child, scurrying off, complete with umbrellas, Mackintoshes and sandwiches; they were utterly respectable and charming, and a complete, happy little unit. I felt a great lump in my throat: I don't know why they were so poignant.

With passes, journalists' press permits, cards and instructions clutched tightly, and with sticker on the hired car, and my grey topper filled with sandwiches, Indian ink and gadgets for my drawings, I was off on my way.

Remarkably smooth traffic regulations. Already at this early hour motors were bumper to bumper in front: it was fun to peer at the old men, bad-tempered and sleepy at this hour, in cockaded hats with lace jabots, their womenfolk having had, before dawn, a hairdresser to their houses to set their coiffures.

Goldsticks [the officers who conduct people to their seats] stationed around the cloisters showed us on our way. They were already frozen blue. One of them asked me if I had heard the good news that Hunt [leader of the successful 1953 British expedition] had climbed Everest. The iced wind blew in circles round the winding staircase that took me to the rafters, and I felt much sympathy for Hunt. My allotted seat was just near the pipes of the great organ. It was by no means an easy place from which to make drawings: only by peering somewhat precariously over the edge of the balcony could the activities below be seen.

But I discovered that, without disturbing my fellow journalists, it was possible to move about fairly freely, and a vantage point from my rook's nest was discovered from which

I could not only see the arrivals coming down the nave, but much of the activity in front of the high altar.

Feeling nervous, cold, and rather sick, I buoyed myself up by eating barley sugar (very sustaining) and chatting to nice Christopher Hussey of *Country Life*.

One has seen many woodcuts, and pictures of all sorts, of the earliest kings and queens being crowned; particularly detailed are the prints of the first Queen Elizabeth's procession. In all periods, painters have had a shot at recording the ceremony; with the improvements in the technique of photography the scene has become almost familiar. Yet this spectacle today transcended all preconceived notions. The ceremonial seemed to be as fresh and inspiring as some great play or musical event that was being enacted upon a spontaneous impulse of genius. Perhaps it was the background of lofty vaulted stone – like a silver forest – that made everything seem so particularly surprising.

The words of the service struck one's ears with an impact that had the pure audacity of a poem by Rimbaud. The music sounded pristine and sifted.

The colours red, gold and smoke-blue always beguiled one's eye by the unexpected. The brilliant gold carpet was the perfect floor-covering for the slippered feet of the pages, the train-bearers, and the scarlet-, blue- and gold-clad heralds, for the bishops and clergy in white and gold. Black Rod made way for a messenger; a mote of light caught a gold sequin fallen on the carpet, on a jewel in a bishop's ring; the sun came out and lit up a posse of scarlet uniformed goldsticks. It was all living and new: it was history, but of today and of the future. It was something that is pulsating and vital to us, and an essential part of the life we believe in.

The guests presented great contrasts in their national and traditional garments. The peeresses en bloc the most ravishing sight – like a bed of auricula-eyed sweet William – in their dark red velvet and foam-white, dew-spangled with diamonds. Lady Haddington and the Duchess of Buccleuch in huge diamond 'fenders' were particularly outstanding but, most beautiful of all, was young Debo Devonshire, sister of Nancy Mitford, with her hair dressed wide to contain the Edwardian cake-like crown, in Georgiana, Duchess of Devonshire's eighteenth-century robes, quite different in cut with the straight line from shoulder to shoulder.

Willie Walton's 'Orb and Sceptre' blazes out on the organ as the other royalties arrive and the procession begins: the minor royalties, and the foreign royalties and representatives of states. Norway, Greece, Nepal, Japan, Ethiopia, Morocco, Thailand, Peru; the sultans under Her Majesty's protection; Queen Salote of Tonga, a great big warm personality. Is Russia here? Then the Princes and Princesses of the royal blood: the mother of the Duke of Edinburgh, a contrast to the grandeur, in the ash-grey draperies of a nun. The manipulation of the long velvet trains is in some cases too under-rehearsed: Princess Marie Louise, agonisingly old, but still athletic, is obviously very angry with her fatuous lady-in-waiting for making such a balls-up with her train. The Gloucester boys, too, give their mother a moment or two of anxiety as they tug and mishandle her train. Likewise the attendant of Princess Alexandra is at fault; for that matter, so is the Princess's dressmaker, for he has made her a confection that is far too fluffy and unimportant for the occasion. Her mother, the Duchess of Kent, has the dignity of a carved wooden effigy. The Mistress of the Robes [Helen, Duchess of Northumberland, Mistress of the Robes to the Queen

Mother], of towering height, is minimised by the enormous presence and radiance of the petite Queen Mother. Yet in the Queen Widow's expression we read sadness combined with pride.

A posse of church dignitaries portends the Queen's procession followed by the Knights of the Garter and the Standard Bearers. After them the Prime Ministers of the Commonwealth and the Lord High Chancellor. The dour old Scot, Canning, with his lean face, exposed skull and dark crimson cape, does not intend to play second fiddle to anyone; yet, quietly and legitimately, the Archbishop of Canterbury overshadows him with consummate tact. That great old relic Winston Churchill lurches forward on unsteady feet, a fluttering mass of white ribbons at his shoulder and white feathers in the hat in his hand; Mrs Churchill, close by, grimaces a recognition as Montgomery and his page, Winston Junior, pass her by.

Then, most dramatic and spectacular, at the head of her retinue of white, lily-like ladies, the Queen. Her cheeks are sugar pink: her hair tightly curled around the Victorian diadem of precious stones perched straight on her brow. Her pink hands are folded meekly on the elaborate grandeur of her encrusted skirt; she is still a young girl with a demeanour of simplicity and humility. Perhaps her mother has taught her never to use a superfluous gesture. As she walks she allows her heavy skirt to swing backwards and forwards in a beautiful rhythmic effect. This girlish figure has enormous dignity; she belongs in this scene of almost Byzantine magnificence.

She moves to the Chair of State. Then the archbishops and bishops, having placed the Bible, Chalice and the Regalia on the altar, come to present the young Queen for recognition to the east. '*Vivat! Vivat!*' shout, surprisingly, the boys from Westminster School: trumpets sound to split the roofs and shatter the heart. Then, likewise, the Queen faces her people to the south, west and north. '*Vivat! Vivat! Vivat!*' and each time the trumpets blow the recognition as the solitary figure bows humbly at each shattering volley.

The Queen takes the Coronation Oath, kisses the Bible, and, after the Creed and the Communion Service, the Archbishop says the Prayer of Consecration. The choir begins the marvellous anthem 'Zadok the Priest' during which the Queen is divested of her crimson robes, her diadem and Collar of the Garter, and, in preparation for the Anointing, puts on a simple white shift. Four Knights of the Garter hold a canopy of cloth of gold under which the Archbishop anoints the Queen with holy oil in the form of a cross. Then the presentation of the Spurs, Sword and the Orb, and, on the Queen's fourth finger of the right hand, the Ring. The Queen's hands are those of an artist, a ballerina, a sculptor or surgeon. When the Sword has been presented, then offered to the altar, Lord Salisbury redeems it for a bag containing one hundred silver shillings, and thenceforth holds it naked and erect.

The crowning is superbly dramatic: the expression on the small face of the Queen is one of intense expectancy until, with magnificent assurance, the Archbishop thrusts down with speed and force the Crown onto the neat head. At this moment the hoarse shouts of 'God save the Queen' break out. The peers put on their coronets and caps of state, and the peeresses, with long, gloved arms looking like wishbones, hold up their coronets. A fanfare of trumpets, a blaze of violins, an eruption from the big organ, and the guns are shot off from the Tower down the river. This is a great moment, immediately to be followed by the enthroning and glorification of the new monarch. While anthems are sung, homage is paid by a strange concourse of old and young alike. As a simple communicant rather than as Queen of England, she kneels to take the holy wine and bread. Thence she goes to St Edmund's Chapel where, divested of the garments delivered to her during the solemnities, she is arrayed in the robe of purple velvet.

Long delays, pauses and waits, but always something occupies one's attention. A new arrival of uniformed dignitaries. A procession forms, and Mr Winston Churchill comes from his pew to line up for the final exodus. He turns on his heels to admire the peeresses. 'Yes – a very fine bunch of women, a most magnificent sight,' he seems to be saying as he gives them his appraisal. He turns back to see if things are ready. No. Again he turns towards these wonderful women. Also waiting to take their allotted place are the great figures of the war, Lords Alanbrooke, Halifax and Portal.

There is an unfortunate hold-up when the Queen Mother is about to proceed from the Abbey. Someone has mistakenly allowed minor members of the clergy to go before her; a herald is sent to inform her of what has happened. She smiles patiently as she waits.

The Queen's maids of honour were selected from the aristocracy, chosen for their height and appearance as much as their titles and suitability. They had been sworn to secrecy on the subject of their dresses, all made to complement the Coronation robes. They had practised and practised, sometimes in the Abbey, so they would not put a satin-slippered foot out of place.

At these rehearsals the Queen's place was taken by the Duchess of Norfolk, who was roughly the same height as the Queen, about five feet three. (I shall have to look up centimetres in my diary to find out how tall that is in metric measurements, but actually I don't think the Queen does litres or centimetres, so I shall leave that hanging in the air. I know she always likes to use the old-fashioned version of the Lord's Prayer' . . . which art in heaven . . . them that trespass against us,' and so do I. Mystery is at the heart of prayer, and, frankly, the stranger the language the better.) Lady Anne Coke, later to become Anne Glenconner, was one of the chosen maids of honour. In her glorious memoir, *Lady in Waiting,* she describes taking part in the service in the Abbey on that heart-stopping day.

The Queen looked absolutely ravishing. She had the most wonderful complexion and her eyes were glistening, and finally we, and the nation, set eyes on her Coronation dress under her Parliamentary train of crimson velvet, which, by now, we were very familiar with. The dress was exquisite: designed by Norman Hartnell, of ivory silk, covered with embroidery of the rose, the thistle, and all the different emblems of the British Isles and Commonwealth.

I have often been asked whether the Queen seemed nervous. She didn't: she was as calm as she always is. She knew exactly what to do. She had seen her father being crowned, and although she had been quite young, I am sure she would have remembered everything.

Once the Queen had got out of the carriage, we gathered up her crimson train, using the silk handles as the velvet rippled over our hands. The Duke of Norfolk stood on the steps of the Abbey in his ducal robes, just as he had done in May 1937 at the late King's Coronation. He had greeted the young Princess Elizabeth that day, and now, sixteen years later, he was receiving her as Queen Elizabeth II. After greeting the Queen, the Duke stepped back and the six of us waited behind her while the Duke of Edinburgh went inside and put on the robes of a Royal Duke, and the peers carrying the Regalia got ready. The Duke of Norfolk had worked out it would take the Queen fifty-five seconds to walk from her spot, marked by a single red thread stitched into the blue carpet, to the Gothic Arch, at which point the trumpet fanfares would start.

It was fifteen minutes from when the Queen arrived to when she walked into the Abbey, signalling the beginning of the ceremony. As I stood behind her, I felt so unbelievably lucky. There I was, just happening to be the right person, in the right place, at the right time, quite literally attached to the Queen. Before she set off, a hush fell around the Queen, who stood in front of us, ten yards away from the Great West Door. Then she turned to us and said, 'Ready, girls?'

We nodded and off we went after her, disappearing into the Abbey. This was a very nervous moment because as the Queen set off we realised that she walked slightly slower than the Duchess of Norfolk, whom we had practised with for so many weeks. All of a sudden we were having to adjust our pace, but as we were all so in tune with each other, having walked together through so many rehearsals, we adjusted as one.

Fifty-five seconds later, when the Queen reached the Gothic Arch, the state trumpeters sounded, and the congregation stood up in unison. As we followed the Queen up the aisle, the choir sang Hubert Parry's almost seven-minute-long

anthem, 'I Was Glad', the choir boys now focused and reso-
nant, their voices ringing out the glory of the occasion.

The service had started perfectly, with the Archbishop
presenting the Queen to the congregation in the Recognition
– during which the Queen curtsied to all four sides of the
Abbey, a beautiful gesture and a rare one (though she does
bow twice to the peers at the State Opening of Parliament).
From there, the Queen took the oath, and was presented
with the Holy Bible before the most solemn part of the
service began: the Anointing. The Anointing is considered
the most vital part of any coronation, because, without this
sacred moment, the new King or Queen cannot be crowned.
So significant and so holy is it that, despite the traditional
canopy set up around her, held by four Knights of the
Garter, the cameras were diverted so she was hidden from
view, with only a handful of people, including me, able to
witness it.

Afterwards, the television cameras were allowed back and
the canopy removed. As the choir sang 'Zadok the Priest',
the Queen was de-robed by the Lord Great Chamberlain,
with help from the Mistress of the Robes, and a simple white
dress put on over the Coronation dress.

Time ran away with itself as the Queen was robed in a
cloth of gold, then presented with spurs that, as a female
Sovereign, she would never wear. We stood in the same place
while the different blessings and presentations took place,
ending with the Lord Great Chamberlain fastening the
poppers on the Queen's robes, then standing bolt upright,
showing off his handsome profile once more.

After the Queen had received the Regalia, it was time for
the Archbishop to crown her. In one movement, the 8,006
people in the congregation rose to their feet. This was the

moment the world had been waiting for. I am certain that every hair stood on end, every person held their breath, as the Archbishop held St Edward's Crown high above the Queen's head, his arms outstretched. As soon as the Archbishop placed the crown on the new Queen's head, the distinct silence that had fallen broke, replaced by 'God save the Queen!' ringing out in a wave of jubilant cries. There was a flurry of movement as all the peers and peeresses put on their coronets in a sweeping gesture.

Fanfares of trumpets added to the continuous cheers. Outside, the crowds shouted too, and the salutes could be heard, fired by artillery, the low boom of gunfire in the distance.

The rest of the service was a blur. After the enthroning and the homage, a full communion service commenced, and I remember singing 'All People That On Earth Do Dwell' with particular enthusiasm before the recess when we made our way to St Edward's Chapel. Inside the Chapel, the Queen took off St Edward's Crown, which weighed over four and a half pounds. That must have been a relief. There, she changed from the Robe Royal into her train of purple velvet, and the lighter Imperial State Crown – the one she wears at the State Opening of Parliament.

With the relief that the ceremony was almost over, a wave of happiness spread over me. As we followed the Queen down the aisle to Elgar's 'Pomp and Circumstance', the music captured the joyous element of the day perfectly. What was even more exciting than walking down the aisle was the moment we stepped outside the Abbey where we were greeted by the outside world. The sound reached fever pitch, so loud it felt as if the whole nation was entering into one massive long cheer.

Listen to the promises the Queen made, according to the Order of Service for the Coronation, in the Coronation Oath. In these days of fabulous spectaculars on television, or at the Oscars or Golden Globe ceremony, with crashing music and hyped-up hyperbole, it is sobering to see that in the greatest show on earth (well, in a way it was, it is) the solemn promises are quietly made before God as well as a billion people. When another Coronation takes place perhaps that service will not be as exclusively Christian as this one was. The world of different faiths has changed the United Kingdom for ever and for good.

The Queen having returned to her Chair (her Majesty having already on Tuesday, the 4th day of November, 1952, in the presence of the two Houses of Parliament, made and signed the Declaration prescribed by Act of Parliament), the Archbishop standing before her shall administer the Coronation Oath, first asking The Queen,

Madam, is your Majesty willing to take the Oath?

And The Queen answering,

I am willing.

The Archbishop shall minister these questions; and The Queen, having a book in her hands, shall answer each question severally as follows:

Archbishop. Will you solemnly promise and swear to govern the Peoples of the United Kingdom of Great Britain and Northern Ireland, Canada, Australia, New Zealand, the Union of South Africa, Pakistan, and Ceylon, and of your

Possessions and the other Territories to any of them belonging or pertaining, according to their respective laws and customs?

Queen. I solemnly promise so to do.

Archbishop. Will you to your power cause Law and Justice, in Mercy, to be executed in all your judgements?

Queen. I will.

Archbishop. Will you to the utmost of your power maintain the Laws of God and the true profession of the Gospel? Will you to the utmost of your power maintain in the United Kingdom the Protestant Reformed Religion established by law? Will you maintain and preserve inviolably the settlement of the Church of England, and the doctrine, worship, discipline, and government thereof, as by law established in England? And will you preserve unto the Bishops and Clergy of England, and to the Churches there committed to their charge, all such rights and privileges, as by law do or shall appertain to them or any of them?

Queen. All this I promise to do.

Then The Queen arising out of her Chair, supported as before, the Sword of State being carried before her, shall go to the Altar, and make her solemn Oath in the sight of all the people to observe the premisses: laying her right hand upon the Holy Gospel in the great Bible (which was before carried in the procession and is now brought from the Altar by the Archbishop, and tendered to her as she kneels upon the steps), and saying these words:

The things which I have here before promised, I will perform and keep. So help me God.

Then The Queen shall kiss the Book and sign the Oath.

The Queen having thus taken her Oath shall return again to her Chair, and the Bible shall be delivered to the Dean of Westminster.

All along the streets of London massed crowds were standing in the drizzle, waiting eagerly for the procession to pass by. The route back to Buckingham Palace had been published in advance: the best vantage points had long since been nabbed by people camping on pavements, but everyone was cheerfully jostling and making way for each other to catch a treasured glimpse of the newly crowned Queen. Jane Fabb was in the crowds right outside the Abbey. Her memory is taken from *Long to Reign Over Us*, a collection of Coronation memories gathered by Kenneth and Valerie McLeish.

At last, after the escorts had ridden by, the Queen, wearing the Imperial State Crown, came out with Philip, still in his Admiral's hat. We yelled! They got into the coach and juggled a bit with the Orb, which she couldn't seem to get hold of. The Queen looked tired and the crown seemed to press her down; she didn't smile and wave as she had on her arrival, but she still looked beautiful. Philip is gorgeous and much broader than I thought. The Coronation coach is like something out of *Cinderella*, but the gold is a bit brassy.

A little further along the road on the damp Embankment, where sooty plane trees dipped their branches towards the river, and the lamp-posts still bore the traces of war, with shattered glass and peeling columns, young Eileen Cottrell (her memory is also taken from *Long to Reign Over Us*) was watching, wearing her school uniform and madly waving her flag:

> Was it imagination or had she really seen me? Was she really waving just to me? In that fleeting moment I was sure our eyes had met. Was it possible that she had noticed Eileen Cottrell, aged thirteen, from Form 1110 [*sic*] of the Lady Edridge Grammar School?

After the five-mile journey, clip-clopping through the rain behind the eight grey horses, which had behaved immaculately, the heavy golden coach turned into the courtyard of Buckingham Palace. Was the Queen's face stiff from smiling, her arm tired from waving? Did she catch Eileen Cottrell's eye as the coach rumbled past at a steady pace?

Once, at an event at the Royal Academy, the traffic had suddenly ground to a halt and the taxi-driver who was taking my husband and me to join Her Majesty (and a thousand others) in celebration of her Golden Jubilee advised us to get out and walk. We were now hopelessly late. The evening was hot and muggy, the traffic jam stretched as far as the eye could see. Gasping, we dashed along Piccadilly and turned under the great archway into the Royal Academy just as the royal car swept out. 'Oh, oh!' I cried. 'Oh, Your Majesty!' and I curtsied to the great limousine. At that moment, Eileen, the Queen looked straight at me and her eyes lit up as she smiled her famous smile. Eileen, she *did* see us: I know she did.

Then the next part of the never-ending Coronation Day began. Up the steps and into the Palace, Lady Anne Coke was thanking her lucky stars for the fortune of being a Maid of Honour.

Inside Buckingham Palace there was a similar sense of excitement as there had been in Westminster Abbey, but it was markedly more relaxed. Although it was still formal, there wasn't the feeling of a whole nation holding their breath, and without the television cameras, it was easier to enjoy what was going on. The role of Maid of Honour continued to be one of great privilege because staying at the Queen's side meant we were right there to see everybody.

Prince Charles and Princess Anne were ushered in to see the Queen and, straight away, they dashed under her dress. The Queen didn't mind a bit. She was walking on air, although when she took off her crown and placed it on a table designated for the job, Prince Charles made a beeline for it, diving on it with great enthusiasm. Somebody – it might well have been my mother – got the crown from the clutches of the Heir Presumptive, and put it back on the table.

Just as in the Abbey, time ran away with itself. Soon I and the other Maids of Honour were following the Queen down one of the long, wide corridors of the Palace, on our way to be photographed. The Queen was so full of excitement that she started running so we all ran with her. Equally spontaneously, she sat down on a red sofa in the gallery, her dress billowing and settling down around her. We sat with her, and when she kicked up her legs for total joy, we did the same. It was the happiest of moments.

The Duke of Edinburgh had wanted his friend Baron to

take the photographs, but the Queen Mother was very fond of Cecil Beaton so she had overridden him. The Duke began to make a great deal of fuss, being frightfully bossy again, telling us where to stand and when to smile. Cecil Beaton was very commanding behind the camera. He was well known for taking a dislike to interfering comments, and the more the Duke of Edinburgh tried to have his say, the tetchier he became.

The Duke persisted, either not realising or not caring that he was disrupting the photographer, and eventually Cecil Beaton snapped. He put down his camera, glared at the Duke of Edinburgh and said, 'Sir, if you would like to take the photographs, please do.' He then gestured to the camera and started to walk away. The Queen looked horrified, as did the Queen Mother, and realising he had gone too far, the Duke of Edinburgh moved off.

When the photographs were finally over, the Queen stepped on to the balcony and we went with her. This felt like one of the most momentous parts of the whole day. The crowd was enormous – there wouldn't have been enough space to put a pin between the people – stretching right down to Admiralty Arch and covering St James's Park. As soon as the Queen walked out, the crowd cheered so loudly I could physically feel the noise hitting us on the balcony.

As I stood there, it struck me that the cheers marked the beginning of a new Elizabethan age. We'd been through the war and we were still suffering from it, but this day was one to celebrate.

The Queen was visibly moved by the reception and her eyes shone as she took in the nation's support. Along with the crowd below, we lifted our eyes heavenward to watch the planes as they flew over the Palace, dipping their wings towards the Queen. The pilots were among those who had survived the war. And not only had they survived but they had saved us all from peril. And, as if we were one, we all knew it. Their actions had enabled the day to take place, so the flypast was a magnificent tribute, simultaneously a look to the future and a reminder that we had escaped, that we were free and at peace. It was confirmation that we could all, as a nation, put the war behind us. I could see and feel the Queen's pride as we all shared a distinct feeling of unity and hope.

Cecil Beaton has a different memory from Lady Anne. He doesn't report the snappy response to the Duke of Edinburgh's organisation of the group photograph in his diary. Their recollections vary, but only slightly. This is how history is made, different people reporting the same event from their own standpoints. You can get a good idea of how it all was from Beaton's frantic marshalling of the royal ones to get the pictures he had been commissioned to do for the whole world's press. (He doesn't use the phrase 'herding cats' as that would have been lèse majesté, so I shall not use it now.) The strain of this stupendous responsibility took its toll on him that afternoon.

Rain had fallen solidly throughout most of the ceremony. Uniforms were soaked, horses champing; the Golden Coach was now waiting in Dean's Yard in a downpour. The men in cockaded hats and livery were making little effort to keep out of the rain. I made my getaway before the traffic started.

Back home, I found my mother listening to the radio announcer's banal, genteel, rich-fruit-cake voice: 'On this, this great day . . .'

I rushed upstairs, took a fistful of aspirins, then off with my clothes and I was able to sleep for nearly an hour before dashing again to the Palace for the photographs.

I awoke minus my headache and much relaxed. Again managing to avoid the crowds, within a comparatively short while I found myself at the tradesmen's entrance of the Palace, to be shown up to our now almost familiar haven in the Green Drawing Room. My sister, Baba, who in the inevitable absence of Maud [Nelson], my secretary, had kindly offered to help arrange the trains, presented a miserable spectacle, chattering with cold and rain-soaked. Thank God the others – the electricians and assistants – had also contrived to be here. Pat Matthews [Beaton's assistant] was calm and reassuring. From the balcony of the inner courtyard we watched the return of the carriages. Baba was proud that David Smiley, our brother-in-law, was the Field Officer commanding the Escort.

Every window framed the faces of Palace servants, and a group of them raised a tremendous cheer as the Queen Mother came back, waving and smiling as fresh as a field flower. Then, to the sound of distant roars, drawn by eight grey horses the bronze gold State Coach, with its Cipriano paintings and dark-strawberry padded silk, bowled through the central arch and back to home. The Queen looked back over her shoulder and appeared somewhat dazed and exhausted.

Not long after, girlish voices were heard at the end of the Picture Gallery. 'Oh, hello! Did you watch it? When did you get home?' From the mirror-doors of the Green Drawing Room I spied the Queen with her ladies, her excited children; the family asking questions, jokes, smiles, laughter, the high-pitched voices of the Queen and Princess Margaret heard above the others. The Duchess of Gloucester was leaning forward from the hips with almost perilous intent. The Duke of Norfolk, his duties successfully carried out, lolled behind one of the mirrored-glass doors. George Bellew, Garter King-at-Arms, leaned against the brocade walls. The fair, good-looking Duke of Hamilton beamed.

It was now time for the Queen to be on her way to the Throne Room to be photographed by *The Times* – then she would come to me. I started taking family groups. The Queen Mother, dimpled and chuckling, with eyes as bright as any of her jewels, and her younger daughter, with pink and white make-up and a sex twinkle of understanding in her regard, was now sailing towards me, her purple train being held aloft by her four pages; Prince Charles and Princess Anne, who were running around to try and get a hold on it, eventually had recourse to climbing under the purple velvet. No time to lose! Please turn this way, now that; a certain shape was formed, a picture came to life. Quick, quick! All sorts of royalties popped their heads in on me: Prince Bernhard; then the Duke of Edinburgh put his face through a door. 'But you must come! You're keeping the whole group waiting!' Exit Princess Margaret and the Queen Mother. Through the mirrored doors I watched the guests in the long Picture Gallery.

Then the return of the Queen Mother in rollicking spirits, and slow voice asking: 'Do you really want to take a few more?' Suddenly I felt as if all my anxieties and fears were dispelled. The Queen Mother, by being so basically human and understanding, gives out to us a feeling of reassurance. The great mother figure and nanny to us all, through the warmth of her sympathy bathes us and wraps us in a counterpane by the fireside. Suddenly I had this wonderful accomplice – someone who would help me through everything. All at once, and because of her, I was enjoying my work. Prince Charles and Princess Anne were buzzing about in the wildest excitement and would not keep still for a moment. The Queen Mother anchored them in her arms, put her head down to kiss Prince Charles's hair, and made a terrific picture. Then, ashen-faced and like the wicked uncle in a pantomime, Richard Colville, who deals so sternly with all of us who are in any way connected with the press, appeared prematurely and, as if to sound my death-knell, informed me: 'The Queen has already been kept waiting. You must take the Queen now!'

In came the Queen, with her ladies, cool, smiling, sovereign of the situation. I asked her to stand against my 'blow-up' Abbey background. The lighting was not at all as I would have wished, but no time for readjustments: every second of importance. Yes, I was banging away and getting pictures at a great rate; but I had only the foggiest notion of whether I was taking black-and-white, or colour, or giving the right exposures. The Queen looked extremely minute under her robes and Crown, her nose and hands chilled, and her eyes tired. 'Yes,' in reply to my question, 'the Crown does get rather heavy.' She had been wearing it now for nearly three hours.

The Duke of Edinburgh stood by making wry jokes, his lips pursed in a smile that put the fear of God into me. I believe he doesn't like or approve of me. This is a pity because, although I'm not one for 'Navy type' jokes, and obviously have nothing in common with him, I admire him enormously, and think he is absolutely first-rate at his job of making things comparatively lively and putting people at their ease. Perhaps he was disappointed that his friend, Baron, was not doing this job today; whatever the reason he was definitely adopting a rather ragging attitude towards the proceedings. However, I tried in the few seconds at my disposal (like a vaudeville comedian establishing contact with his audience) to keep the situation light and full of movement so that no one could adopt any definite attitude: like a juggler I moved the groups about. Photographs of the Duke alone; he looked extremely handsome. Once I replied, in a cursory manner to the Queen's 'What shall we do now?'

'Will you go into the corner?'

'Go into the corner?' She looked at me with wide eyes and a wide smile. No time for explanation.

Now to the other side of the room: the Queen and her Maids of Honour. Quickly, quickly, because this was just about the end.

'You must be tired, ma'am.'

'Yes, but this is the last thing we have to do.'

While the entire family retired to watch the 'flypast' of the RAF from the balcony (which we watched, too, from the inner balcony), Baba and my assistants toasted the Queen from a glass of champagne from which the monarch had only taken one sip.

A panic-stricken page came in: 'Where are the Orb and Sceptre?' They had been left here on a cushion.

Other groups then appeared. Princess Marina, romantically beautiful and remarkably distinguished but sad, and incapable of keeping her children in a vein of seriousness: they all joked and made staccato noises. It was difficult not to get exasperated with my delightful friends, but they, poor things, were at the end of a long, tiring, possibly unnerving day; they confessed their feet hurt.

It is hard enough to give instructions when taking large groups in circumstances like these, but when one is challenged, and asked for a reason why one's instinct has prodded one to say, 'Move over there,' then chaos ensues. The Gloucesters came in with the two boys pulling their mother's train in every direction. The Duke, in his crown, red and shining of complexion, looked like an *Alice in Wonderland* character.

'Will you stand on that step, sir?'

'But won't I look too tall?'

'Yes, sir, you're perfectly right. Won't you stand down there on that step?'

'Well, if the others are going to be there, won't I look too short?'

I then suggested that perhaps he might open his cape to let me see more of his uniform.

'I don't think I could do that.'

'No, sir?'

'Well, as a matter of fact, I've got the wrong ribbon [wibbon].'

'Which ribbon, sir?'

'This wibbon wight across here.' His eyes protruded and lips quivered.

But the Gloucesters were chivvied off quickly for the Queen was available again for a few more pictures to be taken, this time sitting at a table on which were placed my by-now rather sad-looking 'Étoile d'Hollande' roses and the wilting 'Jackmanii' clematis from Reddish.

Now that's all.

For better or worse I'd had my chance.

I felt somewhat dissatisfied; the sensation of achievement had escaped me all day long. Now I wondered if I had got any worthwhile pictures. Except with the Queen Mother and her grandchildren, I felt I'd never become airborne. The bulk of my pictures had been a smash-and-grab affair. I couldn't imagine they would be successful. Not only was I depressed, but rather alarmed. If the results weren't sensationally good, the press would attack me bitterly for having failed with such a fine opportunity. Yes – a unique opportunity had been afforded me. Had I misused the trust?

The rain poured. Still the crowds roared and the Queen reappeared on the balcony. Baba and I went home utterly whacked. But I had now to wire a description of the Abbey proceedings for syndication to Australia and Canada. Luckily I had written a considerable amount of local colour material beforehand; even so, the chore took me longer than expected, and the cables were late relaying through my accounts. No sooner were these sent off than Siriol Hugh Jones arrived with a shorthand-typist from *Vogue*. Siriol suggested an article was not necessary: that 'Notes from the Abbey' would be more spontaneous. I agreed with relief. When the 'Notes' were finished, we drank champagne and talked over the day's events with excitement. After midnight I went to the Massigli party at the French Embassy. I ate enormously; I drank a lot. At three o'clock in the morning I rang up the studio to hear that they were delighted with the colour pictures of the Queen; they thought I, too, would be pleased. I went to sleep relieved.

Early-morning visit to the studio to be surprised to find that so many of the pictures were excellent. A heavy morning's work selecting the best and getting them to the Palace; by midday a number of them were passed for publication. The rest of the week was a complicated nightmare trying to supply to the press the requisite number of pictures. Messengers were waiting in the various rooms of my mother's house for another messenger who never arrived. I talked myself hoarse on the telephone, and only by a fraction of a minute did I catch the Friday-evening train to make my getaway to the retreat of the country. I bought an evening paper at Waterloo station and one of my pictures of the Queen was printed across the front page of the *Evening News*.

All around the country there were parties and street festivals to celebrate this great day. In Malaya, Malaysia as it is now, the Army School I attended had a fancy-dress parade. My mother had made costumes for my sister and me on her Singer sewing machine, which I still have: I can hear now the thrum of the hand-turned wheel as she stitched, late at night, listening to *Desert Island Discs* as it was transmitted across the Commonwealth. We went as little Norwegian girls, with aprons edged in rick-rack and our long hair plaited up around our heads.

After the Coronation film was shown, it was odd to hear some grown-ups talking nostalgically of those wet grey London streets as home: home for me was the jungle near our bungalow, the bazaars and sluggish yellow river, the airstrip in front of our house and the Chinese grave behind the tin-mine. It was Fraser's Hill, where monkeys whooped as we climbed higher and higher to the cooler air, travelling in a convoy of armoured cars, as the hills and kampongs might be full of bandits.

But what an impression that film made on us! The Duke of Edinburgh, as handsome as any fairy-tale prince, and the bejewelled nobles, the golden carriage and the great glittering crown and then . . . the tiny central character of the Queen herself, moving slowly down the aisle, while crowds roared. Much later, sixty years later, at a party thrown in his honour to celebrate his birthday, I made a short speech telling the Duke of Edinburgh that because of his appearance in the Coronation film he had immediately become the template for all the heroes I would subsequently read about in books: Julian in Enid Blyton's Famous Five, Mr Darcy in *Pride and Prejudice*, and Max de Winter from *Rebecca*. He laughed a great deal. The title 'liege-lord' seemed to me to be even more potent than 'king' would have been. Because I was young it never crossed my mind that not being crowned could be seen as a slight in any way. Prince Philip, Duke of Edinburgh, carried his titles and position throughout his long life with the greatest humility and nonchalance, a tremendous combination.

I think we all wrote essays about our impressions of the Great Day, sitting under swirling fans in our hot veranda classrooms, trying to imagine what it would be like to be in England. Far across the sea, thirteen-year-old Mary McLay wrote an account for Mass Observation, a social research project which gathers records of everyday life in Britain, entitling her composition 'What I did on Coronation Day'.

On Coronation Day I watched the television. We invited fourteen people which included five children. We watched the procession and service in the morning, the five-mile procession in the afternoon and the summary of the Coronation and fire-works at night.

We were given a box of chocolates with a picture of the Queen on the lid and a tin of toffees with a picture of the Queen on horseback on the side. My sister and I have a Coronation mug each and the handle is in the shape of a lion wearing a crown.

My mother made a very special dinner for us, which

included a salad with Scotch eggs and shrimp patties which everybody enjoyed.

It was very late at night when I got into bed and everybody told Daddy and Mummy how much they enjoyed it and how very pleased they were to have been able to come.

By now a trusted BBC reporter, who had covered the funeral of the late King, Audrey Russell stayed behind in the Abbey after the congregation had departed.

In the still after the storm, she had time to note the aftermath of the event as she wandered through the huge almost-deserted church.

It was a bonus to be left behind. My senses were uplifted and I walked up the Nave nearly as far as the High Altar, past rows of empty blue velvet chairs. Already a few cleaners were beginning to tidy up, to straighten the chairs and clear away litter left behind, before the public were permitted to see the setting built into the Abbey for the Coronation, the barriers covered with blue silk damask creating gangways between the rows of seats which filled the entire Nave and rose tier upon tier almost to the ceiling of the Triforium for the congregation of 8,000 people.

A very great deal has been said over the centuries about litter left behind at Coronations (refreshments have always been a problem). Richard Dimbleby, as he left the Abbey, said he was shocked to see sandwich wrappings, toffee papers, morning newspapers ('All this and Everest too'), and even miniature gin bottles under some of the chairs. As I wandered about ahead of the cleaners I saw relatively little mess and have put it down to typical journalistic exaggeration. Admittedly, on that day I had not yet heard how someone had asked the Lord Great Chamberlain if packets of sandwiches could be carried in a coronet. The reply was that 'It is undesirable but permissible.' One peer at least must have regretted taking advantage of this pronouncement, for when he joined his fellow peers simultaneously putting on their caps and coronets he heard a soft thud and, looking down, saw a plastic-covered triangular package at his feet.

I returned to the Annexe. The swirling crowds outside the huge west window were now allowed much closer to the glass and there was a great sea of faces looking in at emptiness: the Queen had left the Abbey to drive through the wet streets to Buckingham Palace.

The heavy curtains leading to the robing rooms were now pulled back. Greatly daring and feeling like Alice going through the looking-glass into another world, I went in. The now empty dressing rooms had a faintly theatrical look with big mirrors and strong electric lights. The Queen's robing room looked very tidy and quite bare save for an arrangement of golden roses set on a small table near the looking-glass. In the room shared by the Queen Mother and Princess Margaret there were some sheets of discarded tissue paper about, and a beautiful spray of Odontoglossum orchids nestled in an open cardboard box on the dressing-table. Was this a gift sent direct to the Abbey? More likely, a case of second thoughts . . . 'How beautiful, but no, not to be worn on this occasion.'

I could hear the sound of some clearing up, the chink of silver and the clatter of plates, and exploring further discovered a small octagonal dining room in the royal private apartments. It was here that the Queen and the close members of her family had enjoyed what was later described to me officially as 'a very simple packed lunch brought from the Palace'.

A footman was clearing a large round table, covered with a white damask cloth. In the centre of the table was the perfect still-life of flowers, a simple bunch of philadelphus in a small basket, a few petals already dropping from the little cup-shaped flowers. The fragrance was reminiscent of orange blossom.

The table was laid for ten, perhaps twelve, people, and chairs were now pushed back; there were crumpled table napkins around, empty glasses and quite a lot of crumbs. I believe it would be plain to anyone where the Queen had been sitting at that round table, and the young footman shyly confirmed it when I asked if I was right. Characteristically, Her Majesty's chair was set quite straight, her table napkin had not even been unfolded, there were no crumbs and a wine glass was still three-quarters full of champagne.

4. The Queen on Tour

The scale and splendour of royal tours, either here or overseas, cannot be exaggerated. Planning and mapping, arranging lists and protocols, timetables and presentations are all stage-managed to a degree that would leave you breathless. Sometimes it will be the one and only time the Queen visits a country or island. Sometimes, as in this vivid memoir from R. J. Prickett, it will be a return to a place that has a special memory for the Queen, in this case Treetops Hotel in Kenya, where she had learned of the death of her father the King more than thirty years before. Prickett was a British civil servant who left the service of the Kenyan government in 1968 after twenty-two years as a forester and game warden. He became assistant hunter at Treetops. The Queen had not visited since the day she found out that she was no longer a princess but a reigning monarch. Now, in 1983, much had changed, but even more was wonderfully familiar to her.

When Princess Elizabeth, in 1952, had excitedly waved to a small group of people and shouted, 'I will come again,' she had no idea it would be so long before she could keep that promise. She had enjoyed what she described as her most thrilling night and was totally unaware that she was no longer a princess but an uncrowned queen. From the moment she was informed of the fact by her husband, in the Royal Lodge, Sagana, she must have realised that she could no longer be a carefree princess, able to wander at will, but must be a monarch, reigning over an Empire upon which the sun never set. How well she subsequently ruled, and how deeply she was to be revered by people in what was changing, even then, from Empire to Commonwealth, by a process of evolution beginning in bloodshed but ending in respect, is, perhaps, best illustrated by an incident that occurred along the Airport Road outside Nairobi when she returned to Kenya in November 1983. She was on an official five-day visit, having been invited by Kenya's President Moi during his state visit to Britain some five years earlier.

The welcome the citizens of Kenya gave to Her Majesty that day was remarkable, with every inch of the road from the city centre lined with singing, chanting, flag-waving children, and millions of cheering adults of many races, for Kenya today is very much a multi-racial country. The flags of both Kenya and Britain were much in evidence. For hours officials had been going around with huge bundles of them, placing one of each in the hands of the children, regardless of whether they were African, Asian, Arab, Somali or European. It was certainly a day of rejoicing long to be remembered.

Countries which do not have a monarch, and which do not belong to a commonwealth, often fail to grasp the hold those two institutions have over the minds of their people and, failing to understand, are often jealous and try to belittle their significance. A gentleman of that kind stood near as the royal car approached. A little African girl was jumping up and down with a Union Jack in one hand and the Kenya flag in the other, waving them both enthusiastically. The gentleman pointed to the Union Jack and exclaimed: 'What have you got that for? Don't you know they were your colonial masters?' The little girl jumped higher still, and waved her two flags more enthusiastically than ever, and shouted: 'But she's our Queen! She's our Queen!'

Prickett went on to recall the arrival of the royal party at Treetops.

It is a steep climb through the forest before the track reaches the Treetops car park. We heard the vehicles of the royal party stop for a while where there is a small pool, and that meant Her Majesty was late. The press were later to assert that she was late because she was loath to make a return trip to Treetops. We who were there know that it was simply because a big herd of water-buck was drinking and she wanted to stop and watch them. Eventually we heard the two escorting police cars come roaring up the hill. The area of the car park is small and is encircled on three sides by trees, and there was almost a smash as they skidded into it. I heard the police captain standing on my right mutter, 'The — fools', and instinctively I turned around. Almost before I had time to recover, the royal Range Rover, pennant flying, was beside me, and the Queen was alighting unassisted. [The provincial warden, Wilfred Asava] muttered: 'This is your hunter, Your Majesty', and my greatest moment had arrived. I heard myself, in answer to her greeting, saying in a very small voice, 'Thank you, Your Majesty.' Instantly HRH Prince Philip, Duke of Edinburgh, followed with a vigorous handshake so different from the touch that protocol dictates for the Queen.

Seconds later, loaded rifle pointing skywards and held firmly by the pistol-grip, I was walking beside Her Majesty, with Wilfred Asava and the Duke following. My mind was in a turmoil. I felt as proud as a strutting turkey, but was aware of the necessity to watch all sides for dangerous animals. Once, as tourists left the car park, a rhino had come round the first bend like a puffing train, and had only been turned aside by a bullet over the ear accompanied by yelling. I had to guide Her Majesty around the stones and elephant droppings – more than one excited tourist has turned an ankle on the path. And above all I had to listen attentively to all she had to say, though I knew it would not be the foolish prattling of city tourists, who, with an elephant near, so often insist on asking, 'Is that a water-buffalo?' when it is merely a forest hog, and other such inanities . . .

The press had drawn lots the previous evening to decide which of the only two positions allocated to them for the Treetops visit each person would go to. These were 'on the ground' and 'on the Treetops roof' and, after setting up their positions before the Queen's arrival in these two places, they were not permitted to move around. No members of the press were allowed actually inside the building, and those taking up their positions on the roof had to remain there during the Queen's arrival below, while she was inside Treetops signing the visitors' book and looking at Corbett Corner in the lounge, and after she had left the rooftop for her historic walk back to the old site. Not all were happy about this as it would not allow them to hear every word that was said, but they took it in good part and replaced words they could not hear and sights they could not see with the products of their fertile imaginations.

Press and television cameras on the rooftop were able to

obtain pictures in beautiful sunlight of Her Majesty cutting the magnificent thirty-pound [fourteen-kilogram] 'welcome back' cake, which turned out to be a daunting task with a small cake knife. Quickly sizing up the situation at the outset, the Duke had said urgently, 'Fetch the chef,' and 'Call the chef, call the chef,' had echoed along the rooftop from mouth to mouth until it reached Eamon Mullan, Block Hotel's chief executive chef, who was in the background, and who immediately sprang forward to assist. Every published photograph shows him, the Queen and Prince Philip laughing over the ridiculous situation of the too-firm icing and the too-fragile knife.

The members of the press on the ground had the advantage of being able to witness much more closely than their colleagues on the rooftop the walk to the old site – and the buffalo. Those on the rooftop could only see it from a lofty distance.

When the last member of the royal party entered Treetops, those members of the press who had been allocated a place on the ground on the other side of the pool surged across the salt-lick like excited children, led by the assistant hunter Paolo Bindi, an experienced man. Paolo is an Italian. Forty-three years ago [fairly early in the Second World War] I was chasing his people out of what was then Abyssinia and Somaliland. But that is now all well into the past. We no longer talk about it, just as there are things I no longer talk about with my Kikuyu fellow-workers at Treetops, whose people, the Mau Mau, burned down the old Treetops two years after the Queen's first visit. I played a part in that fighting too. Thirty years can heal even the hardest of feelings. We are all good friends now and the past is history.

In the general excitement, everybody had forgotten that

silent spectator of the Queen's return – the dominant old bull Satan, whose companion had been near us at the beginning of the walk. Throughout the ceremony of the presentation he had stood on the salt-lick glowering, totally oblivious to all the noise, and he had no intention of being driven away to allow the Queen to cross later, or the press photographers to advance now. (I once saw such a buffalo bull argue with a rhino until the blood from constant jabbings of the latter's horn ran down his face.) There were two other bulls further back, but they cleared off immediately, and gave no further trouble. It was a ludicrous situation, but deadly serious – a buffalo bull standing up to an armed hunter and a mob of forty members of the press, each weighed down by cameras and incapable of running. Satan would retreat a few yards, then swing around and stand defiant once more.

The situation was reaching danger point, and I raced over to assist Paolo. If mayhem was to be avoided, and if a killing had to be done, then it was absolutely essential that the bull went down clean. However, when stones had been thrown he finally took the hint and departed.

By the time I returned to the Treetops building many precious minutes had been lost. Originally it had been planned that I would hurry up the fire-escape and be ready to explain to Her Majesty the Corbett Corner I had created in the Treetops lounge. Jim Corbett is still remembered and revered all over northern India, and I do not doubt for a moment that Her Majesty has never forgotten that he was her final choice of a guest in 1952, or that India honoured him by calling her first national park after him. I had signed the visitors' book in his old home, and had a lot to tell her. A voice was calling, 'Mr Prickett is wanted upstairs,' but I knew it was too late, for already I could see the royal party returning to the steps. Once again well-laid plans had gone awry.

As I joined the Queen and the Duke to escort them over to the site of the old Treetops, I again took my place on her right-hand side, trying to keep her eager steps in check and away from the worst of the rough ground. She appeared to be wanting to find the path of yesteryear, and kept heading towards the distant forest instead of around the pool and towards the old site as planned. Elephant droppings, stones and stumps were scattered everywhere, but she detected them and trod lightly, and had little need of my guiding hand. Of course she was concerned about the retreat of the forest, and we discussed ways of arresting it at some length, but she also knew that the population of Kenya has more than trebled since 1952, that the tropical rain-forests of the world are but a pitiful remnant of their former splendour, that nearly half a million people have rejoiced seeing the overabundance of animals around Treetops, and that these factors had made environmental change inevitable. I told her many people were concerned, and that plans were afoot to arrest the retreat.

Wart-hogs, bush-buck and baboons were everywhere, and each group we encountered drew admiring comments from the Queen. The baboons had been absent, raiding the crops of the local farmers across the boundary ditch in spite of its electric fence. Today they were present in strength, having forgotten the ripening maize. She asked me about those buffalo bulls, and I described them as just retired old gentlemen. This amused her greatly, and she passed my answer to the Duke, who was walking much nearer the water with Wilfred Asava, calling back, 'Philip, Philip, he says it is all right, they are just retired old gentlemen.' I had noted every stone beforehand, and soon we were on the spot indicated by the press for perfect photography.

The press were lined up with Paolo Bindi behind a thick white rope some thirty paces further on. They had carefully measured the distance the day before, and placed a tiny twig on the ground. Here I halted, and pointed to the new Treetops across the water, and the gesture drew a barrage from those clicking cameras. Then we arrived at the site of the old Treetops, and I suddenly became aware that the dominant old bull, Satan, though driven off the salt-lick to make way for the Queen, had not left the area but stood facing us some fifty yards [forty-five metres] further on. With Paolo Bindi now so near me, I knew that between us we had sufficient fire-power for any emergency. I pointed Satan out to Her Majesty, and Queen and buffalo stared at each other for a long, long minute.

And then a strange thing happened. Satan, who had been resolutely staring at the Queen, suddenly started walking *towards* us, and just as I was beginning nervously to grip the rifle, he stopped at what was now little more than twenty paces away. Then an even more wondrous thing happened. He started to kneel down facing Her Majesty, with hindquarters high in the air, and I remember muttering, with suspended breath, 'He's going to lie down.' The next moment he threw himself sideways, still facing us. I know that buffalo always lie that way, but to me that kneeling down was an act of supplication to the Queen, and maybe his apology for being so rude as to keep her waiting on the salt-lick.

The Queen turned abruptly and I walked over with her to the stones, pointing out the concrete blocks that were mute reminders of the 1954 fire that had destroyed the building and much of the fig-tree. Those blocks had been necessary as a base for the poles that steadied the tree, for two extra rooms had had to be added to accommodate the 1952 royal party, and each block had an eight-inch [200-millimetre] hole in the centre. All this I explained to her while she stood in silence, deep in her own thoughts. I do not think she grieved, though she had loved her father so dearly. But thirty-one years, almost thirty-two, was in 1983 a little more than half her lifetime. The press did not have to twist events to their own conclusions. Finally the Queen turned away and we headed back to the new Treetops.

It was now that the full significance of this historic event suddenly struck me. Over a hundred elephants had stood on and around the salt-lick at 7.30 a.m. that very morning, and Paolo Bindi had had great difficulty getting all the tourists out safely, finally having to use the big bus. In that mighty throng, the biggest that rainy season, there *must* have been some elephants who were present in 1952, and who without those fourteen rangers patrolling would undoubtedly have returned. Even as I thought these thoughts a big herd of those regal antelopes, the water-buck, was trooping down to drink and I pointed them out to the Queen.

On our return walk across the glade the Queen brightened, and we talked of many things. I found myself telling her about Tiger Tops, in Nepal, and the many wonderful animals I had seen there; of Alaska and its bears, and how, when salmon-fishing a small river, I had been confronted in midstream at a bend by a huge Brownie, the very grandfather of all Alaskan brown bears, and how I had been compelled to climb a tree to save my fish. The account of my undignified ascent amused her. I will remember that genuine laugh as long as I live. Then she suddenly stopped, and said that she had only seen those animals in zoos. It struck me forcibly that I, a mere commoner, with limited financial resources, could see them whenever I wished. I had wings, while she, monarch of a nation of 60 million people, and head of a Commonwealth of 1,000 million more, had to bow to protocol. I am sure she enjoyed those few minutes ahead on our own, away from the press and even from the Duke and Asava, and away, even if only for such a brief spell, from the pomp and splendour surrounding her normal life.

All too soon we reached the car park and my finest hour was over. But before this happened something occurred that emphasised the Queen's unfailing charm. As we joined the hard path the remainder of the royal party, press, security people and the Block Hotels top brass came surging behind. As we actually reached the vehicles I dropped back among them, for my mission was now over. For a few paces the Queen carried on, then she turned back, threaded her way through the throng, smiled at me, shook hands, and thanked me before bidding me farewell. Amid frantic waving the last vehicle went down the hill and suddenly the car park was empty. They were gone.

Here in Britain we rather like the huge spectacle of royalty in full glory: Trooping the Colour, the Changing of the Guard, the Opening of Parliament. We are used to it. We tut-tut at traffic disruption and sigh as roads are diverted. We take it all for granted. But far away and long ago, a visit from the Queen was not far short of a fairy tale come true.

After the Coronation in 1953 the Queen and Prince Philip set off on a mammoth Commonwealth tour, leaving their two small children, Prince Charles and Princess Anne, behind. That was the way then: that was how it was done. They started in Bermuda, in November 1953.

There, the *Royal Gazette* had a banner headline: 'Our Proudest Moment'.

This ancient Colony has had the proudest moment in its 344 years of history.

Our beautiful and gracious young Queen and her handsome Consort, who already had our deep loyalty and admiration, have now won our hearts completely.

Queen Elizabeth II, honouring Bermuda by making it her first point of call on her tour of the Commonwealth, has awakened in us deeper emotions than most of us suspected we had. A new surge of love and loyalty, of pride in our British tradition and hope for the future – a new Elizabethan Age under the leadership and inspiration of a gallant young Queen – has risen from our hearts.

Everywhere the Queen and her Consort, the Duke of Edinburgh, went on Tuesday in their one-day tour of the Colony they were greeted by a devoted people. Bermudians are not demonstrative. The cheers and shouts of London crowds were perhaps missing – but our people had lumps in their throats and tears in their eyes that were more truly eloquent signs of their love and the thrill of pride shared by us all.

This was the first visit to the Colony of a reigning Sovereign. We have had Royal visitors before – and they have had a Royal welcome here. But never before has there been such rejoicing. Never before have we had here with us the living symbol of our unity with the British people everywhere – and never before have we felt so deeply all that that means to us and how right we are to glory in it.

I can remember before the Coronation, when other members of the Royal Family visited Commonwealth countries, Princess Marina and the young Duke of Kent came to Malaya, and were received with all the pomp and splendour that could be mustered. Dinners in full evening dress, medals, parades, speeches and presentations: my sister and I watched our mother getting ready to go to King's House where everyone you could think of waited for the royal visitors. 'Don't muss my hair,' she said, as she spread her nails to dry, and we leaned forward to kiss her and smell her scent. I thought she looked like a queen herself, in a white tight-waisted long dress and a choker of what *had* to be diamonds dripping with pearls: they were paste but, gosh, how they glittered! My father wore his regimental white dress uniform with a black patent leather Sam Browne belt over one shoulder, all gleaming with silver chains and a whistle. The impact of a royal visit is inestimable.

In New Zealand, they waited on tenterhooks. The Queen and Prince Philip arrived in December, stayed for Christmas, and left at the end of January. The New Zealand Ministry for Culture and Heritage gathered the following stories, the first from the then little Judith Foy.

I was nine at the time of the Queen's visit in 1953 to 1954. My sister and I were in the Brownies and I remember clearly her visit to Palmerston North. We waited for what seemed like hours at Milverton Park for the young Queen to pass us by. Suddenly an urgent whisper went through the crowd: 'She is coming.' The black car passed us at quite a speed, but all I could say in my young thoughts was, My gosh, she is beautiful . . . [T]here was magic in the air all over the country and people went crazy over the Queen. Large adoring crowds went everywhere and my mother went to wait outside the Grand Hotel to see her come out on to the small balcony. Everyone was calling, 'We want the Queen.' One small voice was heard to cry, 'We want the Duke' – which really amused my mother at the time. She was so involved with the magic of it all also.

A lasting memory of that visit was of the Queen and Duke leaving Palmerston North on the train. They both stood on the back of the guard wagon waving goodbye. One man ran along the tracks after them in a sort of desperate farewell to a loved one. I think everyone felt the same and we went home with a real feeling of isolation and loss. They were wonderful times and the young people of today who insult and throw off at royalty have really lost something of our heritage which in many ways we should be proud of.

Cherrill Suckling, daughter of a dairy farmer, was in Palmerston too. The kindness of a stranger made her memory extra bright.

In the evening the Queen and Duke of Edinburgh drove around the Palmerston North Square from the Grand Hotel where they were staying to their evening reception. I had seen the Queen during her afternoon drive around the city but then we had to go home for my father to milk. We rushed back into town and I was still walking with my mother when we heard the cheering. I ran ahead to the crowd but it was so deep that there was no way I could squeeze myself through to the front. A man standing at the back saw my plight and lifted me up onto his shoulders. I looked down into the floodlit, open car and had a wonderful view of the Queen looking magnificent in her evening gown and tiara – just the way I knew she should look.

I have often wondered if the faceless man who lifted up a little girl that night ever remembered me or could have imagined how gratefully I link him with the glimpse that created such a special picture in my memory.

The teenager Lindsay Watson took care to secure a perfect viewpoint so that when the royal couple drove by she would not miss a thing.

When the Queen and Philip visited Hamilton on the Royal Tour of '53–'54 the City of Hamilton gave a dinner at Cardrona, near the Fairfield Bridge. I made sure I was positioned at the entrance of Cardrona's driveway, and after a long wait, my anticipation was richly rewarded as the royal car, gleaming in the early evening sunshine, slowed almost to a halt in front of me. To my joy and wonder, there, three feet away, was a tiny figure of great regality, smiling and waving. Deep blue eyes, an astonishingly clear complexion, sparkling diamonds, lustrous silk, and a warm and happy smile greeted the gaze of one young enamoured thirteen-year-old – after which, I raced back across the bridge to regale my family with my great adventure!

Audrey Russell, the BBC correspondent who had attended the Coronation and the King's funeral before that, followed the royal tour as a news reporter. She noted that adoration sometimes had unwanted consequences, although I have a feeling the Queen didn't mind a jot.

On the first tour of New Zealand I had the opportunity several times of staying in the same hotel as the Queen. It was particularly interesting to do so at the Law Courts Hotel, Dunedin, for this was the only occasion that the visit was more than a one-night stand. We were there for four nights – and were to be perpetually and pleasantly besieged. Extra passes were issued, a pink card to be allowed to go out of the hotel and a blue one to return. Looking back, I know that the security measures were much more informal and friendly than would be required today. One became acclimatised to the non-stop chant of the crowds outside – 'We want the Queen' – whenever she returned from an engagement. This did not intrude in the daytime, but on one occasion (in another hotel this time, near the end of the New Zealand visit, at Invercargill) the police were unable to move on a small group of misguided loyalists who kept up the racket after 2 a.m. The Queen had to move to the only corner available that was quiet. This was a small 'ironing room' that happened to have a single metal bedstead kept in case of an emergency. Next morning after breakfast the manageress showed me the room – she was outraged that what she called the 'luxury Royal Suite' had to be abandoned in the middle of the night.

The stay in Dunedin taught me that the work of a royal tour never finishes for the principal participants. In between functions someone was nearly always to be seen waiting for the Queen's return to be given a special audience – a delegation with something to say about a worthy cause, or an eminent descendant of someone who won a medal in the Maori wars but was now too decrepit to meet the Queen at a garden party. Last, but not least, there were the red despatch boxes from London, said to be kept to the minimum on tour, but nevertheless to be seen daily in a shuttle in and out of the Law Courts Hotel.

The Queen and Prince Philip arrived in Australia in February 1954 and stayed until the beginning of April. On 2 April, *The Age* newspaper in Melbourne reported on the departure of the Queen and Prince Philip with the headline 'QUEEN BEGINS LONG JOURNEY HOME'.

The Queen's visit to Australia ended a few seconds after 5.20 p.m. today, when the Royal Yacht *Gothic* steamed slowly out of Fremantle Harbour to the accompaniment of cheers from 40,000 people and the sound of the sirens of every ship in port.

It was a brilliant and stirring finale to one of the greatest events in Australia's history.

Four minutes earlier the Queen had left Australian soil, and walked up *Gothic*'s gangway looking as happy, refreshed and composed as on the bright morning of 3 February when this stately ship had brought her to Sydney.

Behind Her Majesty were 57 days packed with more than 250 formal engagements in a tour of Australia that had been a brilliant success.

As *Gothic* was slowly making its way out of the Swan River into the Indian Ocean the Queen left the top deck to make her farewell broadcast to Australia and its people.

'With the sounds of departure still ringing in our ears I want to say to you, my Australian people, how sad we are to be leaving the shores of your wonderful land,' she said.

As *Gothic* slowly edged its way from the wharf to the

channel of the Swan River, 40,000 cheering West Australians sang 'Auld Lang Syne' and waved farewell.

It was a moving scene and hundreds of women brushed tears from their eyes.

5. Portrait of a Queen

Perhaps the Queen is the most painted lady in history. Countless institutions and charities, town halls and guilds, wardrooms and boardrooms have a painting of the Queen in pride of place. Some are the real thing, an original commissioned portrait painted at sittings that the Sovereign has graciously fitted into her crammed schedule, planned months in advance.

Whenever you paint busy or very famous people you may use another person, or sometimes a dummy figure, to stand in their robes or hats or gowns or rooms, which are complicated and slow to paint. During the actual sitting the artist will concentrate on the face and hands, the two things from which we judge the completed work. Some people are easy to paint (the artist the late John Ward used to say, 'I love a big nose: you can hang anything from a big nose'), and some are almost impossible to capture to common satisfaction.

There are bound to be mixed opinions about any portraits of the Queen, including the profiles used on coins and stamps, relentlessly updated and reminding us all of 'time's wingèd chariot hurrying near'. When someone is as famous as Elvis Presley or Marilyn Monroe, we only really want a few of the most fabulous pictures to remind us of them: Che Guevara, in his cap with the red star, a faraway look, a student beard, has only ever needed one. Maybe we get to the stage that we don't even want another different, truer painting or photograph: we have sealed the favoured likenesses into the pantheon, and don't need any further interpretations.

For small branches of charities and churches there would never have been enough money to commission a portrait of the Queen, so the committee would have spread out the chosen tried and tested, fully-approved-by-the-populace pictures of Her Majesty, and picked out a print of one, which, when framed, mounted and hung on the best-lit wall, would be perfect, and would not be stolen.

Two of the most durable and adored portraits of the Queen were painted by Pietro Annigoni. He was born in Florence and painted in the Renaissance tradition. There was a kerfuffle about the first painting, whether it was too chocolate-boxy. Harrumphing went on among those who thought it hardly better than Vladimir Tretchikoff's painting *Chinese Girl*, a people's favourite. Tremendous snobbery abounded. I love the paintings he did and have indulged myself here with two accounts of his sittings with the Queen. Annigoni saw things with a painter's eye: in minute detail, both critical and appreciative. He noticed and recorded things with surgical precision. His rather highly strung, gossipy nature is ideal for a diary. Being a society painter, someone who undertook private and often aristocratic commissions, put him in an easy position to be denigrated by other portrait painters. Artists are as critical of others' works as any creative people are. I find the accounts of his time with Her Majesty captivating.

The first time he was invited to paint Her Majesty was in 1954, after the Queen and Prince Philip had returned from the long and successful Commonwealth tour.

The masters of an ancient City Livery Company had decided to have a portrait of Queen Elizabeth II to grace their historic hall in the City of London, and were looking for an artist to paint it, an artist who would, of course, require the Queen's approval.

Then, one day when I was at Wildenstein's gallery, Tim Whidborne [an artist and pupil of Annigoni] brought me a letter that he had picked up at my studio. I opened and read it. It was from the Worshipful Company of Fishmongers and asked if I would be willing to paint for them a portrait of the Queen. I thought they were some little association who would want me to copy a photograph, but I asked Tim: 'Who are the Fishmongers?'

'People who sell fish. Why?'

'They want me to paint a portrait of the Queen for them,' I said, dropping the letter.

Tim picked it up, read it, and laughed. 'This is serious,' he said, and told me how important those Fishmongers were. Later it transpired that several of the Company's most influential members had been to see my show before deciding to honour me with the commission for the portrait that would hang in their Hall alongside those of kings and queens of centuries past.

After I had gratefully and proudly accepted, the Queen's acceptance of *me* had to be obtained. The Fishmongers borrowed the portrait of Juanita Forbes, completed in 1953, to show her as an example of my work. In any case she had, as I have mentioned, seen my portrait of Mrs Christie-Miller in 1953 and, even as Princess Elizabeth, she had been sent photographs of some of my paintings by ex-Queen Helen of Romania, my friend for many years in Florence.

Once the Queen's approval was given, then only did the

Princess Elizabeth in ATS uniform during the Second World War.

Princess Elizabeth and Prince Philip on their honeymoon: 23 November 1947.

Treetops in Kenya, with an elephant at the waterhole in front of the lodge.

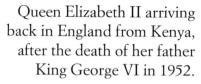

Queen Elizabeth II arriving back in England from Kenya, after the death of her father King George VI in 1952.

The three Queens at the Lying in State of the King, Westminster Hall, 15 February 1952.

The Queen recording her first Christmas Broadcast in 1952, before television cameras were invited to film her speeches.

4 November 1952: The Queen on her way to Westminster before the first State Opening of Parliament since her accession to the throne.

The Queen as Colonel-in-Chief, Scots Guards, on her horse Burmese, taking the salute at the Trooping the Colour ceremony on Horseguards Parade, marking her official birthday in 1970.

The entire Royal Family and foreign royal guests at the Coronation. At the front stand young Prince Charles and Princess Anne.

Norman Hartnell, pre-eminent dress designer of the day, in 1952, with a design for the Queen's Coronation dress.

Queen Elizabeth II, with her Mistress of the Robes and the six Maids of Honour. Lady Anne Coke is third from the left.

The Gold State Coach processing through the wet streets lined by crowds on Coronation Day.

Arriving in Bermuda on her first Commonwealth Tour as Queen, accompanied by Prince Philip in November 1953.

The Rock of Gibraltar towers over the royal procession in 1954.

The Queen and Prince Philip arrive in New Zealand in 1953.

The royal couple arrive at Hyde Park in Sydney in 1954.

Pietro Annigoni working on his first portrait of the Queen in 1954.

The Queen during her visit to Germany making a speech in
Berlin on 27 May 1965.

1964, Ottawa: Prime Minister Lester B. Pearson and wife Maryon Pearson
greet the Queen and Prince Philip on their arrival from Quebec City.

The Silver Jubilee, 1977: The Queen and Major Michael Parker at The Copper Horse in Windsor, as the huge bonfire signals the start of the celebrations nationwide.

One of many street parties held to celebrate the Silver Jubilee in 1977.

During the north-east leg of the Silver Jubilee Tour in 1977 the Queen is greeted by children in Hartlepool.

Crowds of well-wishers acclaim the Queen in Scotland on 24 May 1977: she had been on the throne for 25 years.

enormous importance of the undertaking hit me. It could make or break me. If I failed, all the prestige and goodwill I had earned for myself in Britain would be lost and I would feel bitter about it for the rest of my life. For that reason I wanted as many sittings as possible. I work slowly and would have liked thirty one-hour sessions, but I knew that no other painter had been given more than seven or eight sittings, so I asked for twenty-five. The reply came from Buckingham Palace that the Queen would give me fifteen. Not enough. And yet I knew that I was being exceptionally favoured.

Two months passed before all the details were settled. Then it was decided that the earliest the sittings could start would be October. I returned to Florence and tried to work but, naturally perhaps, my mind was all the time occupied with the daunting undertaking to which I had committed myself. But out of all my preoccupation with the subject came only vague, cliché-ridden, theatrical, and romantic notions about the portrait; and when I returned to London at the beginning of October I still had no serious idea and felt nothing approaching inspiration.

On the appointed day I was at Buckingham Palace half an hour early and was taken straight to the Yellow Drawing Room – a huge and magnificent room, which I later discovered was to be my studio. There Colonel Martin Charteris, the Queen's assistant private secretary, joined me and in reply to my questions as to the procedure when the Queen arrived he explained simply: 'When I come here with Her Majesty to introduce you, just shake the hand that she will hold out to you and make a slight bow. That's all. Don't worry about the rest, because Her Majesty will put you at your ease immediately.'

And that was how it was. From the moment she appeared, dressed in white under a dark blue cloak, the robe of the

Order of the Garter, everything went easily. Not that I was not over-awed and embarrassed at suddenly finding myself alone with the Queen of England. As she stood in front of me, probably expecting me to say where and how I wished her to pose, I was completely tongue-tied. I looked around the great room in the hope that it might give me some inspiration, but it appeared only as a gilded prison full of Chinese ornaments. Desperately uncertain of myself, I asked her to stand just as she was, turned away from the light, and looking into the darkest corner of the room. I began to draw, conscious all the time of the precious minutes slipping away and knowing that the sketch I was making was valueless.

Suddenly – perhaps sensing my uneasiness – she began to talk casually, in French. 'You know,' she said, 'when I was a child I used to spend hours in this room looking out of the windows. I loved watching the people and the cars down there in the Mall. They all seemed so busy. I used to wonder what they were doing and where they were all going, and what they thought about outside the Palace.'

Her words were like a searchlight lighting my way. I saw her immediately as the Queen who, while dear to the hearts of millions of people whom she loved, was herself alone and far off. I knew then that was how I must show her. I asked her to look out of the great window once more and I watched her face light up at the ever-changing scene she surveyed. I began to draw with new zest and at the end of the sitting, after the Queen had left and I was gathering up my sketches and materials, I felt that a great burden had been lifted from me. But there was more good luck to come that day.

Walking through a long gallery, on my way out of the Palace, I saw in the shadowy distance a figure all in white that seemed to be floating towards me. Only when she came close did I realise it was the Queen without the Garter cloak. I stood aside to let her pass and she smiled and was gone. But in the second or two in which I glimpsed her eager young profile against the autumn evening light, she was momentarily transported in my imagination to the open air on a clear spring day.

That evening in my studio I made a rough sketch of a composition for the portrait and sent it in a letter to my wife. Much later I realised that the sketch was fundamentally identical in design with the finished portrait. But the course from the sketch to the finished work was neither direct nor smooth. New ideas kept interposing themselves, the sketch was forgotten, its freshness lost and rediscovered only after many vain and frustrating dead-end journeys.

During the wait for the Queen's second sitting I was still painting the Duchess of Devonshire who, after I had been to Buckingham Palace, asked me how the sitting had gone and I told her 'very well'. Then she asked me if the Queen talked to me and I said: 'Well, yes – perhaps too much.' To my horror she replied: 'Oh, well, I'll let her know. I'm having dinner with Princess Margaret tonight, so I'll see that she's told.'

'Oh, don't do that,' I said.

But when finally the second sitting came along it soon became clear that the 'message' had reached the Queen. She didn't say a word to me while she was posing. Nor did she speak a word during the following three sittings. Of course it was good for my work in those early stages but it was very embarrassing, because I knew that it was not correct for me to open a conversation. However, when we met for the fifth sitting, it was such a terrible morning, foggy, dark and wet, that I could not help remarking that it got on my nerves and made work almost impossible. The Queen smiled and, to my surprise, said, 'It makes me happy, because when the weather is like this my husband won't be flying in his helicopter.'

Her natural way of talking to me about her family, always referring to them as 'my husband', 'my mother', 'my sister', and so on, made a very deep impression on me. Although my diary tells me that, when things were going badly, I was inclined to blame her – 'As a model the Queen does not facilitate my work' or, again, 'The Queen doesn't "feel" the pose and she doesn't appear to be concerned about it' – I now remember only that she was (as I wrote on 1 December 1954) 'kind, natural and never aloof'. In mitigation I can plead only that the dragging out of the sittings over a period of four months meant that for that period my nerves were continuously taut and tense.

In the later stages of the work, that tension might perhaps have been eased by a few words from the Queen saying that she approved, or even liked, the way the portrait was going. But, no doubt because she considered it would be wrong to comment before I had declared it finished, she never once expressed an opinion about its progress. Others in the Palace were not so reticent. Often, when I was working alone after the sittings, servants would find an excuse to come into the Yellow Drawing Room to have a look. Their opinions, which presaged the popularity the portrait was to have with the general public in Britain, were particularly encouraging at times when I felt things were not going well.

The last sitting (I think it was the sixteenth – an extra one generously conceded by the Queen) took place at the end of February 1955. I worked on for a few days at the Palace and then decided to give the portrait its finishing touches at

Tim Whidborne's studio in Chelsea. But before Tim and I could remove it, I had a message from the Queen saying that she and the rest of the Royal Family would like to see it before it left the Palace. So I continued to work on the cloak and the background until one morning it was suddenly announced that the royal private view would take place after lunch that day.

At lunchtime I was quite happily drinking my coffee and munching a few biscuits in front of the portrait when I began to feel renewed doubts about the right eye, doubts that I had allowed to recede while there were so many other details to worry about. Now, virtually everything else was satisfactory, but the eye looked balefully at me, demanding attention. Naturally I was reluctant to start again on a detail that I had thought finished. Especially I was reluctant to try to do anything to so vital a detail as an eye in the short time before the Royal Family would arrive. On the other hand, if I was going to try, I must first be sure what I had to do. Many precious minutes passed before I decided that a little eye-surgery, in painting terms, must be performed and I started immediately. After several moments of panic, when I seemed to have destroyed the entire expression of the face, I knew that I had been successful. But the Queen appeared now to have a black eye!

Normally this would not have alarmed me at all for, unlike oil paint, the medium in which I normally work – oil-tempera – becomes lighter in tone as it dries and the artist allows for this. The Royal Family could not be expected to allow for it. Somehow I had to dry the eye. Frantically, but vainly, I waved a piece of cardboard over it – and heard a box of matches rattling in my pocket. I lit the matches one after another, holding each one for as long as possible and as close to the painting as I dared, and still had the last one in my hand as the Queen walked in, followed by her mother, sister, husband, and children.

Everyone showed a lively interest in the work. The Duke of Edinburgh asked questions about the technique and the Queen Mother told me that the imaginary landscape in the background reminded her of a part of Scotland she knew so well. Princess Margaret, smoking a cigarette in a long holder and enveloped in an aura of sensuality, remarked upon my success with her sister's mouth, a feature, she said, that usually provided great difficulty for portraitists. The Queen herself said that I must be satisfied with my work because everyone in the Palace liked it, and it was clear that she was happy for the same reason.

This happy ending to my sojourn at Buckingham Palace made me sad to leave. I had even become attached to the Yellow Drawing Room, for, although I found its ornate decoration and its chinoiserie unattractive, it had been my studio for many weeks and I had had many bitter and sweet experiences in it. Looking back, it is like a half-dream in which I took part in a light opera, with a military band playing off-stage (for the Changing of the Guard ceremony) and a real queen as the heroine.

How comforting to read about the Queen's natural friendliness and her ability to put people at their ease. Sometimes it's hard to remember that behind the iconic representations of Her Majesty there is a warm-hearted, clever and compassionate soul; an ordinary but extraordinary woman. When John Ward was working on a painting of her at Buckingham Palace in a much smaller chamber than the great Yellow Drawing Room the Queen suddenly said, 'Are you cold?' He protested that he was fine, well, maybe just a bit chilly, and the Queen rose from her chair. 'I think it's cold,' she said, and knelt in front of the fireplace, crackled up some kindling and placed small wood in a pyramid, then a larger log on top and put a match to it. The fire blazed up. 'There,' she said. 'That's better.'

Pietro Annigoni had been made to feel comfortable with Her Majesty during the painting of the first widely acclaimed, and equally roundly criticised, portrait; he was surprised, however, to be asked to paint her again, this time by the art 'establishment' who had been so hostile to his work fifteen years earlier.

Just before I went to Iran to paint the Shah and his empress I had been surprised to get a letter from Dr Roy Strong asking me if I would accept a commission to paint a portrait of Queen Elizabeth II for the National Portrait Gallery, of which he was then the director. I was surprised because most of my portraits of members of the Royal Family had been received with hostility by almost everyone in the art 'establishment'.

Work on the portrait did not begin until two years after Dr Strong approached me. I arrived in London on 19 February 1969, having travelled by train across a snowbound Europe. There was snow in Florence, snow on the Paduan plain, snow in Switzerland, snow in France. And there was snow in the forecourt of Buckingham Palace that afternoon when I reported to Sir Martin Charteris, the Queen's secretary, to arrange details of the sittings. Fifteen years, a knighthood, promotion, and more responsibilities had not affected that gentleman's admirable manner. He was as friendly and helpful to me as he had been when I painted the Queen for the first time.

That night, after trying in vain to rustle up some of my old friends, I dined alone in a Soho restaurant and comforted myself that it was probably for the best, because I had to be in the Yellow Drawing Room, with a clear head, at eleven thirty in the morning for the Queen's first sitting. I arrived early and arranged my things, feeling completely calm and at home in the familiar surroundings. From the windows I looked out along the Mall, where the snow was beginning to melt under a slight drizzle of rain and the slush was building up in the gutters. At ground level the heavy grey sky merged into a thick drape of fog peppered with the watery yellow eyes of still lighted street-lamps. It was a morning to make a saint gloomy, but I felt uncharacteristically confident.

The Queen arrived with Sir Martin at eleven forty. If I had not already felt at ease, her pleasant greeting would certainly have made me so. She recalled sitting for the first portrait and I reminded her that it was fifteen years ago. 'So many?' she said.

Indeed, so many, I thought as I noticed how much she had changed. Everything about her seemed smaller, in some ways frailer and in some ways harder. As she posed her facial expression was mercurial – smiling, thoughtful, determined, uncertain, relaxed, taut, in rapid succession. Often, when something outside the window caught her attention, I felt she was a caged bird longing to be free.

I had decided to work on her portrait in the same manner as I had on that of the Shah and his empress, and when I told the Queen she recalled her own memories of a meeting with the Persian royal couple. She had, she said, been placed next to the Shah at the wedding reception of the Queen of Holland's daughter, and she had found, as I said I had, that the Shah talked all the time of politics and reforms. She had been embarrassed, she told me, by his asking which of our major political parties gave more support to the Crown. Britain and Iran were such very different worlds that she did not know how to answer him. How could she explain that party politics had nothing to do with the Crown?

At the second sitting, a week later, the Queen was very talkative. Looking out of the window at the Changing of the Guard ceremony she remarked, as she had done fifteen years earlier, that as a girl she spent many hours looking with fascination out of the windows at the outside world. Nowadays, she said, she rarely saw the Changing of the Guard, but had seen it several times recently because her mother-in-law was a guest at the Palace and had a room overlooking the courtyard. The regiment being relieved that day was about to leave for duty in Germany. 'They must have had enough of Changing of the Guard,' she remarked sympathetically. 'It's been their lot for the past three years.'

Another week later, during the third sitting, the Guard again dominated our conversation after the Queen drew my attention to a group of soldiers marching towards the Palace gates preceded by a goat on a lead. 'I've never seen them changing the guard,' I said, and the Queen explained that the regiment, the Welsh Regiment, did reserve duty when required.

'The goat,' she said, 'is its mascot. He should be a wild goat really, but this one, like all the others these days, comes from some zoo. It's up to me to present them to the regiment. It's an expensive business because they only live a short time and consequently substitutes have to be provided frequently. The soldiers amuse themselves giving them too many cigarettes and the poor beasts get ill and die.'

At that moment I was having problems with the propor-
tions of the Queen's features – nose to chin, chin to mouth,
mouth to nose – and I heard the tale of the cigarettes as if
I was drunk. Did the goats smoke? Or did they just eat the
cigarettes? I asked myself. But I asked her: 'Do they really
like cigarettes?'

'Oh, yes. But it's now been established that they mustn't
have more than two a day.'

I looked at her incredulously but it was clear that she was
serious, even though she was smiling at the beautiful morning
outside. It was an infectious smile and cheered me at the
end of a sitting that had begun badly for me.

At every sitting the Queen chatted to me in the most
natural way and her disarming frankness never failed to
surprise and fascinate me, even at those times when, for the
progress of the portrait, it would have been better if she had
kept silent. As she posed she could see clearly out of the
window while I, facing her and my easel, had my back to
it. But frequently, when something attracted her attention,
she would say, 'Did you see that?'

'Did you see that car? It went the wrong way round the
monument,' she burst out one day in some alarm. And that
set us talking about traffic problems. 'A few evenings ago,'
she told me, 'a taxi ran into my car and made a large scratch
on it.'

'Strange,' I said. 'In general taxi-drivers are excellent drivers.'

'It's true,' she agreed. 'But sometimes they are too pushing. Philip was driving the car and he especially doesn't like
being pushed.'

Another time she drew my attention to a slight accident
between a private car and a taxi and, as we watched the car
driver and the taxi-man arguing and exchanging particulars,

she remarked, 'In the meantime the clock ticks up and that poor thing in the taxi will have to pay.'

Often she started a conversation by asking me if I had seen a particular news-item or photograph in the morning papers. One day she asked me if I had seen the photograph of myself in the *Daily Express*. I replied, truthfully, that I had not. But I knew that it was a photograph taken with a telescopic lens and showing me looking out of the Palace window, and although I was curious to see it I pretended complete ignorance of it. Another day she told me she had seen a little boy on television who, when asked if he would have liked to go to the moon with the American astronauts, replied, 'No, I think the money ought to be used to feed the poor people in Biafra.' She had clearly been very touched by the story and recalled it with an air of surprise, sadness and amusement, emphasising with the palm of her left hand turned down, the size of the little boy.

It had been arranged that my portrait would show the Queen wearing the mantle of the Order of the British Empire, but it was not until the seventh and eighth sittings that she made her appearance in it for me. Each time she had come straight from another sitting, which, she told me on the second occasion, was for a sculptor who was making a bust for the new *Queen Elizabeth* liner.

'The poor man is rather desperate,' she said. 'He says that my face is extremely changeable.'

I told her that he had my sympathy and I could understand his difficulty, and she smiled, amused, and went on: 'This morning's sitting was an extra to the six agreed upon but he has destroyed the clay head again. He does it every time, takes it up in his hands and' – she imitated his action vigorously with her own hands – 're-forms it.'

As she spoke a red helicopter flew over the Palace, taking her mother to an engagement. To my enquiry, she replied that it had taken off from the Palace garden, and mention of the garden led her to describe to me the rehearsal that had taken place there the day before for Prince Charles's investiture as Prince of Wales.

'It was so funny,' she began. 'We all had to make and remake the steps and movements as if we were really at Caernarvon Castle, where the investiture will take place. There were even five cords, stretched across the ground to indicate where the steps will be, and we had to lift our feet up as if they really were steps.' She laughed and then added in a low voice, 'Rather silly.'

At the end of that sitting the Queen reminded me that it was the last she was able to give me until the following October. I explained that during that period I would be working in Florence on the final painting, and I tried to convey to her how I visualised the finished portrait.

'I see Your Majesty as being condemned to solitude because of your position,' I said, 'and I intend to let that be my inspiration. It goes without saying that, as a wife and mother you are entirely different, but I see you really alone as a monarch and I was to represent you that way. If I succeed, the woman, the Queen and, for that matter, the solitude will emerge.'

She nodded earnestly in agreement and then came to look at the study I had made during the eight sittings. Although I watched her closely, she gave me no idea of her reaction to it until she spoke.

'One doesn't know oneself,' she said. 'After all, we have a biased view when we see ourselves in a mirror and, what's more, the image is always in reverse.'

I explained that the study had, as yet, no definite character and that that would emerge during the autumn sittings. But I had made up my mind to show her in solitude, rather thoughtful and severe, profoundly human, and, at the same time, queenly without recourse to crowns or other symbols of regality.

'I hope Your Majesty has nothing against being depicted without jewellery, including earrings?' I said, and went on to outline what I had in mind. She listened and nodded in agreement again, and before she left she held out her hand to me and said, 'I feel that the inspiration is there. Go ahead. I look forward to seeing you and the picture in October.'

The Queen's portrait now demanded all my time and faculties. So far I had done little more than prepare the large wooden panel on which I had decided to paint it. Now I drew with a brush the outlines of the composition and painted in the principal masses. Then, using the finished study I had made at Buckingham Palace, I began to work on the head of the Queen and continued until I could take it no further without more sittings. At the beginning of October, I had the panel crated and sent to Buckingham Palace to await my arrival there.

On 19 October I left Florence by train and arrived in London next day, an unusually warm and sunny day that matched the reception by a group of my friends at Victoria Station. The following morning I was at the Palace, with Tim Whidborne to help me to unpack the portrait, when Sir Martin Charteris sent for me. Naturally, I assumed, he wanted to discuss the schedule for the Queen's sittings but, instead, he upbraided me about an article in a woman's magazine which reported passages of the Queen's conversations with me and quoted observations about Her Majesty that I had made to the journalist who interviewed me. The Queen, said Sir Martin, was annoyed about it. I was surprised because, although the article was rather silly, I knew that it was entirely inoffensive. However, I had to admit to myself that I had succumbed to the temptation of the publicity and the fee that the magazine had offered me, and in my heart I reproached myself for having done it. But I forgave myself, too.

A sitting had been arranged for that afternoon and I prepared myself to offer my apologies to a withdrawn and silent Queen, but the opportunity to do so never arose. From the moment of her arrival in the Yellow Drawing Room her amiability was so evident that it would have been churlish to mar it with an obviously unwanted apology. She greeted me with a friendly handshake and showed much more than polite interest in the large picture that she was seeing for the first time.

'Did you do all this work here in London?' she asked, and I answered that I had done it in Florence whence I had just returned. From then on we talked almost continuously, covering a great variety of subjects, from the dilapidated state of the curtains in the Yellow Drawing Room to the sorry state of university life in our and other countries.

'I presided over the inauguration of a new university a few days ago,' she told me. 'A modern building with courts like the traditional ones, only larger. The students weren't satisfied, however. They said that they felt like prisoners.'

I told her about the student sit-ins at universities in Italy and France and she replied: 'I don't know about Italy but in France I believe the discontent is justified. A niece of mine, belonging to an obviously traditional family, has returned from the Sorbonne, where she has been studying, with completely revolutionary ideas.'

The Queen's next sitting, six days later, was on the same day as the State Opening of Parliament, 27 October. When I arrived that morning, hundreds of people already lined the Mall but its entrances were barred to traffic and my car was stopped by a mounted policeman. While my driver was explaining to him who I was, a man came out of the crowd and shouted to the policeman, first in Italian and then in English, 'It's the artist, Annigoni! The Queen's artist!' Then he came to the car and introduced himself to me. It was Fantacci of Florence, a gentleman whose principal claim to fame was that his daughter had married the son of the actor, Frederic March.

I was feeling very weary that morning after a night out with some convivial friends and, as I worked alone in the Palace, I was easily distracted by the activity in the courtyard below and spent much time at the window watching the departure and return of the royal procession. It struck me as remarkable that the Queen had agreed to sit for me on such a day, and I fully expected her to show signs of weariness herself. But she arrived at half past two looking very vivacious and smiling pleasantly, and when I asked if she had had a tiring morning, she answered: 'Not really. If anything was tiring it was the crown, which I had to wear throughout the whole ceremony. It's so heavy my head is still feeling the effects.'

She seemed to be enjoying her frankness and added suddenly: 'This morning I think I have made the dullest and most boring speech of my life. But it dealt with such dry material. One tries at least to put a little expression into one's voice, but it's not humanly possible to produce something even remotely lively.'

Looking out of the window a little later the Queen saw

a Chinese family posing on the Queen Victoria Memorial for a photograph, and this provoked a discussion about the split between the Communist giants, China and Russia. Then, somehow, the conversation switched to drug-taking by young people. The Queen mentioned that the daughter of someone she knew was an addict and went on to ask if I had seen a newspaper photograph of two young English boys who had just been released by the Russians after serving a sentence for peddling drugs.

Three days after the opening of Parliament I worked on the portrait at the Palace during the morning, as was my usual practice, and then went back to my own studio to do other work in the afternoon. Imagine my embarrassment, then, when Sir Martin Charteris phoned me to say that the Queen had waited in vain for me to turn up for that day's sitting. On the memorandum hanging on my studio wall the sitting was clearly marked 'cancelled', in my secretary's writing. Obviously there had been a misunderstanding but there was nothing I could do except apologise to the Queen through Sir Martin, bewail, to myself, the loss of a sitting, and wait four more days for the opportunity to make my apologies to the Queen in person.

Her response was most unexpected. When I told her how much I regretted the loss of the sitting she was amused and smiled broadly.

'For me,' she said, 'it was just the opposite. I was surprised at not finding you here, especially as they told me you had been seen in the Palace shortly before. But I was, after all, very glad to have a free hour. I was able to do many things that I had put off. Usually, if I have a free afternoon, the fact becomes known, and then this one or that one thinks that it is a good opportunity for them to be received. No one knew anything about the other day!' she added gleefully, like a girl who has successfully played truant from school.

In my absence she had looked at the portrait and remarked that it had progressed considerably. But now, too much talk and too little light hampered further progress, and at half past three, when the sitting ought to have ended, I boldly asked if she could allow me a few more minutes.

'Yes, yes. It's all right for me but I don't know about you with this light,' she said. 'I'm looking at the gardeners down there. They've put everything down and off they go. They simply look at their watches and go off at half past three. Not because they've finished what they had to do, but just because it's half past three.'

Again conversation took over and the better part of those extra minutes passed with each of us pronouncing judgements on the subject of work and workers in an age in which technology has taken the element of personal satisfaction out of the work that most people have to do. Before she left, the Queen looked at the painting and commented, 'Bit by bit the portrait is being done.' I took the opportunity then to mention that I would soon be ready to paint the chain and insignia of the Order of the British Empire, which, I had learned earlier, had to be borrowed because she did not possess them. After she had gone, the footman who came to conduct me out of the Palace also looked at the portrait and commented, 'Did you work around the mouth? I'm sure you did, because the portrait has now taken a step forward. It's very much better!'

Two days later I was in Milan for an exhibition, at the Levi Gallery, of my lithographs of Venice, and the following day I went on to Turin for the opening of a small one-man show at the Minima Gallery. Afterwards I had a few days at home in Florence and then returned to London and the Palace. The painting, which I had not seen for two weeks, now appeared to be lacking in contrasts, so I spent the morning strengthening contours and heightening the chiaroscuro.

At two thirty the Queen arrived and for the first quarter of an hour she posed in complete silence. Then the impatient wail of an ambulance's siren shattered her peaceful composure and my concentration, and she began to talk, first about the siren – 'Some days we've counted twenty or more' – and afterwards about the *Apollo 12* mission to the moon. She was following the adventure avidly on television and, during that and the next two sittings, gave me a run-down on its progress. We agreed that, although it filled us with wonder and admiration, it did not move us emotionally. Technology and inhumanity, I reflected, seemed to advance side by side. Men without God either put themselves in capsules of miraculous technological perfection or they disintegrate. Everything, however, will end in dust and there will be only God to dispose of the dust.

The next day, when she sat again, she told me that the astronauts had landed on the moon exactly as planned. She had been up early especially to watch the television and was still watching, shortly before coming to me, when the set broke down. Perhaps, I thought, that was lucky for me, because she was clearly so preoccupied with the moon that she might easily have forgotten her appointment with me. But now, suddenly, she had other news for me.

'Joseph Kennedy is dead,' she announced abruptly. 'After so many years of terrible suffering. At one time he was American ambassador in London. He was a very ambitious man. I don't know how he managed to earn millions and millions of pounds,' she said, eyes round and eyebrows raised in genuine puzzlement, and added thoughtfully, 'Not even a word of regret in the press. So sad.'

For a while she talked about ambassadors but somehow came round to *Apollo 12* again. And she was still full of it at the next sitting, a week later. She had watched the return of the space capsule to earth and there had been some technical hitches.

'One can see that it's easier to land on the moon than on the earth,' she remarked.

To facilitate my work when the Queen was not with me, I had the British Empire robe draped on a dummy figure that was crowned with a wig belonging to her. Now that I was painting her hair from life, I noticed how closely the wig resembled her own hair in colour and style, and commented upon it.

'Yes,' she said, 'it's an excellent imitation and it also cost a great deal!'

A pause, and then she said suddenly: 'I am anxious to hear the Palace police report about the Oxford undergraduate who came, uninvited, to Charles's birthday party. I am curious to know what explanation he has given.'

I looked at her, puzzled, and she went on: 'Yes, an Oxford undergraduate got out of college the other evening and presented himself here at the gates first and then, having been refused admittance, found a way to climb over the garden wall and joined a group of young people who had been invited to the party.'

'But didn't he give an explanation when he was discovered?' I asked.

'I saw him,' the Queen replied, 'and he was so drunk that he couldn't say anything apart from a few incivilities.'

I suggested that it might just have been bravado and she

agreed. She had heard that he was an excellent student, she said, and she hoped that he would only be severely reprimanded and frightened, because she certainly did not want him to be sent down.

According to my schedule the next sitting, the sixteenth, should have been the last and the Queen remembered, but with her usual thoughtfulness she asked if I needed more and acceded to my request for two. That settled, she took up the pose that gave her a view along the Mall. The weather was bad – it had snowed the night before – but there had still been a large crowd of people watching the Changing of the Guard that morning. Many of them, I told the Queen, were American sailors.

'Poor Americans!' she exclaimed. 'They do have their problems. There is now this story of the massacre in Vietnam . . . They who believe they are perfect, or at least that they do things better than anyone else . . . Yes, they do many wonderful things . . . On the other hand, there is so much puffing up and political speculation even in this story of the massacre . . . as if there can be war without cruel and horrible incidents.'

As she spoke I remembered the slaughter committed by my countrymen in Addis Ababa after the attempt to kill General Graziani [on 19 February 1937 20,000 to 30,000 Ethiopians were killed by Italian occupying forces], and I said to myself, 'Let him who is without sin cast the first stone.'

During the last stages of the painting I worked for at least six hours every day at the Palace. The two extra sittings proved of little value. The portrait was already defined in a way quite different from that I had envisaged. The Queen was restless and nervous and I became exasperated as the truly royal image that I aimed for eluded me. I longed for silence but the Queen wanted to talk and in the end I gave myself up to conversation. Among other subjects, she talked of Dr Roy Strong, who had been the prime mover in the matter of the portrait.

'He is very energetic,' she said, 'and does everything he can to promote interest in and collect money for the National Portrait Gallery, which is very good, but recently I've had a struggle with him over the acquisition of a miniature of Elizabeth the First. I wanted it because it was Elizabeth, he on account of the artist. I don't think he should have been so difficult, but in the end I won – by paying more!'

Before she left for the last time I thanked her for the many sittings and she replied, almost shyly, hoping that they had been enough. Then she left the room to the music of the slow march from the band in the courtyard below. I did not think she was entirely satisfied with the portrait and I myself felt that yet again I had created a royal portrait that was going to be liked by some and hated by others. And so it proved when, on 25 February 1970, the painting was shown at a preview, attended by the Queen, at the National Portrait Gallery.

The Queen looking out of her windows in the Palace, noticing everyday things: why does this come as a surprise? We think that we are the ones who do the staring and noticing and commenting: perhaps it never occurs to us that the Queen is watching the world back, maybe from a completely different standpoint but with interest and perception. From her letters written at an early age it's noticeable that she is curious about everything, and sees a great deal more than we who are less restricted do. Not restricted: sometimes it's hard to choose the right words for the massively different life she leads from ours. Of course the Royal Family lets its hair down, dances and sings and dresses up and fools around. We see the carefully edited pieces, and crowd to inspect them: the filming of the Royal Family at home, making barbecues and playing with the dogs, dancing reels at Balmoral, riding in Windsor Great Park. But it is all prepared and planned and edited and eventually vetoed.

Patrick Anson, 5th Earl of Lichfield, professionally known as Patrick Lichfield, was the Queen's cousin. He captured some of the most wonderful moments of happiness and ease within the Royal Family because he was one of them (and because he was extremely funny, talented and a workaholic). I bought one of his pictures for my son and daughter-in-law, of the Queen in dark glasses and a summer dress, leaning on the rails of the Royal Yacht *Britannia* and roaring with laughter. The lovely photograph that was released when Prince Philip died was taken by the Countess of Wessex showing such genuine smiles and relaxation: taken by a member of the family. Do you have to be related to get a good shot of the Queen?

I have known John Swannell, and been photographed by him, for a thousand years. He has photographed the Queen about five times; each time he was invited to do so. For the official portrait for the Golden Jubilee the Palace invited six photographers, including Lord Snowdon and Patrick Lichfield, to contribute: Lord Snowdon dropped out saying he didn't want to be one of six (but he had been married to Princess Margaret after all) and the resulting pictures were a great success. John admired Lichfield's photograph; his own was warmly received.

Swannell was invited to seize the moment when a huge

banquet was taking place, and the photographers were given a few precious moments to grab a picture. With his customary thoroughness he had an idea he thought would work: the Queen superimposed on the battlements at Windsor Castle as the sun set. He was told that the royal couple would be walking down the corridor on their way to the banquet and would be happy to slip into a side room and have a quick photographic session.

The Queen and Prince Philip duly came in, and John, having photographed them both, asked if the Queen would mind if he took her alone, straight on, then from slightly above (him standing on a chair) and then from below (him crouching on the ground). The Queen didn't mind, but time was running out and he hurriedly tried to explain how he was going to assemble the picture and he needed all the angles as he didn't know where the sun would set . . . and they were gone. He used the picture taken from below, and behind Her Majesty he put the beautiful sunset he had taken on the battlements of the Castle. He was hugely disappointed when his picture was rejected: the Queen, ever a stickler for protocol, said she would never be on the battlements wearing a tiara. He asked that his disappointment be conveyed to the Queen as he had really loved the shot. The PR lady said no she couldn't possibly pass on that message but John said, 'Please.' Later he was invited by the Queen to photograph St George's Hall at Windsor to use as a backdrop for the photograph instead of the battlements, as it would be perfectly fitting for her to be in a tiara inside and in that great hall: she had heard of his disappointment and understood.

He was invited back ten years later, this time for the Diamond Jubilee; not six photographers this time, just one: him. He put a great deal of thought into what might be the picture that would capture this tremendous occasion for the public. Could he come to the Palace and look round first? He could, and did. (He would eventually bring two assistants and be allotted about half an hour.) On his recce he noticed a large portrait of King George VI; by positioning the Queen in front of the painting, and propping a huge looking-glass up in front of her, he would capture her and her father twice in one picture. The Queen asked, as this shoot took place, if he would do another set-up, this time without the King. John duly took the memorable picture of the Queen with her back to the window through which can be seen the gold and grey Victoria Memorial. The photograph was spread all over the papers, but John was saddened that the picture with the King hadn't been chosen, as he thought it was really the best. Much later, the 'Palace PR woman', as John called her, told him that far from disliking the photograph with the King's portrait the Queen had loved it so much that she had had it framed and hung it in her bedroom.

6. The Diplomatic Queen

With Buckingham Palace and Windsor Castle, Sandringham and Balmoral, there is no shortage of splendid places in which to welcome dignitaries from all over the world. The Queen is the ultimate diplomat, and a big part of her 'job' is to represent Britain as hostess to statesmen, and also to visit them abroad. Nothing fazes her: she has encountered and experienced every possible kind of social occasion, no matter how grand or informal. She checks every banqueting table, every bedroom and every reception room before the guests arrive: these are her own homes as well as being great palaces and castles of the state.

In 2012, for the Diamond Jubilee, the House of Commons presented a 'Humble Address' to the Queen, and different Members gave tributes, telling their own stories, including Jack Straw, who encountered the Queen's diplomatic skill when he served as Foreign Secretary.

Of the many privileges that go with the best job in the British Cabinet – that of Foreign Secretary – the greatest is that the whole office is expected to accompany Her Majesty the Queen on state visits abroad. During my five years as Foreign Secretary, I went with Her Majesty to, among other places, Germany, France, Malta and Nigeria. Those visits gave me the opportunity to witness at close hand the extraordinary preparation, dedication, commitment and time that Her Majesty and Prince Philip devoted to these sometimes very difficult public engagements. The pace that the Queen and the Prince set for these visits would have tired somebody half their age.

In Nigeria, the arrangements for the day-to-day engagements showed a little flexibility – to be delicate about the matter – and Her Majesty and Prince Philip had to accommodate that flexibility. She had taken part in one engagement at which I thought she did stunningly well. I said to her afterwards, 'Ma'am, if I may say so, that showed extraordinary professionalism.' There was a pause. She looked at me and said, with a benign motherly smile, 'Foreign Secretary, it should have been professional. I've been doing this for long enough.'

As Home Secretary and then Lord Chancellor, I had a rather less public duty – that of administering the oath of homage, which all new bishops of the Church of England have to make to the Sovereign, and have done since the age of Henry VIII. Through that prism, I was able to observe the profound seriousness with which the Queen treats her duties as head of our established Church, as well as her encyclopaedic knowledge of the parishes and personalities of the Anglican communion.

As Member of Parliament for Blackburn for the past thirty-three years [Straw was speaking in 2012], I have seen the excitement and, more importantly, the sense of recognition that visits by Her Majesty and other members of the Royal Family have brought to the people of my area, as they have to every constituency and to people of every ethnic background and religion. These are but a handful of examples of the extraordinary, exemplary way in which Her Majesty has led our nation over the past sixty years.

Of the three most recent of the Queen's dozen prime ministers, one was in nappies and two were not born when she acceded to the throne in February 1952. I guess that I am one of a diminishing band of Members who can recall that day and period. Food and clothes rationing were still in operation and, much more importantly for a six-year-old, so was sweet rationing. There was an acute housing shortage. Vast areas of our great towns and cities were still bombed wastelands, Britain was almost exclusively a white society and I can still recall, in the second year of infant school, the map of the world that our teacher had permanently fixed on the wall and to which he pointed with great regularity. It showed a quarter of the world's land mass painted pink to signify the British Empire.

Six decades on, the world is a very different place, and so is the United Kingdom. We are now a heterogeneous society, with people from many religious and ethnic backgrounds proud to call themselves British. The Empire has gone, to be replaced by the Commonwealth. The rate of social, industrial and technological change has been breathtaking. But through all this change, there has been the Queen – constant, reassuring, providing a sense of security and stability in an uncertain world, yet, remarkably, remaining in touch.

No less splendid (and equally draining I would think) are the state visits here at home. I only say draining because part of me wonders whether I would have read all the research notes, and remembered all the special names and how to pronounce them, and been prepared for unusual ceremonies. I know the Queen is always fully briefed, but there is hard work behind the magic of majesty. Andrew Duncan, sounding rather jaded by the end of the following piece, gives an inkling of the splendour during an important state visit from President Saragat of Italy in 1969. Britain was hoping to join the EEC, a move much desired by the politicians and possibly much of the country. *O tempora, o mores!*

State visits are produced in Britain by the Lord Chamberlain's office, with aplomb and dedication, almost as if they were a finale for the apocalypse. There were two during the year. President Giuseppe Saragat of Italy from 22 to 30 April; and the President of Finland, Dr Urho Kekkonen from 15 to 19 July. Both showed how people who care about tradition and ceremonial and who have the setting, money, and dramatis personae to match their own entrepreneurial ability can make republicans wilt under the nonchalant weight of history play-acting, and even old-time Hollywood envious with the lavishness of the show.

A special programme, about seventy pages long, is printed, a superior time-table showing all aspects of the ceremonial and people involved, with alternative arrangements for wet weather.

Usually there is a set routine with coaches, horses, welcoming committees, morning dress, bands, soldiers, police, roads temporarily closed to traffic, familiar duties such as wreath-laying, dinner at the Palace, and lunch with the Prime Minister. A full cast list for the first day appears over three columns of the Court Circular published in *The Times* and the *Daily Telegraph*, and then gradually recedes in importance.

For President Saragat there was a special treat, an experiment that had not taken place since King Manuel [of

Portugal] visited Edward VII in 1909. As a concession to London traffic and a convenience to the Queen, the state visit took place at Windsor. Princess Margaret, in shocking pink, and Lord Snowdon, met him and his daughter, Signora Santacatterina at London airport and drove in two of the royal Rolls-Royces, followed by nine other cars, to Home Park, an expanse of playing field, fringed with cherry blossom, below Windsor Castle.

A royal pavilion had been erected in the middle of two rugby football pitches (which had involved the moving of the Berkshire seven-a-sides to another pitch a few days earlier), and on it stood a posse of dignitaries – the Lord Lieutenant, Prime Minister, Foreign Secretary Michael Stewart, Home Secretary James Callaghan, chiefs of the three services, chairmen of the county and borough councils, and Chief Constable of Thames Valley Police. They were moved into line by a small bespectacled man with a clipboard, Ronald Hill, secretary in the Lord Chamberlain's office. A red mat was placed in front of the dais, and kept swept, because the field was muddy. To the left, a row of VIPs in morning dress, or military uniform, sat on collapsible wooden chairs placed on a red carpet. Some had blankets on their knees. To the right, there was a press enclosure. And in front the Guard of Honour took up position.

Quarter of a mile away, two hundred schoolchildren waited in a temporary car park. They and a few adults were the only outside witnesses to this self-perpetuating affection to international goodwill, this merry frolic. It seemed a little odd, even narcissistic. Salutes fluttered in constant yo-yo profusion.

'Don't they look splendid, absolutely splendid,' said Lieutenant Colonel Eric Penn, comptroller in the Lord Chamberlain's Office, referring to the Irish Guards, stiff-backed, tall, handsome, father of one of Princess Anne's boyfriends, a man of exquisite courtesy combined with unmilitary romantic gestures. His wife, Prudence, had a personalised number plate on her MG – PRU 365 – because, it was said, he loved her three hundred and sixty-five days of the year. His own Bentley was PEN, followed by another number.

As the Queen arrived, he handed her a list of names in the ceremonial line-up, which she studied while Prince Philip chatted to Harold Wilson and Michael Stewart.

'He's coming,' she said finally to her husband.

Prince Philip took note, turned his back, and continued talking. The Queen played with her gloves and watched the President's car coming down the road, into the field. He was a small man in an ill-shaped suit covered by a grey overcoat, looking dumpy and businesslike among the splendour of a British state occasion. He spoke to the Queen in French, beamed happily as the commanding officer of the Guard, Major Richard Hume, announced, in Italian taught to him by the embassy: 'The Guard of Honour of the First Battalion of the Irish Guards is present and ready for your inspection.'

This accomplished, Signor Saragat was accompanied to the first of eight open carriages by the Duke of Beaufort, Master of the Horse. He clambered in, next to the Queen, and a two-mile procession to the castle began, watched by several thousand people lining routes specially decorated by the council. Behind them came cleaners with shovels and bins to pick up horse manure. 'It was something we hadn't had to cope with before, and I appreciated the problem during the rehearsal,' said town clerk George Waldram. 'We tried to follow up at a discreet distance.'

'Pronto, pronto, pronto,' screeched an Italian journalist

into a telephone, attempting to browbeat the bland British post office into allowing him to relay a report of this historic British pageantry to Rome.

At the castle, Signor Saragat met other members of the Royal Family and was made a Knight Grand Cross of the Civil Division of the Most Honourable Order of the Bath. He saw the Queen Mother in the afternoon, was presented with loyal addresses from the council, walked round the gardens, and in the evening was guest of honour at a state banquet in the Grand Reception Room for one hundred and fifty-four people.

They sat at the Queen's longest table – one hundred and sixty-seven feet of solid mahogany, eight feet wide, that had been in preparation since eleven thirty in the morning. The candelabra had to be placed in position by three men standing on the table, and the gold plate and cut glass were meticulously wiped before being laid out.

The menu of asparagus soup, *flétan au vin blanc, caneton à l'orange*, and *ananas glacé royal* were washed down with Hattenheimer Mehrholzen 1964, Mazis Chambertin 1961, Louis Roederer 1961, and Dow 1945, and digested to the sounds of appropriate music from the Scots Guards: 'Wine, Women and Song', 'Nights of Gladness', 'Mary Poppins', 'Highland Mary', and 'Blaze Away'.

I think that what Andrew describes as 'international swank' else-where in his book, writing about state visits, will be with us for a long time. It attended the princesses of Japan when they made yearly visits across the country from Kyoto to Edo in the Middle Ages, their massive retinue taking six whole days to travel through a single village: it will be with us long after we are gone. We cannot stand dullness: we are all showbiz enough to long for pageantry once in a while. Look at what we love: Oscar ceremonies, red carpets, Mardi Gras parades, carnivals in Rio, the Cannes Film Festival, New Year's Eve fireworks, Indian weddings, ticker-tape welcomes . . . People like swank.

Not all visits are state visits, and sometimes statesmen and stateswomen drop in to see the Queen more informally.

In April 1956 Nikita Khrushchev and Nikolai Bulganin visited Britain. At the time Bulganin was the Premier of the Soviet Union and Khrushchev was First Secretary of the Central Committee of the Communist Party. They visited as official guests of Her Majesty's Government at the invitation of Sir Anthony Eden, the Prime Minister, from 18 to 27 April. On Sunday the twenty-second they had an audience with the Queen at Windsor (Khrushchev might have been using English inexpertly in describing it as a palace). According to the intelligence report written of the visit, Khruschev was rather bowled over by the Queen: 'Khrushchev told the Prime Minister, with every appearance of sincerity, that he had been deeply impressed by the Queen. He said that if ever the Prime Minister were to hint to the Soviet Government that the Queen would like to visit the USSR an invitation would be sent at once, and they would give to the Queen and her court all the honours that were their due.'

Khrushchev recorded the Soviet visit to Windsor. At the end of this extract he muses on the remarks made by an Englishwoman he met on their subsequent tour of the country, who spoke with sympathy about the Queen's responsibilities:

The next day we had an appointment to visit with Queen Elizabeth. We didn't have to wear any special sort of clothes. We had told Eden in advance that if the Queen didn't mind receiving us in our everyday business suits, it was fine. If she did object, then it was just too bad. We had some preconceived notions about this kind of ceremony, and we weren't going to go out of our way to get all dressed up in tails and top hats or anything else that they might have insisted on for an audience with the Queen. I remember once in Moscow we were watching a documentary film which showed Anastas Ivanovich Mikoyan [a Soviet politician] all decked out as our official emissary in Pakistan. We all roared with laughter at the sight of him. He really did look like an old-fashioned European gentleman. I might mention that the fancy airs required of ambassadors by foreign diplomats were not alien to Anastas Ivanovich.

Anyway, we arrived at the Queen's Palace on a warm, pleasant day. According to Eden, April is the best time of year, with the least rain. There were throngs of tourists sightseeing on the Palace grounds. Eden told us that we would find the Queen to be a simple, but very bright and very pleasant woman. She met us as we came into the Palace. She had her husband and two of her children with her. We were introduced. She was dressed in a plain white dress. She looked like the sort of young woman you'd be likely to meet walking along Gorky Street on a balmy summer afternoon.

She gave us a guided tour around the Palace and then invited us to have a glass of tea with her. We sat around over tea and talked about one thing and another. Her husband showed a great interest in Leningrad. He said he'd never been there and dreamed of going someday. We assured him it was a very interesting city and said we were very proud of it. We also told him that it would be easy for us to make his dream come true. We offered to invite him to Leningrad any time he cared to come and said he could visit us in any capacity he wished – as a government representative or as a commander of the army. He thanked us and said he'd take us up on our kindness when he had the opportunity to do so.

The Queen was particularly interested in our plane, the Tu-104, which flew our mail to us while we were in England. Actually, part of the reason we had the Tu-104 fly to London while we were there was to show the English that we had a good jet passenger plane. This was one of the first jet passenger planes in the world and we wanted our hosts to know about it. The Queen had seen the plane in the air as it flew over her Palace on its way to land. We thanked her and agreed that, yes, it was an excellent plane – very modern, undoubtedly the best in the world.

I was very impressed by the Queen. She had such a gentle, calm voice. She was completely unpretentious, completely without the haughtiness that you'd expect of royalty. She may be the Queen of England, but in our eyes she was first and foremost the wife of her husband and the mother of her children. I remember sometime later during our trip around England I met an English woman who said, 'So you met the Queen. What did you think of her?' I answered that we'd liked the Queen very much. The woman shook her head sadly and said, 'I feel so sorry for her. She doesn't have an easy life.'

'Why do you say that?' I asked.

'Well, she's a young woman. She'd probably like to live the normal life of a woman her age, but she can't because she's the Queen. She lives in a fishbowl. She's always on display, and she has to make sure she bears herself in a manner suitable to her royal position at all times. It's a very weighty responsibility, and it makes her life hard. That's why

I feel great sympathy and even sorrow for her.' I liked this woman. What she said about the Queen was a very human and feminine reaction. Maybe Nekrasov [N. A. Nekrasov, the nineteenth-century poet] was right when he said, 'Who in Russia Lives a Carefree Life?' that not even the tsar had it easy. The same thing applies to Queen Elizabeth II.

The Queen has met all the American presidents who have served during her reign, except Lyndon B. Johnson. She may have met more US presidents than anyone else alive, from Harry Truman, whom she met while still a princess, in 1951, to Joe Biden, whom she met recently in Cornwall at the 2021 G7 Conference.

The Queen has made several visits to America throughout her reign, including a state visit in 2007 when she went to Virginia and Jamestown. From the American publication *Indian Country Today* on 26 May of that year the headline read: 'Inclusion of Virginian Indians in Jamestown Anniversary Makes History'.

This moving encounter takes a step aside from too much pageantry and formality and relies on a historical truth: the Virginian Indians welcomed the English as long ago as the beginning of the seventeenth century. The Queen must have been very touched by the gift of the copy of Pocahontas's brooch. (They spelled brooch 'broche', which phonetically makes more sense).

The eight chiefs of the state-recognized Virginia Indian tribes stood in line near the Capitol steps 3 May, awaiting the visit of Queen Elizabeth II of England.

The occasion made history since the event, set to coincide with the 400th anniversary of Jamestown's founding, included Virginia Indians as dignitaries invited to meet the Queen as well as the state's General Assembly – and marked the first time Virginia tribes were represented in a Jamestown anniversary.

As Queen Elizabeth II approached the Capitol steps, Chief Ken Adams of the Upper Mattaponi Indian tribe welcomed her.

'Your Majesty, the descendants of the sovereign Virginia Indian nations who greeted your people in 1607 extend a warm welcome to you today,' Adams said. 'We have the profound privilege of renewing and strengthening our common bonds of history. Just as your people recently greeted us with such honor and dignity, we now return that honor with the Virginia Indian Intertribal Drum and dancers' song of welcome.'

After the welcome, the Queen shook hands with the eight chiefs. Chief William Miles of the Pamunkey Indian tribe gave the Queen a broche encased in a clam shell. The broche was a replica of one that Pocahontas wore when she visited England.

A few years later, in 2010, the Queen was back in America, where she visited the United Nations in New York, addressing the General Assembly for the first time in fifty years. She first addressed them in 1957. Now the UN Secretary General was Ban Ki-moon.

Some speeches can numb the brain if they are too worthy, predictable or dull, but in all the good ones there is a nugget to hold on to, to mull over and ingest.

The formality of Ban Ki-moon's address to Her Majesty shows how much thought and admiration went into his remarks to the Queen.

We are honoured by your presence, Your Majesty. In a changing and churning world, you are an anchor for our age. Your reign spans the decades, from the challenges of the Cold War to the threat of global warming, from the Beatles to Beckham, from television to Twitter. Through the years, you have travelled the world and met its people. You have become a living symbol of grace, constancy and dignity.

In 1957, you first visited this Chamber when the United Nations was still young. Over half a century ago, you told the General Assembly that the future would be shaped by more than the formal bonds that unite us. It would be shaped by the strength of our 'devotion', devotion to the hopes and great ideals of the United Nations Charter: peace, justice, prosperity.

With you at the helm, the United Kingdom and the Commonwealth have contributed immensely to the United Nations. Today, the four largest providers of United Nations peacekeeping troops are Commonwealth countries. Around the world, you are working with us to foster development, advance human rights and promote global security.

In September, we will gather to advance this mission further still by pushing for progress towards the Millennium Development Goals. This is the blueprint of the world's leaders – to save lives of the poor and vulnerable, to combat hunger and disease, to promote gender equality and to provide education, opportunity and decent work to billions of people. We will once again heed your call and devote our full strength to the ideals of our Charter, and to realising a better world for all.

For your dedication, to the United Kingdom and the Commonwealth, and to the United Nations and our common values, we say thank you and welcome. We wish you continued good health and we are happy to have you here today.

I love that: 'You have become a living symbol of grace, constancy and dignity.'

The Queen's devotion to the Commonwealth and the immense strength it has gained through uniting so many different countries is recognised in Ban Ki-moon's moving tribute. No less touching is Her Majesty's own description of this extraordinary gathering of nations, delivered in her Christmas broadcast of 1953: 'The Commonwealth bears no resemblance to the empires of the past. It is an entirely new conception . . . built on the highest qualities of the spirit of man: friendship, loyalty and the desire for freedom and peace.'

As head of the Commonwealth the Queen is not just Queen of the United Kingdom of Great Britain and Northern Ireland, but of sixteen realms. They are: Antigua and Barbuda, Australia, the Bahamas, Barbados, Belize, Canada, Grenada, Jamaica, New Zealand, Papua New Guinea, Saint Kitts and Nevis, Saint Lucia, Saint Vincent and the Grenadines, the Solomon Islands and Tuvalu. Throughout her reign the Queen has visited Canada often. Her father, George VI, was the first reigning British Sovereign to set foot on Canadian soil. She first went there as Princess Elizabeth with Prince Philip in 1951. In Sarah Jane Dumbrille's *Royal Visit to Prescott: Its preparation and staging* on the Queen's visit to Prescott in 1984, I discovered the following story:

Ten-year-old Tina Fisher came all the way from Toronto by train herself to stay with her grandparents, Mr and Mrs Ralph Etheridge, of Prescott, R.R.3, Prescott, so that she could see the Queen. Waiting nearly five hours, Tina, with a bouquet of white carnations, yellow daisies and baby's breath, took up a position in a roped-off area close to the receiving line. With so much security, it was uncertain Tina would be able to present her bouquet until one sympathetic OPP [Ontario Provincial Police] officer told Tina to hold out her flowers to the Queen as she passed. This same kindly officer asked nearby security officers not to interfere with the girl's plans.

And so it was, as the Queen passed, she heard Tina call, 'Your Majesty,' and saw her wave her flowers. Her attention thus drawn to the child, the Queen beckoned Tina to come over. Ducking under the rope, the excited little girl passed through security lines and handed her much-loved Queen her gift – an experience that will be recalled by Tina for as long as she lives.

The Queen has been head of the Commonwealth throughout her reign – a symbolic, unifying role, bringing people together from all around the world. During that time the Commonwealth, has grown from eight nations to fifty-four and now represents two billion people. A huge and important part of Her Majesty's role is to visit Commonwealth countries.

The writer A. N. Dar sums up the Queen's visit in 1961 in an anthology entitled *The Queen's Visit: Elizabeth II in India and Pakistan*:

Twenty-three days through India, twenty-three days on a magic carpet hopping from city to city, each more colourful than the other, each with its own bundle of surprises.

Twenty-three days of a whirlwind tour over an itinerary turned into one long ribbon of teeming millions, of men and women crowded on pavements, of children hanging precariously over tree-tops and waving from the scaffoldings of new constructions.

Twenty-three days of receptions, of costume parades, dance performances and children's rallies, of visits to giant industrial enterprises, atomic reactors and institutes of learning and science.

Such were the twenty-three days Queen Elizabeth and Prince Philip spent in India. But the story of their visit cannot be confined to these twenty-three days alone. For long before the arrival of the royal visitors, India was in a fever. Months in advance old roads were being renovated and new ones laid. Shop-fronts were cleaned up, traffic islands decorated and flag posts dug into road berms [strips of grass besides the road] to fly the Union Jack and the Indian National Tricolour. From small towns and suburban areas thousands of people flocked into big cities to catch a glimpse of the royal visitors as they drove past.

Kenya is another Commonwealth member. Reading about the Queen's visit there in 1983, I was reminded that the Queen's kindness and concern for small children, the infirm and the overlooked shine out wherever she goes. Carefully rehearsed ceremonies, often operating under a different perspective of time, must sometimes be exhausting to attend. I think there may be a knack: focus and be fascinated, and time flies by. Sometimes, as when these children sang to her, I think she might wish that time would stand still.

Mr Prickett, our old friend from Treetops, continues with the following story:

Nyeri Club's great day came on 12 November 1983 when it was decided to invite the Queen to a display of tribal dancing and school singing. I don't know who actually made the great decision but the Vice President of Kenya is one of the club's keenest patrons and a great golfer, and he escorted Her Majesty whenever the President was unable to be present. He comes from the Nyeri area and can often be seen in the Outspan Hotel.

Her Majesty was due to arrive at the club at 5 p.m. During the day she had been busy inspecting a factory eighty miles [130 kilometres] away at Thika, and the road, though tarmac, was good only in parts. And there had been that long climb up *Pole Pole* Hill, which, in Kiswahili, means 'slowly-slowly'. It is so steep that there is no other speed one can go. It was no wonder that, when she did arrive, the Queen looked pale and tired. The Duke was not with her, having left to open a new road around Mount Kenya, a British Government project. As a result the press had gone haring around the mountain, thinking there would be more to see there than in a little country club. They never knew just what they were missing.

Nyeri town turned out in such vast numbers to see the Queen that I had to take Gertrude Annie [his wife] down early in the car, leave her in a good viewing position, then return the car and proceed back on foot the full length of the golf course to re-join her. I do not know where the town obtained the long red carpet linking the road to the club steps but I do know what happened when a dust-devil suddenly struck. Spiralling dust storms are a feature of hot weather in the tropics, and can rise without warning. Two police officers in their immaculate uniforms knelt down and blew away the dust for a considerable distance, then patted the fabric smooth before standing up again and desperately trying to pat the dust and crinkles from their trousers.

When the excitement was at its height, and all the children

appeared to have arrived, the district commissioner commenced handing out flags, Kenyan and British alternately, so that each child could hold one. After Her Majesty had signed the visitors' book she emerged from the clubhouse and sat in the centre of a long line of chairs on the club veranda. Before her were the colourful Wakikuya dancers in their traditional dress, followed by the girls of Tumu Tumu School. The scene was, perhaps, the most beautiful in Kenya, for the last rays of the setting sun were lighting up the snows on Mount Kenya, not so far away. It was a poignant scene too, for she must have thought how vastly different the people before her were from the Kikuyu she had last seen almost thirty-two years before. There are few earlobes hanging almost to the shoulders today, filled with coils of gaudy beads, as there had been then. Though the tribal costumes were genuine enough the wearers spoke very good English, and many would have been working in offices. Though the drums they were beating, the songs they sang and the dances they danced were of the old Kenya, they themselves were of the new, and most would not even have been born in 1952. But it is good to keep alive the old cultures. What has Britain to show today other than a little morris-dancing?

There were no speeches, for speeches would have been a banality. It was the only time I have been present in a mighty gathering of this type in which speeches have not been made. The welcome was in the smiling faces, and in the wonderful words of the songs – words which were so moving that they made the tears glisten on many a hardened cheek. After the tribal dancing came the schoolgirls from Tumu Tumu. Dressed in yellow blouses, brown skirts, and white socks, they danced and fluttered around on the grass like daffodils in a breeze, like rays of sunshine in a day far spent. They were followed by younger children from other schools, singing in a higher pitch to the tune of that old English favourite, 'In An English Country Garden'. The words of the songs were wonderfully fitting for a country that has retained all that is best from the influence of another country so very far away. The poignant words and the gestures went unheard and unseen by the world's press, still in the wake of the Duke opening the new road. For the sake of posterity, and so that they will never be forgotten, they are reproduced as follows:

A Jubilant Salute
Welcome! Karibu!
Oh Daughter of our land!
For you have come back!
Like a beacon our beautiful land
has lured you back.
Welcome back! That mountain booms!
Your Royal Majesty, the Queen,
A gracious and charming sovereign,
A noble and loving mother,
With a smile worth a million,
A mind at peace with everyone,
A heart overflowing with kindness
and tenderness. With open arms
We welcome you back home.
Three decades ago a princess you ascended
Treetops.
A queen you descended to your preordained position,
And a great honour to our land.
Welcome back! The wind echoes in jubilation.

131

We were yet to be born.
May your stay here be pleasant.
And may we cherish the memory
Of this great honour to our Motherland.

Your Royal Majesty,
Britain and Kenya are not new friends.
It was here in Kenya that you visited
Just before Your Majesty became
The head of the British people.
May this bond of friendship between us
Never wither, fade or die.

Your Royal Majesty,
We wish to send you to Britain,
To the children of that great nation.
Take our message of love and friendship.
For far apart as we may seem to be,
We are but the youth of tomorrow.
Today and the world tomorrow
Will be ours to lead.

And now, Your Royal Majesty,
Accept our thanks and humbleness,
As we bid you here farewell.
When back at home, do please remember
Our land – where *jambo* means hello.
Kwaheri is our word for bye.
Karibu means please come again.
Thank you and goodbye, Your Majesty.

Welcome to Nyeri Your Majesty

Your Royal Majesty,
Welcome to this our Motherland,
We are most grateful to you
For agreeing to come to our land, Kenya.
Zebras and buffaloes, lions and elephants,
Cheetahs and bongos, leopards and birds,
Many more you'll see and you'll find out –
Your visit will be wonderful.

How many mountains, rivers and lakes
In this beautiful country Kenya?
We'll tell you of some that we all know that do
exist in Kenya.
Mount Kenya, Elgon, Aberdares, Longonot,
Tana, Chania, Tsavo, Nzoia, Athi,
Lakes Nakuru, Naivasha, Baringo
And the biggest Lake Victoria.

How many races that do
Exist in our beautiful country Kenya?
We'll tell you of some that we all know.
In our motherland of Kenya
Africans and Europeans, Japanese, Americans,
Indians, Arabs, Chinese and Greeks.
We are all guided by one motto,
Peace, Love and Unity.

Perhaps we will never know who thought of those beautiful
words, both in English and Kikuyu. Perhaps they were the

joint effort of many people. Whoever wrote them, they were inspired – fit for a royal occasion.

When the provincial commissioner told me that the Queen had commanded her personal secretary to obtain for her a copy of those words I felt proud and deeply moved.

During 'the Troubles' in Northern Ireland, visiting the Republic was deemed to be too dangerous for the Queen. No reigning monarch had been in Ireland since George V in 1911; in those faraway days Ireland was still part of the United Kingdom. From all that I have heard, the Queen has always had a special affection for Ireland and its people; and when in 2011 she finally went there she was received with immense affection and admiration. The trip was a huge success, due to the Queen's obvious joy at being there and her determination that what she called 'the ties of family, friendship and affection' should be encouraged and treasured. She went out of her way to greet people not actually on the itinerary, stepping aside to praise the gardaí, the police, and greet the grannies. She stole their hearts. At the Irish State Banquet on 18 May, a hundred years after her grandfather George V had toured the country, she made her feelings clear.

What were once only hopes for the future have now come to pass; it is almost exactly thirteen years since the overwhelming majority of people in Ireland and Northern Ireland voted in favour of the agreement signed on Good Friday 1998, paving the way for Northern Ireland to become the exciting and inspirational place that it is today. I applaud the work of all those involved in the peace process, and of all those who support and nurture peace, including members of the police, the gardaí, and the other emergency services, and those who work in the communities, the churches and charitable bodies, like Co-operation Ireland. Taken together, their work not only serves as a basis for reconciliation between our people and communities, but it gives hope to other peacemakers across the world that, through sustained effort, peace can and will prevail.

For the world moves on quickly. The challenges of the past have been replaced by new economic challenges, which will demand the same imagination and courage. The lessons from the peace process are clear: whatever life throws at us, our individual responses will be all the stronger for working together and sharing the load.

There are other stories written daily across these islands which do not find their voice in solemn pages of history books, or newspaper headlines, but which are at the heart of our shared narrative. Many British families have members who live in this country, as many Irish families have close relatives in the United Kingdom.

These families share the two islands; they have visited each other and have come home to each other over the years. They are the ordinary people who yearned for the peace and understanding we now have between our two nations and between the communities within those two nations; a living testament to how much in common we have.

These ties of family, friendship and affection are our most precious resource. They are the lifeblood of the partnership across these islands, a golden thread that runs through all our joint successes so far, and all we will go on to achieve. They are a reminder that we have much to do together to build a future for all our grandchildren: the kind of future our grandparents could only dream of.

So we celebrate together the widespread spirit of goodwill and deep mutual understanding that has served to make the relationship more harmonious, close as good neighbours should always be.

State visits abroad are carefully chosen far in advance. Diplomacy in accepting invitations from different countries in the right order may cause headaches, but these are the proverbial swan's feet paddling madly underwater while progress is serene and unruffled above. Frank Roberts was British ambassador to West Germany from 1963 to 1968. In his book *Dealing with Dictators* he writes of a particularly sensitive set of protocols to be micro-managed so that no slights were perceived by the host nation.

The fact remained that the Queen, by this time, had paid state visits to almost every country in the world, and if HMG did not advise Her Majesty to visit Germany soon, all our efforts in other fields might be wasted.

This was particularly important because of the special position that General de Gaulle had acquired in Germany, partly on his visits, on one of which he had rather surprisingly insisted upon his partial German ancestry, a field in which the Queen could obviously outplay him with ease. American presidents had also been to Germany, and there had been, above all, the most successful visit in the summer of 1963 of President Kennedy, which is best known for his famous phrase, '*Ich bin ein Berliner.*' When I pointed this out to London, I had a sympathetic hearing from the then Foreign Secretary, Rab Butler, whom I had first known as Parliamentary under-secretary in the Foreign Office before the war, and it was rapidly agreed that such a visit should be made. State visits, however, take some time to arrange, and the Queen's visit took place in 1965 under a Labour Government with Michael Stewart as Foreign Secretary.

I had not previously been concerned with any state visits and did not realise the immensely detailed work which went into them, particularly into a visit of such political importance as this one. It was to be one of the longest state visits that the Queen had ever paid, one of ten days, to cover much of the Federal Republic. One of the first problems which arose concerned the Queen's and also Prince Philip's many relations in Germany. There had recently been a state visit from the King of Greece [King Paul] who, with his wife [Queen Frederika], also had many relations among the German princely houses. Since Prince Philip was much involved in these family matters, he sent me a message explaining that there had been great protocol difficulties during the King of Greece's visit when members of the former German ruling houses, who had no position in the current Republican protocol, had found themselves seated at dinners below relatively junior German officials. Prince Philip suggested that I should explain the position to the German President, Herr Lübke, and say that the Queen would understand if her relatives were not invited on any formal occasions.

President Lübke was a very decent man of clear and firm views but without a broad vision. He had been selected in a hurry when Adenauer turned down the presidency himself, and had many good qualities without being on the same high level as other German presidents, such as Heuss himself or Richard von Weizsäcker. He was greatly helped by his intelligent wife. One of his qualities was that he knew his own mind. When I put Prince Philip's suggestion to him he at once told me that this would not do. He came from the Sauerland in the mountains behind Cologne, whose inhabitants are famous for the hardness of their heads. In the Sauerland, he explained to me, it was a tradition when, if I wouldn't mind his putting it this way, a girl of the country came back after it did not matter how many years, her relatives must be invited to meet her; and there was no doubt about the Hanoverian origins of the British Royal Family. He could not therefore possibly fail to invite her relatives to meet her. I found myself between the hammer of Prince Philip and the anvil of President Lübke.

Luckily, by this time I had got to know the late Prince Ludwig of Hessen, who had married a Geddes and knew Britain well. He had a keen interest in music and had translated the librettos of Benjamin Britten's operas. For my purposes the important thing was that he was well in with Buckingham Palace and also seemed to be accepted by other German princely families as an authority whose opinion on anything affecting the British Royal Family should be respected. He produced the solution, which was that the German 'royals' should only be invited when the Queen visited their own particular parts of Germany – the Hohenzollerns in Berlin, the Hanovers in Hanover, and so forth. Any small protocol difficulty could therefore be got round in a way that would not have been possible with a large number of princely invitees at the same party. I think the solution in Bonn itself was to invite only those who were going to be hosts to the Queen on the rare occasions when she was 'off duty'.

This did, however, create another difficulty. Prince Philip's relatives, who were all in western Germany, had come quite well out of the war and were in a good position to entertain the Queen in suitable style in their great houses in Baden-Württemberg and the Rhineland. The Queen's direct relatives were the Hohenzollerns and the Hanovers. The Hohenzollerns had lost all their palaces, and the then head of the house lived fairly modestly in Bremen. The Hanovers had been hit hard by the withdrawal of the Allied forces to the Elbe at the end of the war, since some of their best houses were in the area then occupied by the Russians. The Queen had some breaks in her ten days, dining at Wolfsgarten with the Hessens and at Langenburg with Prince Philip's sister, then spending part of a weekend with Prince Philip's other relatives, the Badens, at Salem.

The Germans discovered a very good solution to what could have been a major problem in a ten-day visit of constantly changing residences. After their first nights on the Petersberg high over Bonn, where HM gave her party for the President, a special train was made up, in which she and her suite went round Germany. This saved a great deal of time and stress, and proved a most successful arrangement. Another problem arising from the length of the visit was the necessity to submit an unusually large number of speeches for the Queen, suitable for the different places in which she had to make them. The third of her speeches was in Koblenz, just before crossing the Rhine to be the guest of the Hessen government at Wiesbaden. She happened to be crossing the Rhine at precisely the spot where Marshal Blücher had crossed on his way to join Wellington at the Battle of Waterloo. Our speech writer in the embassy introduced a very diplomatic reference to the spot where, in a period of Anglo-German military cooperation, a great German general had crossed the Rhine on his way to help his British Allies. There was no mention of Waterloo or the French. This did not prevent the French general in Koblenz from saying afterwards that he had had the greatest difficulty in restraining himself from leaving the meeting in a huff; and I was told that even so good a friend of this country as General Catroux, then marshal of the Legion of Honour, refused his invitation to the Queen's birthday party at the British Embassy in Paris, all because of what they regarded as a veiled reference to Waterloo.

In Berlin, the Queen not only gave reassurance to the Berlin population but took a parade of the British garrison, as she had previously taken a major parade of the British and Canadian forces in the Federal Republic.

For me, one of the most important features of the royal visit was not so much the reception of the Queen in Germany, which I knew would be most enthusiastic, but getting the story back on television to the United Kingdom. Those were the days when British television was still full of films and pictures of jack-booted Nazis and escapes by British prisoners of war, and when some British correspondents in Germany were still under guidance from their head offices in London to report unhappy rather than satisfactory developments in Anglo-German relations. It was therefore important that the British public should see for themselves what sort of people their Allies in the Federal Republic now were. They could hardly fail to get the message that the new German democracy had nothing in common with Hitler's Third Reich.

The Queen ended her visit in Hamburg. The city fathers, who were, as has almost always been the case since the war, socialists, but very much to the centre, arranged for twenty of the leading citizens to be received by the Queen at a special guest house on the Alster Lake in the middle of Hamburg. At that time one of the most famous footballers in the world was Uwe Seeler, captain of the very successful Hamburg and German national football teams and highly regarded for his sportsmanship and good character. I knew he was likely to attract more attention in the popular British press than most other citizens of Hamburg, however worthy. The socialist city fathers were less than enthusiastic to include him, but I stuck to my guns, with the results I had anticipated.

I had originally suggested that HM should start her visit by sailing into Hamburg, but the Federal Government correctly decided that the visit should start in the capital, Bonn. Her Majesty's departure from Hamburg at night with HMY *Britannia* fully illuminated and escorted by British and German naval vessels was an unforgettable sight. The Queen's visit had more than fulfilled our highest expectations, and established a sure foundation for Anglo-German bilateral relations.

In Germany, it is reported, they say there are many queens but only one Queen. The continuing fascination of other nations with Her Majesty and her appearance means that the smallest observation merits a place in the foreign press. *La Repubblica* carried a front-page story on Tuesday, 17 October 2000, during the Queen's visit to Italy. It read:

'Ode to the Queen's Handbag'

There it is. That disturbing object, firmly attached to her left forearm. The secret of her regality is in that little royal, but so ordinary, accessory.

The Queen speaks fluent French, which must have impressed her host President François Hollande when she went to Paris on a flying visit: a tiny part of the city was to be named after her. When I was a model in the sixties I often travelled to Paris to 'do' the collections: not on the catwalks, but to be photographed in clothes from the Paris collections ready for the papers the next day in Britain. I had friends in the Île de la Cité who lived in a glorious little garret, and I can still remember their telephone number: Médicis onze-trente-six.

'*Où sont les neiges d'antan?*' (It's a question that has never been answered satisfactorily. Where indeed are the snows of yesteryear?)

The French capital had a touch of royal fever on Saturday [reported *France 24*], as Britain's Queen Elizabeth breezed through town on the last stop of her official visit to France for the D-Day commemorations.

After the dinner hosted by French President François Hollande at the Élysée Palace on Friday and a city hall reception thrown by Paris's recently elected mayor, Anne Hidalgo, Saturday morning, the Queen was whisked off to a flower market for the unveiling of a plaque bearing her name.

Located on the Île de la Cité, one of Paris's two central islands, the flower market will now be called Marché aux Fleurs Reine Élisabeth II (Queen Elizabeth II Flower Market). The Queen reportedly selected the location herself as one of her favourite spots in Paris. According to French media, the market has sentimental value for her, since the last time she was there she was pregnant with her son, Charles.

Though security for the ceremony Hollande presided over

was heavy, hundreds of tourists and locals lined the adjacent street hoping for a glimpse of the Queen in her pale rose suit.

Many languages could be overheard, but chief among them, unsurprisingly, were English and French.

'She's amazing,' gushed Liz Brooks, a sixtyish British woman on holiday in Paris with her husband and long-time friends from Australia. 'At eighty-eight, she's still so interested in everything. We used to have a house in Normandy, so we're very sensitive to the history of the landings and to the whole French-English connection.'

Brooks said she had met the Queen once when receiving a national award. 'She was marvellous,' she recalled. 'Easy to talk to, very professional. Quite an amazing lady.'

Younger fans of the Queen were also on hand to behold the spectacle, which was projected on a big screen set up next to the flower market for those unable to get closer to the action.

'It's probably the last time we'll get to see her in France,' said Marie, a twentysomething Parisian accompanied by her boyfriend. 'I think it's important to see her once in your life. She's the last great monarch of Europe.'

Marie admitted to a bit of royal envy. 'I love the fact that she's England personified. Here in France, we elect presidents that come and go every five years, but the Queen remains the symbol of her country no matter where she goes.'

7. The Queen Reigns

The Queen is above politics. She does not rule, she reigns, and through the daily boxes that follow her wherever she is in the world she is up to date with all that goes on in the country and the Commonwealth. She has acquired more inside knowledge than can be imagined, throughout her long reign, and from countless meetings with heads of state, weekly conferences with her prime ministers and thousands of letters from the general public, who write to her when all else has failed. The Queen's Speech is all part of the pomp and circumstance of government, and here Cecil Beaton, with a painterly eye, describes the first time she went to open Parliament, in 1952, before she was crowned; at the end, the photograph he refers to is one of the most famous of them all.

I went to the Opening of Parliament. It was the first time that this ceremony was to be performed by the young Queen.

I always enjoy watching my fellow human beings, but now, in their traditional fancy dress – a fancy dress that has been tried, developed and improved until found flawless – the show could have gone on for ever. Ancient men with tired eyes, wrinkles, thinning hair, and all the sad outward aspects of age, appeared perfectly cast as unique and remarkable characters, in these marvellous scarlet, black and white clothes. Grand soldiers or officers of state were stiffly encumbered with gold thread embroideries as if they were in their natural everyday habit.

Indoors all quiet until suddenly, outside the high windows, various rumbling noises told one that the Queen was arriving. The cheers of the people sent a tremor through the bloodstream. One expected, but did not hear, an organ to roll out a volume of noise. It was the continued insistent silence that made all the more impressive the moment when the tall double doors were thrown open to reveal the young Queen standing with her gloved hand held high on that of her Consort. A moment's pause, then in a slow, ambling march the procession passed towards the throne where the young lady would make her first speech to Parliament.

The Queen wore gold and stolid white. The long red velvet train, miniver-edged, splendid against the gold and scarlet setting, her stance, with the rigid little head and the well-curled hair around Queen Victoria's crown, was marvellously erect. She has inherited many of her mother's graces but, most important of all, she has acquired her frank serenity: her eyes are not those of a busy, harassed person. She regards people with a recognition of compassion – and a slight suggestion of a smile lightens the otherwise cumbrous mouth.

There was nothing formidable about the general mood, which encouraged an ease and sense of relaxation in the spectators, and the procession moved so slowly that one felt tempted to talk to those passing by. The Duke of Edinburgh appeared somewhat hollow-eyed, his complexion pale, and hair beginning to thin.

When the procession moved out of sight, one could only imagine the ritual when Black Rod, with the ebony hand at the end of his wand, shouts, 'Open, open!' to allow the doors of the Chamber to give entrance to the Queen.

Then we hear the relayed voice of the Queen, in high, childlike tones, thanking the Lords and the Members of the House of Commons for their sympathy expressed on her Sovereign father's death. She hopes to follow her father's example, being sure that Her People would accord her the same loyalty and understanding. In the year to come she hopes to visit some of Her Colonial Empire, prays for an armistice in Korea, promises that Her Government would take full share in the work of NATO, aims to strengthen the unity of Europe, and considers the scheme for Federation in Central Africa. The task of placing the national economy on a sound foundation, curbing inflation and reducing expenditure, must also be undertaken, while every encouragement shall be given to the fishing industry. She prays that the blessing of the Almighty may rest upon Her Government's Councils.

Then, no doubt greatly relieved that her vocal ordeal is at an end, she smiles with added sweetness as the procession returns. Smiles to the left and right, and the sea of spectators billows down in curtseys and bows. The Queen and her Duke are through the double doors whence they came; the doors are shut.

The Queen departs. A clash of steel, horses' hooves, and again the distant thundering of cheers from the people lining the streets.

The old fur coats are helped onto shoulders of skinny peeresses. Some wrap their trains round their goose-fleshed arms, and the party breaks up.

London was in its usual blue haze, the bare plane trees dripping with tassels like Victorian bobble fringe. Big Ben struck twelve, military orders were shouted in rasping, retching voices, guards sloped arms, a brass band brayed, the crowds jumped on their toes, nannies ran with their charges to follow the bobbing sea of bearskins, and the ordinary flow of traffic, so severely inconvenienced, again began to move. Already the newspaper men were selling the earliest editions with their posters, 'The Queen's Speech', and the photograph of the monarch in her coach, laughing and jerking her hand at the crowds. The flashlight had caught the brilliance of the Queen's laugh, the glitter and the movement of the coach exemplified by the pear-shaped pearl swinging at her ear.

Elaborate procedures frame every appointment of ministers in a newly elected government. After the general election of 1964 and the Labour victory, Richard Crossman was appointed Minister of Housing and Local Government. Crossman was a tremendous diarist: candid, perceptive and critical. His description of 'kissing hands', the formal installation of a government minister, shows what a strain these ceremonies can be on the participants.

I continue to have this curious sense of fiction, the feeling that I am living in a Maurice Edelman [Crossman's fellow Labour MP and a political novelist] novel. All this business of being a cabinet minister is still unreal to me. And this feeling has been particularly strengthened by the fact that every time we left Downing Street or moved along Whitehall there was always a crowd of people watching, cheering, clapping as we went in and out – it's as if we are taking part not in real life but in a piece of reportage on the British constitutional system.

Undoubtedly the most fantastic episode in this novel was the kissing hands and the rehearsal. It took place last Monday when we new ministers were summoned to the Privy Council offices to rehearse the ceremony of becoming a privy counsellor. I don't suppose anything more dull, pretentious, or plain silly has ever been invented. There we were, sixteen grown men. For over an hour we were taught how to stand up, how to kneel on one knee on a cushion, how to raise the right hand with the Bible in it, how to advance three paces towards the Queen, how to take the hand and kiss it, how to move back ten paces without falling over the stools – which had been carefully arranged so that you did fall over them. Oh dear! We did this from 11.10 to 12.15. At 12.15 all of us went out, each to his own car, and we drove to the Palace and there stood about until we entered a great drawing room. At the other end there was this little woman with a beautiful waist, and she had to stand with her hand on the table for forty minutes while we went through this rigmarole. We were uneasy, she was uneasy. Then at the end informality broke out and she said, 'You all moved backwards very nicely,' and we all laughed. And then she pressed a bell and we all left her. We were privy counsellors: we had kissed hands.

It was two-dimensional, so thin, so like a coloured illus-tration in the *Sphere*, not a piece of real life. It's the thinness of it that astonishes me still; and this is true not only of kissing hands but of cabinet meetings.

There are all kinds of rules about speaking to the Queen, some enough to put you off ever daring to utter any words at all to Her Majesty: don't speak until you are spoken to;

always address her as 'Your Majesty' first, then 'ma'am' to rhyme with jam; don't talk too long; don't think that it is up to you to finish the conversation, as the Queen will do that. There is something about her shifting her bag from one arm to another to signal to a lady-in-waiting to steer you away, as you may have become a crashing bore unintentionally. And you will have made an obeisance, a bowing of the head from the neck only if you are a man, a curtsey if you are a woman, but not too deep: not the court curtsey I was taught when we were young, one knee behind the other and sinking down to the ground with eyes lowered, because it is now considered out of date and unnecessary. A shame, as I had practised it to perfection just in case I was suddenly summoned to the royal presence ('We must get Joanna Lumley here now. She will know what to do'). After meeting the Queen, you invariably go over and over it in your head, editing out the gaffes you may have made, which the Queen will be sure to have neither noticed nor cared about, and rewriting your gleaming moment of history in your own book of precious memories. Over the months and years of her reign the Queen will have met thousands and thousands of people for whom the moment is etched for ever in their mind: some, like Richard Crossman, met her many times, as politicians do, and his insight into the woman behind the protocol is wonderfully revealing.

In 1966 he travelled to Balmoral for a Privy Council meeting.

After the Privy Council we went for a drink in the drawing room. It has a wonderful long picture painted on slate in which Landseer has a really jolly sketch of the young Princess Royal [Princess Victoria, the eldest child of Queen Victoria] riding home from a stag hunt with Prince Albert benignly bending over her. What a splendid painter he would have been if he'd just left all his paintings half finished like this one. During the drinks the Queen was extremely good at keeping things going but I noticed this time even more than last how shy she can be. When we walked back into the drawing room I was carrying my papers and she was carrying hers. I put mine down on a side table and she held hers tight in her hand. Somebody tried to take them off her and she said, 'No, I must go and get rid of them.' But she stood there for three minutes without a drink, with the papers in her hand and with nothing to say. If one waits for her to begin the conversation nothing happens. One has to start to talk and then suddenly the conversation falters because both are feeling, 'Oh dear, are we boring each other?' She has a lovely laugh. She laughs with her whole face and she can't just assume a mere smile because she's really a very spontaneous person. Godfrey Agnew [Clerk of the Privy Council] was right when he said to me that evening that she finds it difficult to suppress her emotion. When she is deeply moved and tries to control it she looks like an angry thundercloud. So, very often when she's been deeply touched by the plaudits of the crowd she merely looks terribly bad-tempered.

When Margaret Thatcher, accompanied by her husband Denis, was summoned to the Palace and asked to form a government, she was anxious to follow protocol to the letter. An awesome ability to absorb data and to manage on very little sleep made her a formidable character; Lord Shackleton, a Labour peer and son of the great Antarctic explorer Sir Ernest Shackleton, told me that she was the only person who read all the parliamentary papers from every party and could quote from them. I sense that Mrs Thatcher appreciated Her Majesty's firm grasp of politics and command of detail.

I can remember an odd sense of loneliness as well as anticipation when I received the telephone call which summoned me to the Palace. I was anxious about getting the details of procedure and protocol right.

At about 2.45 p.m. the call came. I walked out of Central Office through a crowd of supporters and into the waiting car, which drove Denis and me to the Palace on my last journey as Leader of the Opposition.

The Audience at which one receives the Queen's authority to form a government comes to most prime ministers only once in a lifetime. The authority is unbroken when a sitting prime minister wins an election, and so it never had to be renewed throughout the years I was in office. All audiences with the Queen take place in strict confidence – a confidentiality vital to the working of both government and constitution. I was to have such audiences with Her Majesty once a week, usually on a Tuesday, when she was in London and sometimes elsewhere when the Royal Family was at Windsor or Balmoral.

Anyone who imagines that these meetings are confined to social niceties is quite wrong: they are quietly businesslike and Her Majesty brings to bear a formidable grasp of current issues and breadth of experience. And, although the press could not resist the temptation to suggest disputes between the Palace and Downing Street, I always found the Queen's attitude towards the work of the Government absolutely correct.

Prime ministers come and prime ministers eventually go. I remember them all, some vaguely, from when I was very young, and some still very clearly. The Queen will have formed her own opinions of not only their time in office but of the people themselves; from what I have read about their audiences with her, she is interested, never openly critical, and extraordinarily well-informed. No matter how young or old or experienced you are, you will be meeting the best of the best, and would be wise to remember it. Tony Blair describes 'kissing hands' at Buckingham Palace after the landslide victory that brought him and the Labour Party to power in 1997:

As we drove through the gates of Buckingham Palace there were more crowds, frantic to get a sight of the new prime minister. I could tell Cherie was very excited. As ever, I just wanted to get on with it. By now, I was straining at the leash of the convention, tradition and ceremony that delayed the doing.

I was shown into a little antechamber, outside the room where the Queen was. I suddenly became nervous. I knew the basic protocol, but only very vaguely. It is called 'kissing hands', the laying on of the Queen's authority to govern. She was head of state. I was *her* prime minister. A tall official with a stick stood by me. 'I should tell you one thing, Mr Blair,' he began (note 'Mr Blair' until I had been appointed), 'you don't actually kiss the Queen's hands in the ceremony of kissing hands. You brush them gently with your lips.'

I confess this floored me. What on earth did he mean? Brush them as in a pair of shoes, or touch them lightly? While I was temporarily disconcerted, the door opened and I was ushered in, unfortunately tripping a little on a piece of carpet so that I practically fell upon the Queen's hands, not so much brushing as enveloping them. I recovered sufficiently to find myself sitting opposite her. I had met her before, of course, but this was different. It was my first audience. There is much to say about the Queen. At this encounter, I noticed two things: she was quite shy, strangely so for someone of her experience and position; and at the same time, direct. I don't mean rude or insensitive, just direct. 'You are my tenth prime minister. The first was Winston. That was before you were born.' We talked for a time, not exactly small-talk but general guff about the government programme, the conversation somewhat stilted. Then Cherie was brought in to pay her respects, and the Queen relaxed more as they chatted. (Contrary to popular belief, Cherie always got on well with her.) Cherie was explaining very practical things we would need to do with the children, and how strange it would be for them to live in Downing Street, and the Queen was generally clucking sympathetically. I fear I sat there looking a trifle manic, unsure how or when to end the conversation, focusing on what I would say on the steps of Downing Street and feeling, through lack of sleep, more than a little spaced out. The Queen understood it all, of course, and kept the conversation going for just the right length of time; then, by an ever so slight gesture, she ended it and saw us out.

'This way, Prime Minister,' said the tall chap with the stick as he ushered us down the stairs to the waiting car.

8. At Home with the Queen

It's a sort of dream to be asked by the Queen to come for lunch, or even stay for a night at one of the royal residences. What would it be like? What would you eat, or say or wear? Would the Queen really laugh at your jokes? Would it be nerve-racking? Close friends of the Royal Family have quite rightly remained silent about their time in the Queen's company. The evangelist Billy Graham was courteous but tight-lipped when questioned about his private visits. However, he felt he had to share the story of the pheasants when he and his wife Ruth visited the Queen at Sandringham; those stuffed birds may still be standing under glass somewhere in Montréal.

No one in Britain has been more cordial toward us than Her Majesty Queen Elizabeth II. Almost every occasion I have been with her has been in a warm, informal setting, such as a luncheon or dinner, either alone or with a few family members or other close friends. Out of respect for her privacy and that of her family, I will say little more.

Her official position has prevented her from openly endorsing our Crusade meetings. But by welcoming us and having me preach on several occasions to the Royal Family at Windsor and Sandringham, she has gone out of her way to be quietly supportive of our mission. She is unquestionably one of the best-informed people on world affairs I have ever met. Part of that knowledge comes from the weekly in-depth briefings she is given by the prime minister, of course, but I have always found her highly intelligent and knowledgeable about a wide variety of issues, not just politics.

Once, when visiting the Royal Family at Sandringham in 1984, Ruth and I walked past a woman wearing an old raincoat, wellingtons, and a scarf; she was bent over fixing some food for the dogs. We thought at first she was one of the housekeepers, but when she straightened up, we saw it was the Queen!

At the end of that visit, a doorman came up to the car just as we were departing. He had a box under his arm, which he handed to our friend Maurice Rowlandson, who had come to pick us up.

'A brace of pheasants from Her Majesty the Queen, for Mr and Mrs Graham,' he said.

All the way back to London we debated what to do with them. Maurice suggested we take them to the hotel chef to be prepared and roasted. In the end, however, I decided that would be a waste. I asked Maurice to arrange for them to be stuffed by a taxidermist. Eventually, they arrived at our Montréal home in a glass case – truly pheasant under glass! Later Maurice admitted that shipping the case from England and getting it through US customs had been one of the greater challenges of his life.

The terror of saying the wrong thing is heightened in the presence of royalty. A kind of Tourette's syndrome threatens to take over your tongue, and even when well-prepared it seems possible that you might disgrace yourself and insult the company you keep.

The playwright Noël Coward, ever a friend of the Queen Mother, recognised this. Suave and sophisticated to a high degree, and not one to blurt out profanities, he was nevertheless aware of the danger.

I've just got back from my royal weekend with the Queen Mother. She was charming, gay and entirely enchanting, as she always is. The Queen came over to lunch on Sunday, looking like a young girl. It was all very merry and agreeable but there is always, for me, a tiny pall of 'best behaviour' overlaying the proceedings. I am not complaining about this, I think it is right and proper, but I am constantly aware of it. It isn't that I have a basic urge to tell disgusting jokes and say 'fuck' every five minutes, but I'm conscious of a faint resentment that I couldn't if I wanted to. I told the Queen how moved I had been by Prince Charles's investiture, and she gaily shattered my sentimental illusions by saying that they were both struggling not to giggle because at the dress rehearsal the crown was too big and extinguished him like a candle-snuffer!

Apart from being an extremely fine screen actor, Dirk Bogarde was a prolific letter-writer. He had long been a hero of mine before I got my first postcard from him, in which he thanked me for praising him in a column I used to write for *The Times*. He wrote books and diaries, letters and postcards, often illustrating them himself, and his slightly waspish nature was honeyed by this charming and generous trait. He set up a correspondence with a woman in America he had never met, writing to her for five years. Their correspondence had started when she saw a photograph of him standing outside a house she had lived in during the 1930s. He describes to her his initial reluctance to lunch with the Queen, something you or I would jump at (well, when the invitation came my way one golden day, I did jump at it . . . but that is another story). Watch how he mellows as the royal magic overwhelms him. On 31 May 1968 he wrote:

I have to go and have lunch with HM on the 6th. One D-day (in 1944) was bad enough. I simply dread it. I'm no good at this kind of function. I tried to get out of it but to no avail. Was asked to go in April, by her equerry, Patrick Plunket, with whom I was in the war. Managed to wriggle clear by pleading that I simply had to work. I wasn't but managed to make it stick. He fixed me for June. He was very shocked when I tried it again, and when I told him to get me excused, he explained patiently, but with a certain amount of grittiness, that I was 'commanded' to appear for lunch, and that the Queen was disappointed about the last time. I bet. Don't suppose she knows who I am even. This set of lunches is all a part of Philip's 'democratisation' (if that is a word!) of the royals. They get to meet the People at the lunch table.

Oh, hell. I suppose it'll be a famous footballer, a jockey and a district nurse and tinned pears and custard. And I don't know anything about corgis much, and absolutely nothing at all about horses. It'll be a sparkling lunch.

A week later, on 7 June, he described attending the lunch:

I set off to my dreaded lunch . . . half hoping, well, hoping entirely really!, that it might be cancelled because of the news [of the assassination of Robert F. Kennedy] . . . but alas! her standard was streaming high in the summer breeze. I will admit, although I feel a bit guilty, that sweeping through the great gilded gates in my own car, in my best dark suit, was quite fun. And the tremendous Present Arms I got from the guard, and the smashing wink I received from the guard commander under his busby sent the Japanese tourists absolutely frantic with their Nikons and Pentaxes . . . Flashes popped like flak bursts! Kennedy quite forgotten. Although perhaps the Japanese don't share our grief to the same extent?

However. As we made a wide curve across the gravel to the red carpet and the distant figure of Patrick waiting for me, Louis, my driver, immaculate in his new cap for the occasion and new cockade, turned in his seat, and with a deferential cough, signalling a question, he asked what he should call me *after* lunch. I told him that it really was only that, and no kneeling and sword tapping . . . and he sighed wistfully.

Patrick was rather glum-faced, I thought . . . 'So glad you got here in *time* . . . Don't look so disagreeable, you're not going to the block, you know.'

Miles of corridors and carpets . . . like an annex of St Peter's. And then the private apartments, wide windows open on to sunlit lawns, great trees, the shimmer of the distant lake. The room comfortable, small; turkey carpet, fat chairs, great jardinieres stuffed with tall clumps of Nicotiana (white) much as Vivien [Leigh] used to have at Notley in the summer. Maybe she pinched the idea from here? A sort of country-house atmosphere, with a tray of glasses and crystal decanters . . . some other drinks in bottles. Very informal. Patrick told me that I was to call her Your Majesty at the introduction and then forget it . . . ma'am from then on; an informal, private affair. There were only three other guests . . . and not one footballer! Julian Bream the guitarist (classical not electric), Max Aitken of the Beaverbrook Press . . . looking neat and simian . . . I was momentarily astonished to see him present after all the unpleasant attacks he makes on the family in his papers; however . . . and a nice gentleman who was once my commanding officer, years ago in Catterick, and was now something very high up in the War Graves Commission . . . we had not met since 1941 . . . so that was quite relaxing over Tio Pepe. I must confess that I had a swift amused thought that I had come quite a way since those days as an inept Signals corporal. And a long way too from bangers and beans in the pub opposite my first rep[ertory] theatre.

Then she came in . . . among a scattering of the familiar corgis, with Princess Alexandra just, apparently, back from Germany where, poor girl, she had been reviewing some regiment . . . They were laughing very much about something, and Alexandra straightened her hat and put her gloves in her pocket.

The first thing that strikes one is her astonishing prettiness: not at all apparent from a million press photographs or newsreels. And she is quite tiny . . . neat and elegant. A simple, sleeveless black dress and a whacking great diamond clip on her left shoulder. Pearls and the handbag. But she didn't for one second look like the cook she so often does in those floating silk coats and hats like chamber-pots-inverted, which she is forced to wear in public. It seemed a terrible pity that they had never seen her as smart, chic, relaxed and jolly as she was that morning. My good fortune I know. For that alone I felt rather smug . . . and enjoyed my lunch. A simple affair, eight of us (with the lady-in-waiting and a pleasant colonel from Sussex). No vastly important conversation, general chit-chat really as we went from smoked salmon, inevitably, to a lemon soufflé, which was pretty well risen but molten glue inside. There was a hock, a claret . . . and we all used just the one set of eating irons, simple silver knives with George III stamped on them, and wiped on your bread between courses. Sensible. And I set up three of each at home. Middle class?

Afterwards back to the sitting room again for coffee . . . the sun striping the faded turkey carpet . . . sparkling on polished wood and the brass fender: in the empty fireplace, a neat pleated paper fan.

Naturally we talked about the Kennedy business, and agreed how dreadfully difficult it was to find words for yet another telegram of condolence. The official one was all right, but the personal one far harder. I said what I'd sent and she thought it correct. And then about Paris and the events of last month, and how good it was that there were no longer any cobblestones left in the streets of London . . . it was all very relaxed and pleasant; she stood there in the windows, the sun on her face, her eyes a startling cornflower blue (something else that doesn't show on photographs), one foot comfortably out of a shoe, the corgis lying about on the terrace with their shot-rabbit legs, and I suddenly fully real-ised, looking across to the lake and the lawns and the summer trees beyond, shimmering in the afternoon, just what Shakespeare had meant by 'this sceptred isle'. At three she looked at her watch, said that she was going to the Thynne wedding at St James's [Christopher Thynne was marrying Antonia Palmer, daughter of one of the Queen's ladies-in-waiting], and was I? And I said not: I'd been invited but had declined because I was so dreading lunching with her and one event in the day was enough, and she laughed and said I really ought to come because she had heard that the Rolling Stones might be there, and she rather longed to see them . . . By this time, of course, I was so enchanted and under her very potent spell that I nearly changed my mind. But really couldn't face it and drove out into the town of half-mast flags very contented with my lot and a confirmed Royalist. If she and Philip really had power of any kind and really could rule, I'm damned sure I'd stay; in fact I know I would . . .

As one of her Archbishops of Canterbury, George Carey was required to pay homage to the Queen. Imagine the solemn scene on 19 April 1991: his outstretched hands held by the monarch, the oath declared and repeated. Remember the Anointing under the canopy at the Coronation, the vows and sacred promises made; all live on through the Queen's daily life. Those of us who worship sometimes, or not at all, must reflect on how lucky we are to have as head of state someone who so devotedly keeps her word.

Nice touch about Mr Kinnock snaffling rather more than he should at dinner.

On 16 April 1991 Eileen and I were driven to Windsor Castle, where I was due to pay homage to Her Majesty. We were shown to a highly impressive suite of rooms overlooking the long drive leading through the park, and two valets immediately busied themselves unpacking our cases. Later were amused to find that we had been given separate bedrooms, our underclothes had been packed neatly in gauze, and my white ecclesiastical 'rochet', needed for the homage, which I hunted for frantically, had been put on a hanger alongside Eileen's nightclothes – my valet obviously thought I wore it to bed.

Homage is a form of commitment made by bishops and cabinet ministers on taking up office. One is required to kneel before the Sovereign, who places her hands outside the new archbishop or bishop's hands, and one remains in that position until the oath is administered by the Home Secretary and repeated by the bishop. It was a moving and special moment, and is a ceremony that the Queen takes very seriously. Dinner followed with Prince Philip and Princess Margaret and a few guests, including Neil and Glenys Kinnock. At one point, when Eileen was serving herself from the meat dish being offered to her, the waiter quietly murmured in her ear, 'Please don't take three pieces, Mrs Carey. Mr Kinnock has taken three, and there won't be enough to go round.' It was reassuring to be reminded that economy reigns at Windsor as well as elsewhere.

Following dinner all the guests were taken on a personal tour of the royal art collection and library by the Queen and Princess Margaret. Among the exhibits was a collection of Her Majesty's childhood drawings and diaries. She told us with great amusement of one bishop who was so astonished at the extraordinary feat of a princess doing something ordinary that he exclaimed on seeing her childish script, 'Did you write it in your own hand?' To which the Queen said, 'In what other hand could I have possibly done it?' More moving to me was to see for the first time the original treatise of Henry VIII's Defence of the Faith against Martin Luther, and the reformer's defiant response. There was a special poignancy in seeing documents that led to such momentous changes in the Church and the nation long ago – including my own new office.

My meetings with the Queen from that moment on brought home to me the sacramental manner in which she views her own office. That God had called her from birth to fulfil her responsibilities as Sovereign was very evidently her conviction, and it was founded on a firm Christian faith, which also took the form of duty – not in the sense of a burden, but of glad service. She, like her great namesake Elizabeth I, viewed her role as being an 'instrument' in maintaining a noble service to all her subjects.

In Alan Titchmarsh's fascinating book *The Queen's Houses* he describes in riveting detail what it is like to attend a state banquet. He observes all the tiny things that might escape the notice of the dazzled onlooker: on this occasion, even knowing how the Queen stops her skirt blowing in a gust of wind, a lesson Mrs Obama, First Lady of the United States, had yet to adopt. The Obamas were famous already, and the eyes of the world were on this state visit, the old country welcoming the new.

Alan Titchmarsh is a most unusual man. Well known and loved as a gardener and broadcaster, he is also a wonderful poet, and I suspect a mathematician and philosopher too. Gardening does that to you. Here he makes us feel as though we too are guests, walking just behind President and Mrs Obama, through all the royal pageantry of a state banquet.

In her compelling book, *Becoming*, Michelle Obama writes of the Queen's friendly informality: it must have been a first encounter neither would forget, although they met several times after this grand state occasion. Mrs Obama tells of the overwhelming size and splendour of the Palace, which is fifteen times the size of the White House: she called it breath-taking and incomprehensible. Teeth were sucked in the press for her putting her arm around the Queen's shoulders (but admiration for the First Lady of the United States was such that there was a tinge of envy and admiration as well); only she knew that Her Majesty quietly slipped her hand on the small of her back in return.

The state visit of US President and Mrs Obama in May 2011 is a good example of the brilliantly choreographed, set-piece theatre, full of pomp and ceremony but run to a precise, rehearsed schedule, which characterises a typical state visit and its climax, the state banquet.

The Queen and the Duke of Edinburgh were on hand to welcome them at the Grand Entrance to the palace. A brief meeting with the Duke and Duchess of Cambridge, married barely a month before and just back from their honeymoon – and Kate's [the Duchess of Cambridge] first role as a member of the Royal Family – in the 1844 Room (named in honour of a state visit by Tsar Nicholas I in 1844) was followed by a ceremonial welcome on the West Terrace. Stepping out from the bowed front of the Music Room into the blustery sunshine, the President and the Queen stood two steps in front of the Duke of Edinburgh and Mrs Obama, who was holding her skirt down lest the gusts of wind should render her reminiscent of Marilyn Monroe in *The Seven Year Itch*. (The Queen has her dressmaker sew tiny weights into her hems to discourage them from lifting.) As the Guards band played the American national anthem a 41-gun salute reverberated over the music from the guns of the Kings' Troop Royal Horse Artillery lined up in Green Park nearby. Twenty-one guns is the standard salute for heads of state but an extra twenty are added when the salute is given from a royal park. The President and the Duke of Edinburgh, accompanied by the major commanding, inspected the ceremonial Guard of Honour of the 1st Battalion Scots Guards before the massed ranks moved off to the sound of the pipes and drums.

The Queen and the Duke then took the presidential couple on a tour of American-themed items from the Royal Collection, which had been assembled in the Picture Gallery, including a photograph of HMS *Resolute*, timbers from which were used to make the desk in the Oval Office in the White House. A trip to Westminster Abbey to lay a wreath on the Tomb of the Unknown Soldier was followed by a visit to Prime Minister David Cameron at 10 Downing Street and a game of table tennis against Southwark schoolboys, the Cameron-Obama axis being soundly beaten – which required a 'high-five' to cement the Special Alliance. A return to Buckingham Palace saw a courtesy call by the Leader of the Opposition and then it was time to get into white tie and tails ready for the state banquet, the President and the First Lady retiring to their suite in the Belgian State Apartments. This suite of interconnecting rooms was named after Victoria and Albert's uncle, Leopold, King of the Belgians, on the ground floor of the west-facing garden wing at the foot of the Minister's Staircase. These rooms also formed the suite used by Edward VIII during his brief tenure at Buckingham Palace before his abdication in 1936.

As the presidential couple got ready there would have been a purposeful bustle below stairs and in the ballroom where the table had been laid (preparation for the dinner had begun some three weeks before). Since 1914, all state banquets at Buckingham Palace have been held in the ballroom, a vast room 36.6 metres long, 18 metres wide and

13.5 metres high (120 x 59 x 44 feet). When it was first built between 1853 and 1855 it was the largest room in London. The first event staged in the ballroom was a ball to commemorate the end of the Crimean War. In the centre of the room a huge horseshoe table had been constructed, a giant jigsaw puzzle of interlocking bases and tops, all adjustable to fit the numbers required – 172 on this particular night. For a state banquet the top of the horseshoe, where guests of honour sit, is usually 8.5 metres (28 feet) across. It can seat fifteen, and is dressed with damask festoons, a tradition dating back to George IV's Coronation banquet in 1821. The table is covered with several fine damask linen tablecloths with the royal cipher of George IV woven at intervals, all sewn together to ensure they lie flat, altogether extending over 60 metres (200 feet). At Windsor Castle a magnificent single 50-metre (175-foot) long mahogany table stretching the length of St George's Hall, dating from 1846, with 68 separate leaves and seating 160 people, is used for state banquets. It is left without tablecloths and polished to a high shine by staff standing on it using what appear to be padded croquet mallets.

At Buckingham Palace, with the tablecloths laid, the table settings can begin. The setting out of the table usually begins two full days before the banquet. The first to be set out are the table napkins embroidered with the Queen's monogram, folded in a Dutch-bonnet style by the Yeoman of the China and Glass Pantries. Candelabra holding over a hundred ivory candles a foot high are placed at intervals, each candle topped with a miniature shade. They rest on mirrored stands, which reflect the candlelight and the gleam of gilt plate from the table settings. The very grandest, richly chased silver-gilt candelabra, depicting sculpted figures enacting stories from mythology, stand over 1.2 metres (4 feet) tall and hold twelve candles each. They are, like so many of the treasures on display, part of George IV's Grand Service of banqueting plate and cost nearly £3,400 each in the early nineteenth century (approximately £240,000 today), a staggering sum. They are placed on either side of the 'top' table, just as it intersects with the two arms extending down the room. Over thirty flower arrangements take the royal florist and a team of arrangers the best part of thirty-six hours to create and are displayed on the tables around the rooms. The flowers used for the Obama visit were predominantly roses, then in season, and the heady perfume permeated the air throughout the banquet.

The individual place settings measure 45 centimetres (18 inches) across and are laid according to the dishes being served. For the Obama banquet more than two thousand pieces of cutlery had to be individually polished and laid with perfect precision (according to the Butlers Guild, it should take about fifteen minutes per place setting to get it absolutely right). Two knives and two forks were provided for the fish course (sole with crayfish and watercress with a béchamel sauce) and the meat course (new season's lamb from the Queen's Windsor farm with roast potatoes, roast radish, courgettes and green beans), a dessert spoon and fork for the pudding (vanilla charlotte with morello cherries eaten from Minton plates) and a butter knife. Fresh fruit is always displayed on the table (typically grapes, pineapples, plums and nectarines), each fruit or leaf polished to perfection, and a silver-gilt knife, fork and spoon also provided. The fruit is eaten from Tournai fruit plates, cut with a knife and eaten with a fork. Until recently a soup spoon had also been included but the soup course was abolished as the banquets were dragging on too long and the soup had taken at least twenty minutes to serve, consume and clear away. Four guests share a salt dispenser, pepper caster and a mustard pot between them.

Six glasses are always set before each guest, one each for the white wine, red wine, water and port; there are two champagne glasses, one for the toast and one for the pudding course. The thousand or more glasses on the table come from a set made at Stourbridge for the Queen's Coronation in 1953 and are engraved with the EIIR cipher. All were cleaned, rinsed and polished immediately before laying to maintain their sparkle. The Yeoman of the Royal Cellars will have warmed and decanted the port (Royal Vintage, 1963), and checked the red and white wines and champagne (Veuve Clicquot Ponsardin Vintage) are at the right temperature. With the rising temperatures as a consequence of global warming, the alcohol content of British wines has now reached drinkable levels and that night a Fitzrovia Cuvée Merret rosé 2004 from the British winemaker Ridgeview was served. For the state banquet for the Irish President in April 2014 a Ridgeview Grosvenor Blanc de Blanc 2009 was chosen: 'Alluring and zesty, a sort of rustic Bollinger', according to wine expert Jancis Robinson. Some five thousand bottles a year are bought for the more than three hundred events held at Buckingham Palace and Windsor Castle. The more expensive wines served on state occasions are stored in the government cellars under Lancaster House.

A booklet was provided for every guest, bound with a red, white and blue ribbon, the colours of the American flag. Inside, the timetable for the evening was printed, with the wine list, the menu (it is always in French, the language of gastronomy), the music played (selections from *South*

Pacific) and a list of every guest attending. At the back a seating plan folded out neatly with a coloured dot denoting the guest's seat, so anyone in doubt knew exactly where he or she would be seated.

Around the room tables covered in red fabric fringed with gold interspersed with tall buffets displayed the treasures from the Royal Collections, plate and china that is in many instances priceless. The gleaming plate, jugs, wall sconces, platters, dishes, tureens, basins and tankards in silver, silver-gilt and gold on display date largely from the time of George IV, who created the most lavish, theatrical backdrops of any monarch to the business of royal entertaining. At Carlton House in 1811, as the Prince of Wales, he created one of his most spectacular *coups de théâtre*: a miniature waterfall fed a stream, lined with mossy banks, alive with swimming goldfish and studded with aquatic flowers, which ran down the centre of the dining table. The buffet at the Obama state banquet displayed a porcelain dessert service made for William IV between 1830 and 1837, at the Rockingham factory in Yorkshire, celebrating Britain's overseas territories and William's own naval background. The service, originally consisting of fifty-six large pieces and twelve dozen plates, may well have been the most ambitious commission ever produced by an English factory.

With the table dressed and the chairs measured by rod to be at the correct distance, the Queen will have begun her pre-dinner check. Like any concerned hostess, she checks that all is well and her eagle eye can spot anything – a chair not in line, a candle not ramrod straight – a fraction awry. Below stairs (the kitchens were relocated directly beneath the ballroom when it was built) twenty chefs under Royal Chef Mark Flanagan had been hard at work preparing and cooking.

At the appointed time the Yeoman of the Guard, in their Tudor uniforms and carrying halberds, processed into the ballroom and took up their positions guarding the entrances, two standing directly behind where the Queen would sit. More discreetly the American presidential protection officers had stationed themselves around the building, earpieces connected to a command and control centre. The Queen with the President and the Duke of Edinburgh with the First Lady led the procession behind the sword-bearer, everyone governed by strict rules of precedence into the ballroom. With all the guests seated the speeches began. That night there was a rare glitch. The band of the Scots Guards high on the balcony started to play the national anthem before the President had finished speaking. He gamely laboured on with his toast as the music played: 'To Her Majesty The Queen, to the vitality of the special relationship between our peoples, and, in the words of Shakespeare, to this blessed plot, this earth, this realm, this England.'

With the toasts finished, the food service began. A hundred footmen under the direction of the Palace Steward are controlled by a system of traffic lights. When they turn from blue to green they pour in from all four corners of the room to serve the next course. When a zapper controlled from directly behind the Queen signals that she has finished they appear once more to clear the plates. Whether a guest has finished or not, that course is over. Queen Victoria was notorious for bolting her food and her older and slower courtiers managed to eat very little of their meal before it was removed. Petits fours, handmade chocolates and coffee are handed round before the end of the banquet is signalled by the arrival of the twelve pipers processing around the table, led by the Queen's Piper, Pipe-Major Derek Potter. The thirteenth Queen's Piper since Queen Victoria began the tradition after falling in love with the bagpipes in Scotland, his job, for four years until his retirement, was to play under the Queen's window at nine o'clock each morning she was in residence. The tradition continues.

In 1973 the Prime Minister of Australia, Gough Whitlam, and his wife Margaret were invited to stay at Windsor Castle with the Queen. Margaret dwells lovingly on the dresses and furnishings, which is exactly what countless readers of her book *My Day* would appreciate. Examining other people's rooms and possessions is a quality I share with Mrs Whitlam: she so obviously treasured every minute of her time there, despite feeling rather ropy, that it makes her account a pleasure to read. I love her small asides ' . . . it sounds strange but looks fabulous . . .', 'So much less formality here in England than in Australia . . .'

21 April Windsor Castle, England

It is the Queen's birthday at Windsor Castle and a drizzly cold day typical, I'm told, of English Easters . . . well, that's what it looks like from my cosy bedroom in the private apartments.

Our spirits, however, remain high with the excitement of this visit.

The Prime Minister and I arrived at six last evening. The drive from London was so speedy that we had to 'waste' a little time detouring around the town and Great Park to effect a punctual entrance.

Driving through the gateway, our car swung to the right and along to a smallish entrance in one of the stern stone towers. We were met there by Sir Martin Charteris (private secretary to the Queen) and Mr Bill Heseltine (the Queen's Fremantle-born press secretary), among others, and also charming Miss Mary Morrison, lady-in-waiting to the Queen, who was deputed to put me 'in the picture'. We went up a short flight of steps and almost immediately into a suite of rooms called the Ministers' Suite.

There is a little entrance hall, and off it to the left a simple bedroom and bathroom. Straight ahead is a wide sitting-room and to the right a large double bedroom and bathroom. All the rooms are carpeted in a deep blue-green, the simple bedroom (or dressing room, really, for the master) has dark green self-striped wallpaper and carnation-red covers and curtains.

A suitable large bouquet of red carnations decorates the room and more than half-a-dozen amusing pictures from the Royal Academicians' annual presentation to the Sovereign hang on the walls.

Prince Philip pointed this out during a late-night tour of the art treasures of the Castle, and said that he had chosen the ones for this room as being suitable (they varied from nude figures to colourful crowd scenes).

The sitting room, in which I chatted with Miss Morrison while the PM was whisked off to his talks with Her Majesty, is almost squarely above the Long Walk – or long drive really – which goes straight for three miles to Ascot! Nobody drives a car along it – it's for the Queen's carriage.

The sitting room has two pale, gold-covered armchairs around a small fireplace at one end, and a red brocade-covered Madame Récamier-type sofa at the other end. There are three writing tables – and a large one centred between the windows – along the wall opposite a longish buffet laden with decanters and mineral water.

On a little side table are fruit and plates. The walls are papered in striped fuchsia – it sounds strange but looks fabulous – and the long curtains are white with a green band trim and tie, and there are gold tulip ends to the curtain rods. The small chairs also have red upholstery and the room is bright with lamps and flowers. White blossoms mix beautifully with orchids, and there is a large bowl of bright tulips on the top of the large desk.

Everything is beautifully warm – so much so that that night it was necessary for me to remove the pale pink eiderdown, the paler pink silk comforter and one of the cream blankets from my downy bed.

Everything is so temptingly arranged at Windsor Castle that I had a second bath within four hours. I had bathed at the Berkeley Hotel before leaving London, but I was unable to resist the nicely drawn bath in my pink-and-white-papered bathroom before dinner at 8.30 p.m. In the bathroom, too, are more works of art, framed lithographs of flowers and a flower painting by Charlotte Selina Skule. Here also is a practical touch. A cork bathmat is placed under the towelling mat, which in turn covers the green carpet. A cork seat on the white-painted chair is wrapped in a bath sheet and the chair is placed beside the ever-inviting bath. Heated towel rails, of course!

How can I record all of my impressions and experiences? What first? Drinks before dinner . . . dinner . . . the food . . . who was there? What they wore? Where was it?

So much less formality here in England than in Australia, in one way.

A little sitting room, with vast portraits and a French carpet, was the meeting place about 7 p.m., before we all changed for dinner.

Prince Philip met me, and Miss Morrison and I started off our pre-dinner drinks with a plain ginger ale as my stomach was still very wobbly from the tropical tour. Then in came the Queen Mother, Queen Elizabeth, in a lovely blue printed silk dress with an aqua cardigan draped over her shoulders. Another curtsey, and we sat chatting until the Queen herself and our PM joined us.

Her Majesty looked marvellous in a deep cherry-red wool dress pinned with a superb sapphire brooch. She looked prettier than I ever remember – certainly younger than the forty-seven years she is today.

Her Majesty sipped a tomato juice, Prince Philip had a gin and tonic. Princess Margaret then joined us wearing an unusual blue knitted dress with her hair swept up in what I believe is a French roll. Lord Snowdon appeared soon after, looking, as the Princess said, 'as though he'd just come from the stables'. His jeans and denim jacket did look rather operational.

About 7.40 up we went to change, withdrawing curtseys being required. It was then I had my extra bath before slipping into the seemingly suitable black, white and gold dinner dress.

I really had no choice, as it was the only dinner dress I'd brought. Anyway, on the tick of 8.30 we reassembled for another drink – this time sherry for Her Majesty, brandy and ginger ale for my tummy. I began to feel better.

The Queen Mother arrived in a lovely white and gold dress. She really is a pretty, feminine person of enormous warmth. Next, Princess Margaret in a deep red velvet pinafore, scoop-necked, over a glittering high-necked red and blue striped long-sleeved evening sweater; the skirt was flared. Every bit a princess. Then the Queen wearing aqua lace re-embroidered in silver and gold, gold slippers, diamonds at her throat and pendant diamond earrings.

Her Majesty's hair was more bouffant than I can ever recall it, and a little shorter I think. Rather chic.

Would that I could say I enjoyed every bit of the meal, but here again I had to play with food, push it around my plate, sip my water or wine and talk to keep my mind off my wobbly tummy.

The dining room was very grand – red and gold mainly with a vast ceiling. The dinner service was pale green, pale gold and white (Sèvres), given to Her Majesty and Prince Philip as a wedding present by President de Gaulle. Prince Philip admits to being very fond of it and having no intention of letting it be added to the official Royal Collection. He intends giving it to one of the royal children.

Three courses only at dinner. Sensible, beautiful and delicious. First, fresh salmon, boiled potatoes and cucumbers in sour cream; then turkey with what seemed to be a million vegetables. Well, let's count . . . tiny carrot slices, cauliflower, potatoes baked in a cake, cream sauce, gravy and a salad, which I didn't investigate but which Prince Philip enjoyed with his plate of cauliflower as a main course – he had plenty of salmon first.

The sweet was pineapple bombe covered with spun sugar – right up our Prime Minister's alley. White wine and/or red – the white I had was German and delicious. Only three glasses were set: for wine, water and port, but more were added as required. There was coffee at the table before we left the room.

And, as we finally left, NO curtseys, quite different from Government House, Canberra. But of course, there I was with Her Majesty constantly, not leaving her as I did on this occasion.

What an entry for my diary this visit has been, one I will long look back on with the utmost pleasure.

Roy Strong was the director of the Victoria and Albert Museum in 1978 when he stayed at Windsor Castle on 6 and 7 April, a man of tremendous artistic ability. You can almost see him pursing his lips at the stuffed animal he sees in front of 'the marvellous Gainsborough of Queen Charlotte': he can't quite bring himself to identify it. Slightly been-there-done-that though his account is, I think he was delighted to find a special treasure had been unearthed for him to see at the end of the tour of the state apartments.

We arrived in our decrepit vehicle at Windsor Castle. It was a glorious spring day, the hedgerows had suddenly burst into green and the sky was cloudless. I think that it must have been a long time since such a battered and dusty vehicle had arrived at the Castle. There was a flurry of footmen and the Master of the Household, Sir Peter Ashmore, greeted us and then, inside, Lady Abel Smith, a woman in her sixties, practical and easy, a typical lady-in-waiting. Up the stairs into the Grand Corridor and into one of the York Tower guest rooms, all of which overlook Royal Mile down to the Royal Lodge.

The bedroom was like sleeping in the Wallace Collection, polished but impersonal somehow. We warded off a small army of valets and maids who always, in an excess of zeal, want to unpack and press everything so that you can find absolutely nothing as a result. The bathroom had Hugh Casson drawings. The sitting room was comfortable with a lovely Landseer of a dog, a sketch of Victoria and Albert for one of the great pictures of them, and the back view of one of Albert's sisters standing on a terrace. There were a few books on a chest of drawers. I opened one, it was inscribed 'Elizabeth 1943' and another had a small bookplate which read rather sharply 'The Queen's Book'.

After ten minutes we were fetched by another posse and taken down the Grand Corridor to the White Drawing Room, which Princess Margaret said the Queen had made 'squashy', i.e., down-filled sofas and armchairs. This was the only room which seemed a little domestic. The *TV Times* was visible on a side-table and a 'squashy' large stuffed animal by the fireplace, which did strike an incongruous note sited as it was beneath the marvellous Gainsborough of Queen Charlotte in her vast pannier skirt.

Her Majesty entered the room with the Prime Minister. They, of course, had been closeted having their weekly audience, although this time surrounded by a blaze of publicity over HRH [Princess Margaret] and Roddy [Llewellyn, who was then having a relationship with Princess Margaret], which had reached its peak in the press that day with 'Would she or would she not retire to private life?' and, also, coincident with the revision of the Civil List with its royal allowances. In fact rarely can Windsor Castle have been surrounded by such a blaze of publicity. The Queen, as we all know, is intensely shy and I don't think that we exchanged a word beyond salutations. Julia did talk about the dogs, one of which rolled over, at which point HM radiated. She really loves those dogs and at that fleeting moment the character behind the layers came shining through.

Changing for dinner was a flat-out twenty-five-minute break. This time we reassembled in the Green Drawing Room, very 'unsquashy' and formal. More guests arrived, mostly Household, like a Windsor canon and his wife, and the Royal Librarian. More drinks followed. HRH appeared in white, surely by Hartnell, with sparkling embroidery at the neck and hem. HM wore something floating in shades of violent orange and salmon pink with a vast diamond bracelet, necklace and earrings (one of those dresses designed to be 'seen' a mile off) and Prince Philip was in his Windsor uniform with its red collar. HM later put on her specs in the Royal Library, which, like those worn by American blue-rinse ladies, hung on a cord around her neck. 'Where's your specs?' yelled Princess Margaret.

At that moment the children surfaced. Prince Andrew, tallest and thinnest of the boys, is now seventeen and living up in his butch appearance and sensuous lips to his 'Randy Andy' image, and David Linley, the duplicate of Tony Snowdon. He is as tiny as his parents and about the same age as Prince Andrew. A tutor was with him to coach him to get through his O levels. When asked by the Prime Minister what he wanted to be, Princess Margaret replied, 'A carpenter,' to which she added, 'Christ was a carpenter.' We then proceeded to the State Dining Room and sat at a vast table, everyone placed according to precedence, all the surplus men relegated to a horseshoe at one end. I sat between Audrey Callaghan, a cosy lady, and the canon's wife. The table was lit by four vast silver candelabra inter-spersed with bowls of spring flowers, the usual printed menu card and printed statement as to what porcelain was being used. At the end the Queen led out the ladies, the gentlemen remaining for about ten minutes and then we all moved off for a tour of the state apartments.

There is something magical about Windsor, especially that Grand Corridor, which curves its way around the courtyard and, therefore, seems to go on for ever. And then one passes picture after picture one has known for so long, the Zoffanys, the Gainsboroughs of George III's daughters, the framed phalanx of the whole family, the Wilkies and Leslies from Victoria's early life, the pictures of her Coronation and first Privy Council meeting. We pressed on through the redone chapel, all white and gold, seemingly an antechamber but behind a curtain lurked the altar. This now has its double doors restored, which, flung open, led into St George's Hall. Before those were reinstated, the Hall had here James Gunn's state portrait of the Queen in her Coronation robes beneath a canopy of state. The Hall had animal pictures, Stubbses and Landseers, pushed behind the chairs ready for a Wildlife Fund rally, for which an exhibition was being mounted in the Waterloo Chamber.

So we swept on in a dilatory, dawdling manner through room after room, past the Wests of George III's family, Vermeer's *Lady at the Virginals*, hung too high, on through the State Bedroom where the bed badly needed repairing, through the Charles II rooms with their ceilings by Verrio and carving by Grinling Gibbons. The tour culminated in the Royal Library, where Robin Mackworth-Young (the Royal Librarian) had mounted the usual exhibition with a bouquet of manuscripts for me on the founding of the Victoria and Albert Museum, including the Duke of Devonshire's memo to Queen Victoria asking that the Museum should be called not the Albert Museum but the Victoria and Albert Museum!

James Pope-Hennessy was writing the official life of Queen
Mary. He went to Balmoral in 1957 and reflected on meeting
the Queen. Here he paints rather a gloomy picture of what
seemed to him a trying encounter.

The library door flew open, and the Queen marched in
accompanied by several dogs. She walked briskly across the
room and held out her hand.

'You're staying up here, I understand?' she said, with a
curt smile, taking cover behind the long brocaded stool
which was standing in front of the fire.

'Yes, ma'am, at a mill-house belonging to the Farquarsons,'
etc., etc., etc.

She lapsed into dead silence, so I tried again, standing
near her behind the stool.

'I've never been to this part of Scotland before.'

There was a three-minute silence, during which she looked
at the lowering sky out of the window. I thought she hadn't
heard; but as it seemed a new technique of conversation I
remained silent too.

'It's rather beautiful, isn't it?' she remarked, still looking at
the sky. I then remembered Tommy Lascelles [private secretary
to the Queen until 1953] telling me she always looks out of
the window before making a decision. At this point Mr Maclay
[the Secretary of State for Scotland, John McLay] ambled up
to speak to her, and the Queen Mother came into the room,
dressed in a grey and pale pinkish red tartan, beautifully
scented. The Queen, who was wearing no scent, was dressed
in a (?Stuart) tartan skirt, a little olive green tweed jacket and
a complicated raspberry-coloured blouse; on her left lapel was
a large thistle in diamonds, the flower being a mauve cairngorm.
Her brogues were brilliantly polished and reflected the light.

Adeane [Sir Michael Adeane, the Queen's private secretary] came up with two sheets of typed paper and handed them to her. She seized them firmly, glanced at them and gave them back with the nod of a head-girl checking the afternoon's hockey team.

How odd that he remarked on the Queen not wearing scent, as he gives a detailed description of her clothes and the Queen Mother's obviously more genial greeting. Perhaps he felt ill-at-ease: perhaps the Queen was shy.

The Royal Family usually spends the summer holidays at Balmoral, and the Prime Minister is invited for a short stay. Semi-formal, semi-homely, it can be daunting, as it is a new way of being, a way we simply aren't accustomed to: friendly, but not tracksuit-bottoms friendly; relaxing, but slightly edgy, as you may not be able to lie on that sofa with your shoes off. Just when you think you have got the measure of it (you haven't) it's time to leave. Tony Blair writes candidly about the experience. I wonder what was in that drink he enjoyed so much.

Balmoral Castle was built in the 1840s by Prince Albert for his wife and queen, situated between the villages of Ballater and Braemar. It is magnificent, the grounds simply stunning, and although the September weather is normally awful up there, it can be quite pleasant. On a sunny day, there is no more beautiful part of the world than that part of Scotland. The Castle itself is very Victorian. There are no huge chambers or halls, the rooms are of moderate size, and some of the toilets are still the old water closets; not many are en suite, as they say.

I have to say I found the experience of visiting and spending the weekend a vivid combination of the intriguing, the surreal and the utterly freaky. The whole culture of it was totally alien, of course, not that the royals weren't very welcoming. But I never did 'country house' or 'stately home' weekends and had a bit of a horror at the notion.

The walls are hung with Landseer pictures of stags, scenes of hunting and of course Queen Victoria's Mr Brown. There are footmen – in fact, very nice guys, but still footmen. When I arrived for the first time on that Sunday, the valet – yes, you got your own valet – asked me if he could fold my clothes and generally iron the underpants and that type of thing, and so disconcerted me that when he then asked me if he could 'draw the bath', I lost the thread completely and actually thought for a moment he wanted to sketch the damn thing. Using the bathroom on the other side of the corridor was a singular act of courage, sneaking open the bedroom door, glancing right and left and then making for it at speed.

There was a routine to everything. There was a proper afternoon tea, and the Queen would pour with, needless to say, a proper strainer, and a kettle was kept bubbling away so that the pot could be filled up. Breakfast was likewise straight out of Trollope, or, perhaps better, Walter Scott. Eggs, bacon, sausage, kidneys, tomatoes, kedgeree and kippers, all kept on a hotplate. Breakfast was huge. Lunch was huge. Dinner was huge. If you indulged thoroughly, you could have put on a stone in a weekend, but the royals never did. I always noticed that they ate very little.

The blessing was the stiff drink you could get before dinner. Had it been a dry event, had the Queen been a teetotaller or a temperance fanatic, I don't believe I could have got through the weekend. But this stuff – I was never quite sure what it was – was absolutely what was needed. It hit the spot. It was true rocket fuel. The burden and the head got lighter. The courage returned. The easy conversational intercourse with the Royal Family seemed entirely natural. The first two annual visits were, nevertheless, trying at all levels.

Think how many people you have had to stay in your own home and then multiply it by a thousand. I know there are private royal apartments within royal residences, but when people come to stay you must look after them, and the most generous hosts are those who make you feel that nothing matters too much, and that above all you are welcome. The first time Adrienne Clarkson stayed with the Queen was at Balmoral. In 1999 she was the newly appointed Governor General of Canada: her husband came with her, and it was a private visit in that only a few other guests were there, and they were fourteen at dinner.

The gathering of the governors general of the Commonwealth at Windsor in 2002 was on a different scale, and a small disaster lay in wait for her. I wonder if she lay awake at night for years afterwards reliving the bathroom fiasco.

Many people expect that the Governor General of Canada will have a close relationship and frequent conversations with the Queen. In fact, this is a formal, constitutional, and politically neutral relationship, and is treated as such by both the Governor General and the Queen. Before I was installed, but after the announcement was made, John [her husband, John Ralston Saul, the writer] and I were invited to Balmoral, in Scotland, to meet the Queen and some members of the royal household. It's an extraordinary estate of some twenty thousand hectares along the River Dee, and the Queen seems to be most comfortable there; she drives her own four-wheel drive to tour the property, and tries to have a barbecue if it isn't pouring with rain, which it is ninety-five per cent of the time. She exudes intelligence, intensity, and shrewd appraisal, which are dissimulated behind a flashing and often disarming smile. Spending any length of time with her makes one realise that she is the consummate professional who knows exactly what she is doing.

The Queen is a thoughtful host. We had bagpipes after dinner, and every single piece that the piper played was a Canadian composition or was connected with a Canadian regiment. We were determined to begin this thoughtful tradition at Rideau Hall [the official residence in Ottawa of both the Queen and the Governor General]. We did not hear one note of 'Scotland the Brave' while we stayed at Balmoral.

The dinner was a small one, with about fourteen people, including members of the Royal Household, among them the Queen's private secretary, Sir Robin Janvrin, and one of the Queen's ladies-in-waiting, who was Scottish, and some guests, including the assistant headmaster of Eton College. The conversation flowed amiably, with the Queen pointing out rather gleefully that she is a generation younger than her husband, Prince Philip, even though they are third cousins.

I was interested to see that since we were having lamb chops they were (as I had always been told in good etiquette books) picked up between thumb and forefinger to finish them off. And also that the Queen powdered her nose at table. In Canada, we had always been brought up to believe, from the time we were little girls, that we were never supposed to do anything to our makeup at the table, so I am simply passing on the information for those who like to keep up-to-date with royal etiquette.

After dinner, we chatted in the small drawing room, ate chocolates and found that all of the household were people who, without visible effort, could keep conversation going – even if their guests had been from the moon. At a certain point in the evening, one of the Queen's aides-de-camp whispered in my ear that it was time to leave. According to royal etiquette, the guests must leave before the Queen can, so we all bade her good night. She said goodbye to us because we were informed that she never comes to breakfast with visitors.

The next time we met was on the occasion of the celebration of her Golden Jubilee, when all the governors general of the Commonwealth – about two dozen – were invited to Windsor Castle for the night of 17 April 2002. Windsor Castle is as large as most small cities in Canada, but it seems to be where the Queen prefers to live when she is in the capital. We all arrived in time for tea with the Queen and Prince Philip and were introduced to each other, and then were free to circulate and discuss the differences between our countries. Naturally, I homed in on the governors general of Australia and New Zealand, as their countries have the same kinds of population and are industrialised, and generally have the most in common with Canada. The governor general of Barbados told me that he drives around his country in one day and admired my stamina for being able to travel in Canada.

We then went upstairs where our bags had been taken, and John and I were informed that we were staying in the apartments that the Queen Mother had used whenever she was at Windsor. The apartment was larger than the second floor of Rideau Hall, with the bathroom at one end and the bedroom and sitting room at the other. The long corridor in between had mysteriously locked doors all the way down. I decided that I had better have a bath, even though we had only forty-five minutes to get ready for drinks before dinner. I began to run water into the big mahogany-encased bathtub and went back into the bedroom to make sure that my things were ready to hop into for dinner. I got distracted, and suddenly I remembered that I had left the water running. I raced down the hall and to my horror saw bathwater brimming over the mahogany and flowing onto the broad-loomed floor. I turned off the taps, leaned against the wall and thought, This is not what my parents brought me up to do. I called my aide-de-camp, the super-cool Lieutenant Jeremy Sales – appropriately, it now seems, of the navy – who came in, stared at the water flowing into the green carpeting and said laconically, 'Oh, well, I'll inform them immediately.' I ran back to the bedroom area to get dressed, and by the time I went back to the bathroom, Jeremy had the maids and footmen mopping up the water. All I could think, as I saw that water being squished up from the carpet, was that I had drowned the honour of Canada.

As soon as we went down to have drinks, and before the Queen arrived, I said to the Master of the Household: 'I'm terribly sorry. The most embarrassing thing has happened. I've let my bathtub run over and I'm terribly concerned that it might come right through this ceiling.'

Without missing a beat, the true courtier smiled and said, 'Well, you know, it's something Prince George of Hanover [Prince Philip's brother-in-law] does every time he comes to visit.' Smooth or what?

The Queen's sixth sense and compassion are revealed in David Nott's account of lunch with Her Majesty at Buckingham Palace. In his book *War Doctor* he describes his voluntary work in war and disaster zones, which brought for him almost unbearable memories.

I was invited to a private lunch with the Queen at Buckingham Palace. I am not sure how this came about; I knew the broadcast of my Eddie Mair interview had touched a lot of people, so perhaps someone in the Royal Household had also tuned in. In any event, one day not long after I got back I put on my one and only suit and waved goodbye to Elly [his wife] as I passed through the gates of the Palace.

The contrast between those gilded walls and the ravaged streets of Aleppo began doing weird things to my head. I walked along the red carpet into one of the reception rooms and stood awkwardly with the other guests. I felt a fraud, guilty – I should not be here enjoying this splendour and warm hospitality while my friends in Aleppo are suffering. I looked at the seating plan and found that I was sitting on the Queen's left, which I knew was an honour. But I was perilously close to a panic attack.

I stood dumbly with the other guests making small-talk with Prince Philip. God knows what he must have thought. Finally we were taken through to the dining-room and one of the courtiers showed me to my seat next to the Queen. Etiquette dictates that the Queen will speak to the person on her right for half the lunch and will then turn to the person on her left for the second half. I realise now that I should have been speaking first to the person on my left, but I cannot recall doing so and whoever it was must have thought me extremely rude. I could feel myself staring into space.

The dessert arrived and the Queen turned to me. At first I couldn't hear what she was saying, as my hearing had been damaged by a bomb blast near the hospital in Aleppo. I tried to speak, but nothing would come out of my mouth. It wasn't that I didn't want to speak to her; I couldn't. I simply did not know what to say.

She asked me where had I come from. I suppose she was expecting me to say, 'From Hammersmith,' or something like that, but I told her I had recently returned from Aleppo.

'Oh,' she said. 'And what was that like?'

What was it like? What could I say? My mind filled instantly with images of toxic dust, of crushed school desks, of bloodied and limbless children. And of Alan Henning and those other Westerners whose lives had ended in the most appalling fashion.

I don't know why it happened then, or why it should have been the Queen who breached the dam. Perhaps it was because she is the mother of the nation, and I had lost my own mother. My bottom lip started to go and all I wanted to do was to burst into tears, but I held myself together as best I could. I hoped she wouldn't ask me another question about Aleppo. I knew if she did, I would completely lose control.

She looked at me quizzically and touched my hand. She then had a quiet word with one of the courtiers, who pointed to a silver box in front of her. I watched as she opened the box, which was full of biscuits. 'These are for the dogs,' she said, breaking one of the biscuits in two and giving me half. We fed the biscuits to the corgis under the table, and for the rest of the lunch she took the lead and chatted about her dogs, how many she had, what their names were, how old they were. All the while we were stroking and petting them, and my anxiety and distress drained away.

'There,' the Queen said. 'That's so much better than talking, isn't it?'

9. Meeting and Greeting

In preparing this book, I sent out a message to the wider world: 'Have you met the Queen? What happened?' The response was gratifying. As the treasured magic memories began to arrive, I decided to put them together like a bouquet of recollections, each with its own shining moment.

Charmaine Norris was in Malaysia long after I was there. In the olden days we travelled by ship, a month's journey each way. Flying came later, too late for me but just right for Charmaine's family. The Commonwealth tour of 1972 holds a special place in her heart.

When I was a little girl my dad's company transferred him from London to Kuala Lumpur. I was about seven and remember it fairly well. I was excited to experience the world beyond the walls of Twickenham, but it equally upset me to leave my elderly grandparents behind in Kew. I was told that, 'Malaya was far too far to visit Grandad and Grandma on Saturday afternoons!'

My dad flew ahead. My mum, elder sister Gail and brother Michael and I followed six weeks later. It was the first time I had ever flown. My world opened up in an instant. My homemade rag doll had her own seat next to me on the plane and off we headed to South East Asia.

Upon landing in Kuala Lumpur, we disembarked, and I

distinctly felt the high heat and unbelievable humidity. As I tumbled down the aircraft steps, half asleep, to the tarmac, I became a magnet for the Malaysian mosquitos. This didn't matter, though, because I could see my dad waving in the distance from an old terminal building roof.

Not long after this my siblings and I started our new school called the Garden School in Kuala Lumpur. They were in the upper school and I was in the lower school building. It was such a lovely school, friendly and fun. It was more like a big white house, with ceiling fans everywhere, no real window panes and even kittens that lived in the drains.

More importantly, there was an enormous portrait of stunning Queen Elizabeth II in the hallway. I was so proud of the Queen of England. Every morning, I would look up at her portrait and admire her. I would secretly say 'good morning' to her in my mind. I honestly believed that my mum, Marjorie, was just like her. My very own queen.

About two years later, in 1972, my teacher announced that Queen Elizabeth, Prince Philip, and Princess Anne were to visit our school. Only a drive-by, though, she said, and that we were all to stand outside and wave flags as they passed.

We prepared and practised line-up for months on end. Then the day arrived. Beautiful Queen Elizabeth's limousine arrived. But it didn't pass by. It stopped.

The door was opened and out stepped the Queen of England. The Queen chatted to a few grown-ups. My headmistress, Mrs Mary Arshard, was one of them. I remember the moment like it was yesterday. I was baking hot and my chubby hands were shaking, waving the Union Jack in one hand and the Malaysian flag in my other hand. The Queen smiled and walked my way. She suddenly paused and said hello and asked me if I enjoyed school. I seemed to have lost my voice. I smiled and nodded yes. I offered her both my flags, which she gracefully and so gently took. She thanked me for them.

This was a highlight of my life. It was such a small amount of time, probably less than a minute, but with such an enormous impact. I knew I loved her from photographs and from the TV, but now my love and admiration were set in stone from that moment on. Prince Philip was such a charming gentleman. He followed behind her.

I have seen the Queen in her car, entering Buckingham Palace and visiting Brinsworth House, the Royal Variety Charity in Twickenham, several times over the years. I jump at any chance I get to try and see her because she is full of positivity and life and has the loveliest smile. She always seems to me a gracious, kind and sweet woman. I am proud of her and I genuinely love her. She really is our one and only Queen Elizabeth II.

The restoration of parts of Windsor Castle after its catastrophic fire was celebrated by a series of receptions welcoming people from all walks of life. The excitement of seeing the wonderfully restored building, the music playing, the drinks and things on sticks, a buzz of chatter from the crowd, a sense of ease and relaxation . . . And then suddenly you are face to face with the Queen and Prince Philip. Rachel Dixon from Maidenhead managed her sausage dilemma masterfully.

My husband and I were invited to a drinks party at Windsor Castle to celebrate the completion of the refurbishment of the Great Hall after it was devastated by fire in 1992. We helped ourselves to a drink and a sausage on a stick and strolled down the length of the hall, admiring the beautifully restored building with its stunning coats of arms.

Before long we found ourselves at the other end of the hall from everyone else, admiring the beautiful carved-wood doors – which suddenly opened to reveal the Queen and Prince Philip, who had come to join the party.

I was absolutely overcome with panic – I had just taken a bite out of my sausage on a stick and wasn't sure of the correct protocol when meeting the Queen in these circumstances. I did manage a little bob of a curtsey, and of course she put us completely at our ease. 'Chilly, isn't it?' she said to us, before chatting amicably for several minutes and kindly paying no attention to the fact that I had one hand behind my back for the duration.

I suspect I may be the only person on the planet who met the Queen while desperately concealing a half-eaten sausage . . .

Marie Vallejo sent a charming story about her glimpse of the Queen in Gibraltar. I have been doing my maths and I think that my family sailed into Gibraltar about three weeks after this encounter took place. The army sailing date was usually 1 May, my birthday . . . and Marie's father's birthday was 10 May. Three weeks after that we would have been just about there, before entering the ghastly seas in the Bay of Biscay and docking at Southampton at the beginning of June. She was four years older than I was, and when I landed in England the first thing I remember is the scent of roses.

I grew up in Gibraltar from 1945 after the Second World War until we moved to England in the 1970s. I had been born in London during the war. My mother had been sent to London as a refugee as part of the evacuation of the

Gibraltarians. When we returned to Gibraltar after the war, we settled in a house at the top of Willis Road. The house we lived in was close to the top of the Rock on the way to Moorish Castle and the Second World War lookout. I lived there with my mother and father, my sister, and my brothers.

On 10 May 1954, the Queen visited Gibraltar. I remember this because it was also my father's birthday. I was twelve at the time and I remember that at school we practised singing songs so that we could perform something for the Queen during her visit. I remember hearing that she was staying in the Convent, the official residence of the Governor of Gibraltar, which was where I went to school, and that there was an event being put on at Victoria Stadium for her.

At the time, we were lucky enough to have a good-sized garden. We grew flowers and vegetables and herbs. We lived quite far up the Rock so to stop the apes from coming into the garden and eating all the plants we had put chicken wire up and around the top of the walls to protect them. That year, we had a good spring and we had pink climbing roses, which had wound their way up the walls and through the chicken wire. They were in bloom and looked beautiful.

We were all in the house when the Queen's car and convoy came up the Rock past our house on the way to either Moorish Castle or one of the other points on the Rock. We were looking out of the windows of our house and we could see all the soldiers escorting the Queen's car, as it moved slowly up the steep hill. There were guards and soldiers lining the route and spectators were standing behind them. As they drew closer to our house we saw the car slow down even more and a window drop and then we could see the Queen who was looking out of her window at the roses in our garden. It was only a momentary glimpse, but I remember her being very beautiful and smiling at our roses. After they had slowed, almost to a stop, they drove on and that was it, our passing glance at the Queen. But it was lovely, and I always remember it.

Linda Riding's encounter with the Queen was carefully planned: the flowers in the basket, where she would stand in Salford Quays, and how the photograph would turn out if she was lucky enough to catch the Queen's attention. It nearly ended in disaster.

I had always wanted to meet Her Majesty the Queen to thank her in some way for everything that she had done for the country. So when I learned that she was to open the new BBC studios at Salford Quays, I began planning how I could make it happen.

I booked a day off work and made sure that I arrived at the Quays early enough to explore the site, possible routes the Queen would take and most importantly to get as close to her as I could.

To thank Her Majesty for all of her years of service and dedication to our country, I made what I thought was a lovely, eye-catching basket of flowers to present to her as she passed by.

I also took along my amateur photographer husband so that he could record the meeting – if I was lucky enough to make it happen.

By arriving early, I made sure that I found a great position and the basket of flowers made sure that I was noticed by the various policemen and security personnel who were around to safeguard the Queen. She was arriving by car and I was told by the various officials around that I was in a fantastic position to see her and possibly attract her attention as she walked to the studios.

Sure enough, her car arrived, the Queen got out and she was guided in a direction that would take her past where I was standing. As she approached, her lady-in-waiting noticed the flowers I was holding and suggested to Her Majesty that she come over to accept them. My husband began taking photographs.

The Queen came to me and much to my delight we had a brief conversation about the flowers and why I had thought it so important to make my gesture of thanks. I was somewhat overwhelmed by having the opportunity to talk directly to the Queen and I just assumed that my husband had been able to photograph our meeting in its brief entirety.

It was only after the Queen had moved away from us and the cheering crowds around us that my husband explained that, yes, he had taken lots of photographs of the Queen as she had approached us but that then his camera had locked up and he hadn't been able to take a single shot as I spoke to her and presented her with the basket of flowers. Imagine my dismay. I had just had a most wonderful moment meeting and talking to the Queen but I would have nothing to recall the moment except for the memories inside my mind.

And yet my meeting with the Queen had not gone unnoticed by the crowd and a local news reporter came to talk to me about what I had said to Her Majesty and what she had said to me. I also happened to tell the reporter about my husband's failure to capture the moment for posterity.

It was then that the local media took over the search to find a photographer who actually had captured my brief moments with the Queen. In the days that followed, local press and radio all carried stories about my hopeless photographer husband who had failed to capture the exciting moment that his wife had met the Queen. The story even made it on to national radio and we were interviewed live on-air by Jeremy Vine on his BBC Radio 2 show.

Luckily, in the days that followed, the appeal to find a photographer who had captured my special moment went around the country and I was eventually contacted by a gentleman who thought he might have the perfect picture. Fortunately for me, he was absolutely correct and I now have a tremendous photographic memory of my meeting with the Queen.

And if you look really closely at the photograph, you can even see my husband with his camera to his eye. It may look as though he is taking photographs but I can assure you he was doing absolutely nothing of the sort. However, he has been forgiven and we now look back to that day with great fondness and I look back with great pride at being able to fulfil my ambition to meet Her Majesty and to thank her for her service.

When Farms for City Children opened Lower Treginnis, on the Welsh coast, I was lucky enough to be invited. The charity has the express intention of giving children from inner cities the chance to be out in the countryside, to feed chickens, herd pigs and cows, to groom horses and dig potatoes. There is no television, and children listen to a bedtime story round a fire before going up to sleep in dormitories, a world away from their life at home. Princess Anne is the royal Patron; there could be no one better for the position, as she is a countrywoman through and through, understanding everything to do with farming and animals, and the confidence this experience can instil in children.

Under threatening storm clouds, I lined up with some small schoolchildren as we waited for the Princess to arrive; they could hardly contain their excitement.

'Miss! Will she wear a crown? Will she come in a carriage?' No matter how I tried to lower their expectations without squashing their high spirits, they didn't believe me: she was a princess, she would wear a crown and possibly a pink dress. The rain drummed down as a Range Rover splashed though the mud and stopped in front of us. The Princess Royal got out in gumboots and a long Mackintosh, a scarf over her head. There was a murmur of disbelief from the young visitors, not disappointment exactly but amazement that if you were entitled to wear a crown wouldn't you wear it all the time?

This letter to the *Sunday Express* won a three-guinea prize, on 22 September 1968. Maybe that small girl will read this and recognise herself.

> I was one of the many who went to watch the Royal Family attend Crathie Church last Sunday. Standing next to me was a little girl. She kept asking her father how long it would be before the Queen would come. 'Won't be long now,' said her daddy. 'I suppose,' said the little one, 'she would take some time putting her crown on properly!' In my own excitement, when the Queen did arrive, I forgot to take note of that little girl's reaction when she discovered the Queen wore no crown. I hope she didn't feel let down.

Dreams about the Queen are frequent enough for Brian Masters to have written a book called *Dreams about HM The Queen and Other Members of the Royal Family*. I have dreamed about the Queen. In my dream I was her driver, the vehicle was a jeep and whatever mission we were on she was completely in command, jumping into the seat beside me and telling me which road to take. We were both wearing camouflage gear, chatting easily, me being deferential but not creepy, and she trusted me, as I had obviously been driving her for years. I picked out the following dream from the book because it involves the Queen and vehicles again. Is it the memory of that photograph of her during the war, leaning against an army lorry, that sets up this connection?

I was hitch-hiking on the M1, and had been waiting on an approach road for more than an hour. Then a huge articulated lorry appeared, and chugged to a halt. Thank God, I thought, my luck has changed. When I climbed in, I was shocked to find the driver was a woman. What's more, she looked familiar. 'Where do you want to go?' she asked. I told her I was heading for Edinburgh. 'Oh, good!' she said. 'So am I. We can keep each other company. I'm going to stay at Holyrood House for a bit. I hardly ever go there. It will make a nice change.' I looked at her again, and this time she was wearing a crown, the Imperial State Crown, I think. She had not been wearing it at the beginning of the dream at all, and I don't remember her putting it on. She was sitting on a telephone directory, so that she could reach the steering-wheel. I never mentioned the fact that she was the Queen. It was taken for granted. 'Why are you driving this truck all the way to Edinburgh?' I asked. 'I get so bored being accompanied everywhere, and being met, and all that hand-shaking, I thought I would do something for myself, and by myself. I *can* drive, you know.' Her driving was excellent, and she was not averse to shouting to other drivers not to hog the road.

We talked for a long time about Palace life, and what a

bore it all was. She then suggested we stop at a transport café for a cup of tea. 'You had better take that crown off first,' I said, 'or you will be mobbed.' 'Goodness me, have I still got it on? That's habit for you. How silly of me.' The crown discarded, the Queen and I walked into the café, and ordered tea. When I went to pay for it, the lady behind the counter said, 'No charge, mate. She's a regular.'

When the Queen hosts garden parties hundreds of people attend. Usually several members of the Royal Family are there, and mingle with the guests, providing a memorable afternoon and for some the luck of actually speaking to one of them or, if you are very lucky, to the Queen herself. Tricia Bell's experience was happy in every way: Her Majesty's kindness and interest made her feel as special as she undoubtedly is.

On 6 June 2013, I had the honour of attending a garden party at Buckingham Palace for a reception with the Queen. I was invited in my capacity as the long-standing chair of the Cheshire-based charity Dial West Cheshire.

Dial West Cheshire is a wonderful charity providing award-winning services for disabled and older people in our community. Our invitation followed the charity being awarded the Queen's Award for Voluntary Service.

Our charity was represented on the day by myself, together with three long-standing voluntary members and our two support carers. I needed to use a wheelchair for such a long day and one of our other party members was also a wheelchair user.

From the very start of that day everything went brilliantly. First, the weather was wonderful, sunny, bright and warm.

I didn't take a coat – only an umbrella! The train from Chester was supposed to get us into Euston by 12.30 p.m. but unfortunately just outside Euston there was a delay, which meant we arrived late.

A frantic taxi ride across London to Buckingham Palace was 'different' for us out-of-towners. As we walked around the corner into the main gardens the Queen and her entourage were just coming down the steps. The Countess of Wessex turned right and came straight to our group where she spent some time speaking to us. She was really nice to talk to and seemed interested in why we were there. She was particularly interested because we came from Chester, which she knew well. I often wondered if she told the Queen about us, because at the end of the day, I had a lovely surprise.

You are not allowed to take cameras into the Palace and security is naturally very strict, so we only have the official video as a record of our day. The gardens are beautiful and so quiet and soothing – in the middle of London. It must be amazing to have this retreat in the city.

Inside the Palace is an unusual mixture of old fixtures meeting with new. It was breathtaking.

Afternoon tea is exactly what you would expect. Everything is presented appetisingly and with wonderful cakes, my main weakness! There was plenty to go around and drinks stations were all over the grounds as it got very hot.

We met so many different people from all walks of society that day and it was uplifting to hear their stories. The Palace staff, army and security were just as friendly and helpful. Nothing was too much trouble and they made you feel welcome.

At the end of the day, all disabled people attending were asked to make two columns for the Queen to walk down on her way back into the Palace. My support carer, and husband, Stephen, got me in place and to our amazement the Queen came straight towards us and started to speak to me.

She began by asking where I was from and, like the Countess of Wessex, she talked about Chester, which she obviously knew well. She said what a lovely city it was. Then we talked about Dial West Cheshire and why we were there. She congratulated me on my service for the charity and for achieving the award. Lastly, she asked if we'd had a good day. Needless to say, I just gushed and said that it had been so brilliant. She laughed and wished us a safe journey home. She must have been talking to me for about ten minutes. It was so surreal.

What I did notice most about the Queen is that she's about the same height as me. And she smells lovely – the scent was nothing I could put my finger on, just lingering and comfortable. Her skin is absolutely amazing. Although she was wearing make-up it was not thick and her skin is so smooth and bright. She just seems to shine – and that was after a full afternoon of walking around the gardens meeting people in the full heat of a summer's day. She only seemed to sit down for tea and that was for about half an hour. I really hope that when I get to her age I look as good and have as much stamina.

From start to finish it was the most wonderful day of my life, except for my wedding day, of course.

And how lovely to hear from Tricia that Her Majesty 'smells lovely'. The things that strike people about the Queen are her eyes, her height and the intensity of the moment when you are face to face with the most famous woman on earth.

Marta Lipinska from Poland puts her finger on the skill of

the Queen conversing with people she has only just met. We always hear that the royals say, 'And what do you do? Have you been here long? How did you get here?' and other apparently banal remarks: what is seldom reported is the informed interest shown that encourages the conversation into another channel. The Queen is so widely travelled, so wise, and so experienced at putting the other person first that people are dazzled by the few words they exchange.

The Queen visited Poland in 1996. I was then a local employee of the British Council in Poland and she came to our Warsaw office.

We stood in small groups and the Queen moved from one group to the next. The Queen usually exchanged a few words with someone in the group. She asked about what we were doing, about our job – but not only that. A photographer documented all the group and individual meetings. I have a picture with the Queen: I am standing in one of the groups and the Queen is talking to one of my colleagues.

Looking at this photo, I remember thinking how incredibly professional, and at the same time friendly and totally charming the Queen is.

I remember that before this visit, I thought that since the Queen meets such a huge number of people, from various groups, professions, countries and cultures, it must be humanly impossible for her to be interested in what each of these people do and what they think. But I was wrong.

When the Queen was with us – with each of the groups – each and every one of us had the impression that she was 100 per cent interested in us. She focused her full attention on us. And it was important to us. This is how we felt. She devoted to us lots of her time and gave us her full attention.

It is a great skill. The world would be a much better place if each of us could learn this skill and give all the people we meet on our paths the attention and interest Her Majesty had shown us.

Michael and Vivien Noakes spent a year following the Queen, writing an illustrated diary called *The Daily Life of the Queen*. Michael did the drawings; some places they visited were less glamorous than others. Their observation of the Queen visiting Luton Airport shows a flash of her sympathetic humour.

The Queen, whose own travel arrangements do not involve the tedium of queueing at check-in counters, watches as two passengers go through the formalities. As their bag is whisked away through a hole in the wall onto the new robot baggage-handling system, she says with a grin, 'I hope you see your suitcase again.'

The South African-born former weightlifter Precious McKenzie has won Commonwealth medals representing England and New Zealand, where he eventually made his home. This wonderful series of memories, spanning several years, shows how closely the Queen follows sporting events and with what unfailing interest and admiration she regarded this fine athlete.

I first met Her Majesty after returning to England after competing at the Mexico Olympic Games of 1968. She gracefully invited the members of the British contingent to a reception at Buckingham Palace. The team was smartly attired and lined up to meet the Queen. The Queen's secretary made introductions on our behalf. When it came to my turn, the Queen shook my hand and said, 'You are the weight lifter?' I found that I was unable to speak, overwhelmed by the occasion. She repeated the question two further times, by which time I had recovered my composure and replied accordingly. As a result, we held one another's hands for much longer than any of the other Olympic representatives!

In 1970, I obtained my second Commonwealth Gold Medal at Edinburgh and subsequently met the Queen at Holyrood Palace – my wife, Liz, accompanied me. Her Majesty was pleased to re-make our acquaintance and expressed delight on the occasion.

In 1974, I competed in Christchurch at the Commonwealth Games, and later the same year, Liz and I were invited to Buckingham Palace where Her Majesty invested me with an MBE. While in New Zealand, I had fallen in love with the country and with the New Zealand way of life. As a consequence, our family chose to emigrate to that wonderful country. The Queen had witnessed my appearance on the UK TV programme *Blue Peter*, which had contained coverage of all my cups, medals and so on. Her Majesty was impressed by the coverage and subsequently invited my wife and me to Buckingham Palace for tea and to honour me with a personal farewell. We flew back to England and received a wonderful reception.

I competed at my fourth consecutive Commonwealth Games in Edmonton, Canada, in 1978 where I won a gold medal. The Queen was in attendance, together with Prince Philip. The weightlifting competition was proceeding, at length, and this tends to bore those who are not intensely interested in the sport. However, Her Majesty insisted that she wanted to wait until I had competed in the hope that she could observe sporting history being made. Her anticipation was rewarded when I made the successful lift! At the final garden party hosted by the Queen in Edmonton, I was not initially on the list of invitees. When Her Majesty became aware of this omission, she insisted that I be included. As a result, the local police were employed to seek out my whereabouts in order to ensure my attendance. I was indebted to the Queen for this personal consideration.

In 1990, Auckland hosted the Commonwealth Games, and prior to the opening ceremony the Queen met the volunteers, of which I was one. We were all in a long line waiting to meet Her Majesty. When she arrived in front of me, she held my hand (again for a long time) and enquired how I was enjoying my new life in my new country. I simply replied, 'I love this country, ma'am, as indeed I know you do also.'

I have noticed that members of the Royal Family are often more at ease when talking to 'normal people', not dignitaries or people in high office. Maybe normal people are not eaten up with anxiety about how to respond, or how deep to bow, or if their clothes were the right choice and whether their shoes are shiny. Proud parents of members of the armed forces have always merited special attention, particularly if their beloved has been killed in action.

Here is a last poignant glimpse of a magic moment with the Queen. It is very moving to think of that photograph, far away in America, on the night table, the last thing Septimia saw every night before she went to sleep: the Queen among the treasured pictures of her family. Judith Dear from Lund writes:

I have never met Queen Elizabeth II but my beloved grand-mother, Septimia West Butcher, was chosen, as a Gold Star Mother [mothers who lost sons or daughters in the service of the US Armed Forces], to attend the dedication of the American Memorial Chapel in St Paul's Cathedral in 1958, in honour of her son, Captain John West Butcher, DDS, who died in England during the Second World War.

My grandmother met the Queen, whom she described as elegant and regal, everything a queen should be. The Queen expressed her heartfelt gratitude to all of the Americans who stood with Britain in her time of greatest need and especially to the mothers who had sacrificed so much.

For the rest of her life, my grandmother had several small photographs on her night table: her son, her late husband, her two grandchildren and the Queen.

10. Celebrating the Queen

We love anniversaries. Birthdays come round every year, and they feel fairly special, but a really important celebration to mark twenty-five or fifty years is exceptional. Those anniversaries are given names, too: silver for twenty-five years, gold for fifty and diamond for sixty, as no reign or marriage is expected to go on much after that. But wait! There is now another category: platinum trounces all others, as it recognises seventy years of love and devotion.

I remember the Queen's Silver Jubilee so well. In 1977 I was filming *Sapphire and Steel* with David McCallum at Elstree Studios as the country began preparing the street celebrations, the trestle tables and parties, the bunting and the portraits of the Queen: there were mugs and tea towels and commemorative coins, and it was just what was needed to give us an excuse to put on the glad rags and soak ourselves in a carnival atmosphere. Huge events were planned, none larger than the celebration at Windsor, beside the giant equestrian statue (The Copper Horse) of George III at the top of the Long Walk in Windsor Great Park, which culminated in the lighting of beacons across the country. It was a bank holiday weekend, Monday, 6 June. Hugo Vickers was at the event at The Copper Horse, and he kindly allows us to quote from his unpublished diary. At the end of this chapter Michael Parker fills us in on the details, which are well worth waiting for.

Kate [Trevelyan] asked Sir Martin [Charteris] what the Queen would wear the next day. I believed (and Audrey Russell agreed) that the Queen could not travel in the Gold Coach wearing day dress and hat. She must wear an evening dress with tiara. I would have gone further than that. I would have had her in a simple silver gown with cloak-like sleeves, such as she often wears, a few diamonds and a tiara, and I'd have made the Duke of Edinburgh and the Prince of Wales walk behind her to symbolise the solitary position she holds as head of state. Kate asked Sir Martin and he replied, 'The Queen will be appropriately dressed. I hope you will be also.' He said that it would be a day dress.

When we were on the point of leaving, Lady Charteris asked Sir Martin if he would be coming with us. He said he would not. 'Will you be coming later?'

'I shall be in good company,' he replied. I remember the quick response that his telephone got when it rang. Was that 'a summons from the Sovereign', as Robin Woods used to put it?

So off we went . . . We arrived at the Silver Ring. I carried Walter Annenberg's little chair . . . The VIP enclosure was full of Royal Household and people such as Sir Henry and Lady May Abel Smith, Lord and Lady Maclean, and Mr and Mrs Bruce Forsyth. It was an unbelievable sight. The thousands of people, the huge bonfire, the torchlight procession approaching The Copper Horse from the Long Walk and the Queen in green and headscarf looking so happy. The bonfire actually lit some whole minute before the Queen set light to it as the safety devices to make sure it lit worked too soon. A great blaze went up and some of the flaming straw (or whatever) blew into one of the trees and set it alight. A fire-engine took ages to put it out.

The Royal Family came round the back of The Copper Horse and onto a platform to watch a glorious display of fireworks over the Long Walk and lighting up of the Silver Jubilee Appeal symbol. The Prince of Wales wore his huge beige coat. Prince Andrew was a great hit with the crowd. Princess Margaret looked chic, Lord Linley looked confused. When the Royal Family watched the New Zealand activities, the Maoris sang greetings. There were great jokes and Princess Anne said: 'I know what it means.'

We were well positioned for their progress to the ox [there was a ceremonial ox roasting at The Copper Horse celebrations]. The Queen turned right to us and said, 'Weren't we lucky with the weather? It would have been awful if it had been this afternoon. None of this would have been possible.'

Prince Charles followed, saying, 'Hope to get a piece of the ox now.' We watched them eating the ox and their departure.

One of the seventy thousand spectators was inspired to scale The Copper Horse after the royal party left and give a spirited rendering of 'Rule Britannia' to the universal delight of the crowd. His enthusiasm was too much for officialdom, however, and he was soon escorted to ground level.

When discussing the plans for the bonfire two years previously, Sir Martin had quoted Lord Macaulay on the bonfires lit in 1588 to warn of the approach of the Spanish Armada. I ended my account with a snip from Macaulay too: 'Such night in England ne'er had been, nor e'er again shall be.'

Roy Strong was rather world-weary about the Silver Jubilee. Waspishly, he described the decorations as common, which makes me want to put them up all over the house.

I don't think the Queen had been described as 'skittish' before.

June and July. The Queen's Silver Jubilee.

We spent the Silver Jubilee weekend in the country keeping ourselves to ourselves while the village indulged in a turkey lunch, games, watching a coloured TV set up in the village hall, followed by tea and a Jubilee Cake. One can't help reflecting on how enormously the stature of the Queen has increased in the last two or three drear years. Shy, thoughtful, inscrutable, she remains an enigma to me, which, I suppose, is just as well.

I had travelled up to London to see Nureyev's *Romeo and Juliet*, which was patchy but not devoid of moments of splendour. As I left the Coliseum at about 10.45 p.m. the night sky thundered and crackled with fireworks. I strolled across Trafalgar Square, awash with people, and then down the Mall, where it was surprisingly thinner on the ground. The decorations in scarlet, turquoise and silver I thought were common. Having a cheap Jubilee was one thing but bad taste another. I stood opposite the Palace watching a huge crowd gradually assemble. It was shot through with plain-clothes policemen directing each other hither and thither. The crowd itself was basically middle-class British. Educated voices could be heard. Men in suits passed by with Union Jacks tied to the end of their umbrellas. From time to time cheering broke out followed by the singing of the national anthem or 'Rule Britannia' and then more cheers. The crowd was a young one. As I looked down I suddenly realised that it must have rained, for it was wet underfoot and the night air had a decided nip in it.

Then came the moment everyone had been waiting for. The vast TV lamps suddenly beamed down. At last the coaches swept by, with their postilions in scarlet and their interiors somewhat ludicrously lit up. The surge of emotion and the lump in the throat were almost tangible. More cheers, waving and clapping and then followed a long wait. The guards played military music in front of the Palace. At last the centre window opened and out the Royal Family stepped on to the balcony. The roar below was deafening. The Queen only had to lift her hand a little for a tide of fervour to ripple through the masses looking up. Close to me a group started to sing the national anthem, which was taken up across the tides of humanity. One could not help finding it deeply moving, as indeed was the cry of a Cockney nearby, who yelled up to the Queen: ''Ave a good sleep.'

In my strange role as civil servant I had been issued an invitation for a reception to be given for the Civil Service at Buckingham Palace on 10 June. Only ten people were to go from the Department of Education. I dreaded it, but there was no way out. Alone, no Julia [his wife], and with a flock of zombies. And so it was to be.

It was an odd evening for I knew members of the Royal Family and the Household better than the civil servants. I talked at length to the Duchess of Kent, who described how her young son Nicholas, totally misreading the event, on returning to the Palace on Jubilee Day from the carriage procession had exclaimed, 'I am so glad that Elizabeth and Philip are now married!' and how she had thrown her arms around the Queen, kissed her, and said, 'They *really* love you!' The Queen, she explained, had been totally bewildered and overwhelmed by this huge flood of affection directed towards her.

'What are you doing here?' said Princess Margaret.

'Don't laugh,' I said, 'I'm a civil servant.' We sat down in the great White Drawing Room and talked. Tony [Snowdon], in a fit of pique, had just removed vast tracts of furniture from Kensington Palace. The piano had gone and all the nursery chairs. We discussed Nureyev's *Romeo and Juliet*, which we agreed was patchy, when she caught the eye of the Queen who was just about to disappear through the magic door in the wall with a console table attached to it. 'You're not going, are you?' yelled Princess Margaret.

Her Majesty turned, looking, I thought, rather skittish in tiara, jewelled necklace and mini-crinoline and said, 'Yes. I've done all I can. I ask them what they do. They're DES or TUC or whatever and that's that.' Then, turning to me, 'It's the first time we've ever had the Civil Service. I was surprised to see you.'

'Well,' I explained, 'I *am* a civil servant!' I then went on to tell her how marvellous the balcony appearance had been the previous night and about the crowd below. I felt somehow she ought to know. Apparently there was a second appearance after midnight, just the Queen and Prince Philip. Princess Margaret said that she had to more or less push them out as they failed to grasp the fervour of the crowd.

People celebrated the Jubilee in all sorts of ways, some in large fancy-dress parties, some alone and quietly. At times of great pith and moment, many people turn to poetry, both reading and writing it. Sometimes a poem encapsulates in a few words what might take a page of prose to describe.

Pamela Street sent a poem to the editor of *The Field*, Wilson Stephens. Stephens replied, 'Many thanks for your verses about the Queen for which I am most grateful, they will appear in the Jubilee number of *The Field*.' She must have been so pleased. Here is what she wrote.

1952–1977

Of what today have we to sing
As former glory pales?
What subtle, strangely precious thing
Can quite such reassurance bring
To England in her buffering?—
A Queen prevails.

When fretful subjects thrust and thrash
And law and order fails,
When moneymakers' empires crash
Through building up on borrowed cash,
And life seems brittle, bald and brash –
The Queen prevails.
When politicians mourn and moan
And talk of all that ails,
One woman stands – stands out alone –
With grace and courage all her own,
Integrity surrounds the throne –
Our Queen prevails.

Suddenly twenty-five turned into thirty, forty, fifty years on the throne; and the country prepared for another landmark cele-bration, this time made of gold. A new millennium had arrived, and the catastrophic destruction of America's Twin Towers in the 9/11 attack in New York had ushered in a lasting sense of suspicion and enmity. Grumbles were heard about having another huge nationwide festival so soon after the last (so soon! It's like that song about a man watching his daughter grow: turn around and you're three, turn around and you're four . . . time goes rattling away, and twenty-five long years had passed). The extra bank holiday cheered people up, and after all gold was very special. Long live Her Majesty!

I found this wonderful speech made by the Queen at the grand Guildhall banquet given to celebrate her Golden Jubilee on 4 June 2002. Each speech she makes has a particularly personal touch, in this case the mention of football: the country was on fire, with England playing in the World Cup quarter-finals against Brazil, having beaten Argentina. The tributes to her family make this a speech every proud mother would make; and look how she deflects the glory at the end, so that the focus is not on her, but on her people and on the Commonwealth.

My Lord Mayor, Mr Prime Minister, Ladies and Gentlemen.

Thank you, my Lord Mayor, for your invitation to lunch at Guildhall today. It is a great pleasure once again for Prince Philip and me to be in this historic building to add another anniversary celebration to its long record of national events.

I am more than conscious at the moment of the importance of football. Although this weekend comes about halfway through my Jubilee year, as far as we are concerned, it bears no relation to a rest at 'half-time'. However, I am very glad that the fiftieth anniversary of my accession is giving so many people all over this country and in the Commonwealth an excuse to celebrate and enjoy themselves.

It has been a pretty remarkable fifty years by any standards. There have been ups and downs, but anyone who can remember what things were like after those six long years of war, appreciates what immense changes have been achieved since then. Not everyone has been able to benefit from the growth of wealth and prosperity but it has not been for lack of political will. I think we can look back with measured pride on the history of the last fifty years.

Since the spring of this year I have travelled extensively in this country and in the Commonwealth. It has been wonderful to experience the many special events which have brought together volunteers of all ages and organisations of all kinds.

At every stage along the way, Prince Philip and I have been overwhelmed by the crowds waiting for us and deeply moved by the warmth of their welcome. We are both much looking forward to our visits to Wales next week, then to the other regions of England and in the autumn to Canada.

I am quite convinced that these local celebrations have helped to remind people of the value of such neighbourhood events in building a genuine community spirit. I have seen this for myself in Green Street, for instance, here in the east of London, in St Anne's Cathedral in Belfast and at that gathering of the young people of Berkshire at Bisham Abbey. I hope that these celebrations will remind us of our shared heritage and what it means to be a united people, enjoying the support of families, friends and neighbours around us.

I take this opportunity to mention the strength I draw from my own family. The Duke of Edinburgh has made an invaluable contribution to my life over these past fifty years, as he has to so many charities and organisations with which he has been involved.

We both of us have a special place in our hearts for our

The Queen sitting on a grassy bank with her corgis at Virginia Water.

Her Majesty with Lord Porchester (left) and trainer Ian Balding (right).

Riding out with Terry Pendry, stud groom and stable manager at Windsor, 2006.

Watney recognising the Queen at once: at Vindolanda in 1998.

The Queen and Prime Minister Margaret Thatcher visiting Zambia for the Commonwealth Conference in 1979 in Lusaka.

On her 50th wedding anniversary – the Queen and Prime Minister Tony Blair leave Downing Street for a luncheon at the Banqueting House in Whitehall, 20 November 1997.

The Queen and Prince Philip on the train with Scotland's First Minister Nicola Sturgeon in 2015, on the day she out-reigned Queen Victoria.

President François Hollande of France guides the Queen through the flower market named after her, the Marché aux Fleurs Reine Elizabeth II, in Paris, 7 June 2014.

In Cork, 20 May 2011: an enthusiastic welcome for the Queen on her trip to Ireland.

Buckingham Palace, 24 May 2011: President Barack Obama and First Lady Michelle Obama of the United States with the Queen and Prince Philip before the State Banquet.

Precious McKenzie's small son proudly displays his father's MBE.

The Queen receives Madame Adrienne Clarkson, the new Governor General of Canada. She became Governor General in 1999.

The Queen and Princess Margaret in 1996.

The parachute drop into the Olympic Stadium in 2012: part of the short James Bond film featuring Her Majesty and actor Daniel Craig.

Rob Halford, arch royalist and lead vocalist of the heavy metal band Judas Priest.

Roy Strong, director of the Victoria and Albert Museum, who stayed at Windsor Castle in 1978.

2005 – Terry Wogan is greeted warmly by the Queen; in the background is Vera Lynn, in a yellow jacket.

Billy Graham, the American evangelist, strikes a pose for the camera.

The Queen surveys the grim aftermath of the great fire at Windsor Castle in November 1992.

Archbishop of Canterbury George Carey and the Queen shelter from the rain at a garden party in the grounds of Lambeth Palace, his official residence, 2002.

'Your Majesty – Mummy'
The Queen and Prince
Charles at the Diamond
Jubilee concert in 2012.

The Golden Jubilee, 2002:
Brian May of rock band
Queen on the roof of
Buckingham Palace playing
the National Anthem.

A moment of laughter:
The Queen and Prince
Philip in 2005.

The Queen and Prince Philip, 2002. Happy and glorious.

children. I want to express my admiration for the Prince of Wales and for all he has achieved for this country. Our children, and all my family, have given me such love and unstinting help over the years, and especially in recent months.

Your hospitality at this event, my Lord Mayor, is typical of the spirit of this Jubilee and the kindness shown to me by so many people over the years. I would like to give my heartfelt thanks to each and every one of you – here in Guildhall, those of you waiting in the Mall and the streets of London, and all those up and down this country and throughout the Commonwealth, who may be watching this on television. Thank you all for your enthusiasm to mark and celebrate these past fifty years.

Gratitude, respect and pride, these words sum up how I feel about the people of this country and the Commonwealth – and what this Golden Jubilee means to me.

Two days after the banquet at the Guildhall there was a massive party outside Buckingham Palace, headlined by *The Guardian* as 'One Million Join Party at Palace'. There was a huge photograph of ordinary street houses projected onto the front of the Palace while Madness sang 'Our House'. Crowds milled around the stage beside the Victoria Memorial, gleaming gold against the night sky, and then came the moment we shall never forget: Brian May on the roof of the Palace playing the national anthem on his electric guitar.

Twelve thousand pairs of eyes gazed skywards as the lone figure of Queen guitarist Brian May stood on the roof of Buckingham Palace and launched into a surreal performance of the national anthem.

The long-awaited Party in the Palace had begun and performers and crowds were embarked on a musical odyssey through the past fifty years.

It marked the culmination of a day in which guns were fired in salute from Hyde Park to Edinburgh, hundreds of street parties were held, and the nation was encouraged to take part in a mass singing of the 1967 Beatles' hit 'All You Need Is Love'.

An estimated one million people packed the grounds of Buckingham Palace and the royal parks to witness the Queen light the final Golden Jubilee beacon in a chain stretching around the world and trigger a spectacular display of fireworks at the Palace.

The Queen arrived for the pop concert with the Duke of Edinburgh with half an hour to go and was introduced by Dame Edna Everage as the 'Golden Jubilee girl'.

The royal couple, more at home with classical music, were in time to see Eric Clapton play 'Layla', although the Queen appeared to be wearing yellow ear plugs.

Other members of the Royal Family arrived in time for the opening performances and joined Tony and Cherie Blair in a VIP box. Among them were Prince Andrew and daughters Beatrice and Eugenie, Prince Edward and his wife Sophie, Princess Anne, Prince Charles, Prince Harry and Prince William, who elicited a hysterical response from some quarters.

The twelve thousand fans who succeeded in a telephone ballot for tickets for last night's extravaganza had already enjoyed a jubilee picnic in the Palace gardens as they watched the build-up to the concert.

Afterwards Prince Charles said, 'Your Majesty – Mummy. Ladies and gentlemen, in my long experience of pop concerts, this has been something very special indeed.

'I don't think that any of us will ever forget this evening. It really has been a wonderful celebration of some of the best of British musical talent. Well, nearly all British. And when you're talking about British talent, my goodness, there's a lot of it about.'

After the Jubilee celebrations the *Evening Standard* took a fond look back at the uproarious and exhilarating rock concert, marvelling at how times have changed; how very different from the days of Queen Victoria, who I like to think was looking down benevolently from her marble throne at the happy mayhem celebrating the monarchy.

Monday's rock concert at the Palace associated the Queen with a gloriously heady atmosphere of exhilaration, nostalgia and fun in a way which would have been inconceivable twenty-five years ago – as would have been last night's trans-formation of the front of Buckingham Palace into a light show. It delivered to a global audience of 200 million people an uncharacteristically positive message of national pride – in our music, in our monarchy, but also in ourselves, for being able to organise and present these ceremonial occasions better than any other people on earth.

Now we are in 2012. Ten more years had rushed by, and sixty years of unstinting service to the nation deserved the sincerest appreciation. We pinched ourselves, that we were still here, that *she* was still here, never missing a beat, never putting a foot wrong, for the Diamond Jubilee.

On 7 March 2012 *Hansard*, the official parliamentary record, notes this story told by Dan Jarvis in the Humble Address for the Diamond Jubilee, a series of speeches made by politicians in the House of Commons. I can hear guffaws, smacking of thighs and cries of approval and mirth; politicians often overact on purpose and I think they like doing it.

I recall a story about a mayoress from a town that shall remain nameless, although I will say that it was not Barnsley, who showed the Queen around a refurbished town hall. During the tour, the Queen and mayoress arrived at an open cabinet containing a rather formal robe, which prompted the Queen to ask, 'What is that robe for?'

The mayoress replied, 'This is our ceremonial robe, but we only use it for very special occasions.' A wry smile from the Queen said all that needed to be said.

On the same day David Cameron, as Prime Minister, spoke sincerely about his high regard for the Queen. (All good speeches contain a funny story and his is no exception.) Two million people coming to tea at the Palace over the years is a bit of an eye-opener. When you start assembling data about the Queen's duties and achievements the numbers seem to stretch to the moon.

The reign of Queen Elizabeth has been one of unparalleled change, from rationing through to the jet age, to the space age, to the digital age. At her first investiture as Queen, the very first decoration she presented was a Victoria Cross for heroism in the Korean war. Since then, members of the armed forces – her armed forces – have been in action all over the world, from Aden to the Falklands, the Gulf, Iraq and Afghanistan.

Around the world, dictatorships have died and democracies have been born, and across the old British empire a vibrant Commonwealth of nations has expanded and flourished.

Throughout this extraordinary change, the longest-lived monarch in our history has remained resolutely unchanged in her commitment and studious in her duties. It does not matter whether it is something we suspect she enjoys, such as the Highland Games at Braemar, or things we suspect she might be less keen on, such as spending New Year's Eve in the Millennium Dome, she never, ever falters. She has always done her duty, and that stability is essential for our national life.

While the sands of culture shift and the tides of politics ebb and flow, Her Majesty has been a permanent anchor, bracing Britain against the storms, grounding us in certainty. Crucially, simultaneously, she has moved the monarchy forward. It has been said that the art of progress is to preserve order amid change and change amid order, and in this the Queen is unparalleled. She has never shut the door on the future; instead, she has led the way through it, ushering in the television cameras, opening up the Royal Collection and the palaces, and hosting receptions and award ceremonies for every area of public life. It is easy now to take these things for granted, but we should remember that they were her initiatives. She was broadcasting to the nation every Christmas Day thirty years before we let cameras into this House.

In doing those things, the Queen ended a thousand-year distance that existed between British monarchs and their people. Indeed, while much of her life has been governed by tradition and protocol, the Queen has always taken a thoroughly pragmatic view of such matters. On arriving at one engagement in Scotland, she noticed that the local lord lieutenant was having considerable trouble extracting both himself and his sword from the official car in order to perform the introductions. While embarrassed civic dignitaries cleared their throats, the Queen cut straight through the seemingly insoluble ceremonial problem by walking up to the greeting line, hand outstretched, with the words, 'My lord lieutenant appears to be having difficulty in getting out of the car, so I'd better introduce myself. I'm the Queen.'

That human connection is a hallmark of the Queen's reign. Over sixty years, according to one royal biographer, she has met four million people in person, which is equivalent to the entire population of New Zealand. At garden parties alone, she has invited some two million people to tea. She is, of course, Queen of sixteen countries, and has surely travelled more widely than any other head of state in history. As she herself has been heard to say – it is a lesson, perhaps for all of us in this House – 'I have to be seen to be believed.' All this has given her remarkable insight. Like her previous eleven prime ministers, I have been struck by Her Majesty's perspective on world events and, like my predecessors, I am truly grateful for the way she handles our national interests.

The Queen sailed into the sunlit uplands of becoming the longest reigning British monarch ever in 2015, in excellent health and in admirable style. As she broke this remarkable record, one of her twelve prime ministers, John Major, paid tribute to her in a piece entitled by the *Daily Mail* 'A Monarch of True Majesty'.

Princess Elizabeth was not born to be our Monarch: it was fate that made her so. When her uncle Edward VIII abdicated, her much-loved father became King George VI, and she became heir to the throne.

In 1952, by the age of twenty-five, the young Princess had become Queen. On that day few, if any, could have imagined that she would still be on the throne sixty-three years later, having surpassed Queen Victoria as the longest-serving Monarch in 1,000 years of our history.

Throughout her adult life, the Queen has dedicated herself to public service. You have to be aged over seventy to be able to recall any other face on our banknotes and postage stamps; and of the seven billion people in the world today, only one billion have known another British Monarch.

She is the most widely travelled head of state in history: indeed around the world whenever anyone refers to 'the Queen', they mean our Queen. Her sixty-three years on the throne is, quite simply, an awe-inspiring achievement.

When she took the Coronation Oath in 1953, the United Kingdom was still emerging from the aftermath of the Second World War. Her people had not forgotten the sacrifices of war. Some were still grieving for those who had perished, yet – with characteristic British spirit – they were determined to pull together to lift the nation out of its economic and social gloom. The Coronation inspired the British to put the grim days behind them.

Hundreds of thousands lined the streets and many millions more crowded into the homes of neighbours to watch the procession and ceremony on small, flickering black-and-white television screens.

Street parties celebrated the dawn of a second Elizabethan era and small children clutched treasured Coronation souvenirs. It was a time of hope and cheer – a new start – and no one who took part in the events of that day will ever forget them.

The privations following war were easing, but far from

ended. As a ten-year-old boy, I confess that one of my own personal highlights of 1953 was the end of sweet rationing – followed closely by eggs and sausages. For others, the beginning of Coronation year was less happy, as floods ravaged the east coast and caused huge devastation.

But mostly it was a year of hope and triumphs. On the very morning of the Coronation, news came through that Edmund Hillary and Sherpa Tenzing had reached the peak of Everest.

Some sporting heroes achieved lifelong ambitions. After twenty-eight years of trying, Sir Gordon Richards finally won the Derby on Pinza. Stanley Matthews led Blackpool to victory over Bolton in the most famous FA Cup win of all time. And Len Hutton's England team regained the Ashes at the Oval after years of Australian domination.

Popular culture changed our world: James Bond made his debut in Ian Fleming's *Casino Royale*, while Bill Haley and the Comets introduced us to rock and roll music. It would be another ten years before we heard of the Beatles and the Rolling Stones, and then only on a mono record player.

In the home, very few people knew the luxury of vacuum cleaners or washing-machines, let alone tumble-dryers. Fewer than ten per cent of households possessed a refrigerator, and although the Coronation produced a surge in sales, there were only around 1.5 million households with a television, with what is now BBC1 being the only channel, and the black-and-white image barely visible through the fuzzy screen. It would be another fifteen years before we would see anything in colour. As for mobile phones and the internet, such things would have been beyond anyone's wildest imagination.

For those of us who lived through this time, it seems like another age altogether.

Overall, throughout the Queen's reign, we in the United Kingdom have been lucky. We have known peace above war; prosperity above austerity; and, whatever hardships some may still face, we enjoy a quality of life in 2015 that is immeasurably better than it was in 1953.

The Queen is as popular and revered today as when she was crowned, despite living through a world of enormous change.

Since her Coronation, man has walked on the Moon and explored faraway planets. The world's population has more than doubled. Life-spans have dramatically increased as – for most, but not all – living standards have risen beyond any expectation.

Around the world, politics and economics have shifted the global order. Change in every sphere of life shows no sign of stopping. Even the Royal Family – at the behest of the Monarch – has evolved. But amid all the change, the Queen has remained a constant – both here at home and overseas – for it is not only the people of the United Kingdom she serves: she is Queen to more than two billion people around the Commonwealth.

At the time of her Coronation there were only [not including Britain] seven nations in the Commonwealth. There are now fifty-three. No one should underestimate the Queen's dedication to, and affection for, her Commonwealth family. When consulted about how best to mark her Diamond Jubilee year of 2012, the Queen did not want memorials to commemorate the past: she wished to create a much more human legacy for the future. Thus the Queen Elizabeth Diamond Jubilee Trust, of which I am chairman, was founded.

With her active approval and support we have established two Commonwealth programmes: to end avoidable blindness;

and, each year, to identify a group of young leaders who, we hope, will play a significant role in the future of their own nations and others. This is but one illustration of the Queen's support for the Commonwealth, and her central role as its head.

I attended the first award ceremony for these young leaders, which took place at Buckingham Palace last June.

As each winner approached the Queen to receive their medal – many in national dress – I saw the future of the Commonwealth before me: beaming faces, bursting with pride as they represented their own home territory, full of hope, positivity, and the will and wish to work together in the name of their Queen. It was a truly moving occasion, the memory of which I will long cherish.

The core of the Queen's life – apart from family and long-standing friends – has been duty. Almost every day since her accession, she has received and read state papers. Each week she meets her prime minister in a private audience attended by no one else (except, perhaps, a few corgis).

No notes are taken, no reports made, no subject is off-limits – and its privacy is total.

The Queen's first prime minister was Winston Churchill: it would be another sixteen years before David Cameron was born. As one of the twelve who have occupied that office during her reign, I can say in all truth that – on matters of state – there is no one whose personal judgement I would value above that of the Queen.

It is that unique, informed, experienced, yet impartial insight, which is so valuable to the Government of the United Kingdom, and although it is a crucial aspect of her duties as Monarch, it is one which remains largely unknown.

The Queen does not involve herself in party politics, but

may well offer counsel – perhaps through well-directed questions – that any prime minister would be foolish not to consider with care. All of them soon learn that the Queen, far from being cut off from her people, is very much aware of the shifting tides of public opinion – indeed often ahead of it.

Beyond her duties, the Queen has a private hinterland. No one – apart from her family and close confidants – can truly claim to know her thoughts and wishes. In addition to her expanding family, her affection for dogs and passion for horses are well-known – and widely shared across every part of our country. No one who has seen her walking her dogs in the early-morning rain at Balmoral, or watching her horses race at Ascot, can doubt how deep, or how genuine, these interests are. When her horses win, her joy is absolute.

While we honour this historic landmark, we must not overlook the service of the Duke of Edinburgh, who gave up a promising naval career to marry the young Princess Elizabeth.

Through sixty-seven years of marriage, he has been an unfaltering and indefatigable support to the Queen: a pivotal part of our ship of state. At the age of ninety-four, he continues to play an important role in public life and, I believe, is held in greater affection today than ever before.

How does one sum up our remarkable Monarch? Compassionate, shrewd, well-informed, pragmatic and wise, with an unshakeable commitment to duty – and a great sense of humour.

Throughout her reign she has led by example and served our country well. She has entrenched a popular Monarchy so firmly in the affections of our nation that even the most hostile critics have been silenced.

In an egalitarian age, this is an extraordinary achievement. As a nation we have been very lucky: in a world of change – the pace of which is often bewildering, even frightening – the Queen has provided a stability that is comforting and true.

Nearly seventy years ago, the then Princess Elizabeth broadcast a message to the Commonwealth in which she pledged, 'I declare before you all that my whole life, whether it be long or short, shall be devoted to your service . . .'

In that, and so much else, HM Queen Elizabeth II has never failed us.

On the same day that the Queen became the longest-reigning British monarch, she and Prince Philip were on an engagement in Scotland. Think of the steam train *Union of South Africa* chuff-chuffing out of Edinburgh's Waverley station, taking the Queen and Prince Philip across that glorious upland country-side to Tweedbank station, where in front of thousands of spectators Nicola Sturgeon, Scotland's First Minister, addressed Scotland's Queen.

I want to start by acknowledging the milestone which makes this a historic day for many people far beyond the Scottish Borders. Her Majesty today becomes the longest serving Monarch in Scottish and UK history.

Throughout her reign – supported at all times by the Duke of Edinburgh – she has carried out her duties with dedication, wisdom and an exemplary sense of public service. As a result, Her Majesty is admired and held in affection across the Commonwealth and around the world. The reception she has received today demonstrates that that admiration and affection is certainly felt here in Scotland.

The very first public opening Her Majesty performed, as Princess Elizabeth, was in Scotland – at the Aberdeen Sailors' Home in 1944. Perhaps the proudest possession of the new Scottish Parliament is the mace she presented to us when we reconvened in 1999. Her Majesty has undertaken thousands of engagements across this nation including – last year – the opening of the Glasgow Commonwealth Games. And, of course, her affection for Scotland was shared by Queen Victoria, whose memory she respects so much. In fact, when Queen Victoria became the longest-serving monarch, she was also in Scotland – staying at Balmoral.

So it is fitting that Her Majesty has chosen to mark today's milestone here. And all of us are delighted to be able to share some of this day with her. By being here, she is adding a special touch to what is already a special day – for the Scottish Borders, for Midlothian, and for Scotland as a whole.

But now I want to take you back to the Silver Jubilee, to 1977 and The Copper Horse, which Hugo Vickers wrote about earlier. The Jubilee celebrations were, on that occasion as on so many others, produced by one of the greatest showmen of the twentieth century, Michael Parker (not to be confused with Michael 'Mike' Parker, the friend of Prince Philip). After serving ten years in the Queen's Own Hussars Michael turned his considerable talents to producing large-scale events, tattoos and, extravaganzas, unmatched for their ambition, *joie de vivre* and, some would say, insanity. I have the good fortune to know Michael, and a more convincing character you could not meet; he is extremely funny and charming, and always thinking of something to set fire to or blow up. You will see in this extract from his book why he has earned the nickname the Master-Blaster.

It was a fine early June evening in 1977. I was standing by The Copper Horse, the great equestrian statue of George III, at the top of the Long Walk in Windsor Great Park. And I was feeling absolutely sick with fright.

'Don't worry, not many people will come,' the experts had said. 'They'll all be at home watching it on television.' Well, that turned out to be a very false prophecy indeed. But it was one that I was to hear repeatedly during the next thirty-five years.

People were surging towards me, tens of thousands of them. As the dusk deepened, the hordes began to resemble the waves of an incoming tide. I was feeling sicker than ever because, although I had been working on this day for over a year, I had suddenly realised that I was going to be held to blame for whatever went wrong. Live television coverage would ensure that every last detail was sent around the Commonwealth and the world – there would be no second takes, no question of 'We'll sort that out in the editing later.' This was It!

The main problem was that we were running very late. Poor Raymond Baxter, the BBC commentator, was well into his second book of background detail and there was still no sign of the royal party.

The massive crowds had also delayed the three thousand members of the Sealed Knot Society who were to march – the New Model Army in buff coats and steel breastplates, the Royalist officers resplendent in brocade, lace and wigs – from their campsite in the Home Park. A thousand members of the Lewes Bonfire Society, all bearing flaming torches, were struggling to get through the throng. Both groups were there because I'd thought their numbers would be needed to make the evening work – nothing could now be further from the truth.

Somewhere beyond the crowds, we knew, the Queen and the Royal Family were making their way towards us in order to light the first in a chain of beacons stretching the length of Britain. Such a chain had originally been devised to blaze a warning the length of Britain in the event of an invasion.

These few stirring lines from Macaulay's 'The Armada' describe it perfectly:

For swift to east and swift to west the ghastly war-flame spread,
High on St Michael's Mount it shone: it shone on Beachy Head
Till Skiddaw saw the fire that burned on Gaunt's embattled pile,
And the red glare on Skiddaw roused the burghers of Carlisle.

Now it was being used in a celebration that would join every corner of the kingdom on the eve of the Queen's Silver Jubilee celebrations in London.

In the distance we could hear cheering, so that was promising. At the very moment that I spied the royal Land Rovers, a stage manager from the BBC tapped me on the shoulder. 'Sir, one of our generators has just blown up,' he said. 'Can we please have one of yours?'

I obviously had to say yes, knowing that the BBC needed the light more than I did. But it meant at least half of my site would now be in darkness. Among many other problems, the Massed Bands of the Household Cavalry, splendid in Gold State Dress, would now be sunk in gloom, which would be a challenge for the musicians. Fortunately the director of music had on white gloves, which might show up a bit in the dark.

Fortunately, too, I had brought four Second World War searchlights from Hounslow, which I thought would add to the jollity of the occasion. Enthusiastic, if not very skilful, TA [Territorial Army] operators had been playing the powerful beams on the clouds and trees, not to mention the odd aircraft trying to land at Heathrow (we had already had one complaint from Air Traffic Control). They were now re-tasked and moved around by the TV producer, Michael Begg, to illuminate some of the areas left dark by the missing generator.

Then I caught sight of the Queen, standing up in the State Land Rover and waving happily to a hugely enthusiastic crowd. A note of optimism crept into Raymond Baxter's running commentary, and the cold sinking feeling in my stomach lessened slightly – surely nothing else could go wrong now.

The royal party started at the top end of the line-up of the 'great and good' who were to be presented to them. I was at the other end of the line, ready to escort Her Majesty to the actual beacon lighting. I had only met the Queen once before, for about thirty seconds when she gave me an MBE in 1967, so I was doubly nervous.

At last she arrived at the other end of the line. I bowed. 'Ma'am, it might be a good idea if we got a bit of a move on,' I suggested. The Queen smiled, and off we went in the direction of the beacon. As we rounded a slight corner I saw that the 1948 London Olympic torch, which was to be used to light it, had gone out, and British Olympic Committee officials were madly trying to relight it. I gave a little cough. 'Er, ma'am, it might be a good idea if we were to slow down a bit.'

'Do make up your mind!' (with another smile).

At last the torch was lit. The little boy who was to hand it to the Queen was obviously upset by all the hoo-hah, and started to cry. 'You should be in bed!' the Queen told him cheerfully, as she took the torch.

I had been worried that the vast beacon wouldn't light quickly enough, so I'd got the pyrotechnics boys to stuff it with electrically ignited fireworks and had asked a Royal Signals Major, who I thought looked like a sensible sort, to be on the ignition button.

The Queen went forward and lit the fuse, which fizzed up spectacularly. Unfortunately, the gallant Royal Signals Major, having seen the fuse flare up, pressed the button. The Queen's fuse was burning nicely along the ground when suddenly the beacon, some sixty feet away, prematurely and very obviously caught fire.

'Can't think why you bothered to ask me!' the Queen joked. I groaned. Everybody else thought it was hugely funny.

At last, the two sources of fire were conjoined and the beacon burst into very impressive flames – ah, well, better early than never.

Then we heard, way over to one side of us, the sound of a firework mortar being fired.

'What on earth is that?' the Queen asked.

'Well, ma'am,' I explained, 'we've given each of the beacon sites a very bright flare to use when lighting their beacon, in case visibility is bad.'

But instead of a flare, the firework men had put a maroon into the tube; after a few seconds there was a very loud bang a hundred feet above us.

'What are they meant to do with that? Listen to it?'

I gave a deep sigh, and decided I would have to come clean. 'Your Majesty, I'm afraid it's all going terribly wrong . . .'

It's a well-worn cliché that silences of a few seconds can stretch out until they feel like an eternity, but that's exactly what happened. Being chained up in the Tower for life was the gentlest of the possible fates that flashed through my mind.

But then the Queen's face lit up in her famously glorious smile.

'Oh, *good*!' she said. 'What fun!'

11. Queen of the Stars

Once, at a film première, Gareth Hunt, my co-*Avengers* friend, and I were added to a line-up before the film to bulk up what was rather a skinny cast list: the Queen Mother was coming with Princess Margaret and the razzle-dazzle had to impress. Susan Penhaligon had been imported as well, and as we stood next to each other on the red carpet we discussed the glove protocol: we had been told we must wear gloves, then under no circumstances should we wear gloves, then gloves were de rigueur again. I was wearing some long gloves, but knew I could wrench them off if it looked as though the approaching royal party would be offended. The Queen Mother came slowly down the line, smiling and chatting to some members of the imported celebrities, stopping for a while with Ronnie Barker. Beside the Queen Mother, with a list in his hand, was an elderly Palace aide, who glanced down at the name before that person was presented. Closer, closer: then my turn. As I dipped into a curtsey, I heard the agèd one reading out a name. I went into the curtsey with my own name but as I arose I was announced as Carole Lombard, a long-dead American film star. The Queen Mother looked at me keenly: I didn't want to make a correction, but I am pretty sure she knew who Carole Lombard was and that it wasn't me. She gave me a faint smile and moved on to Susan Penhaligon, whose name utterly confounded the oldie one; and the log-jam built up behind them as Princess Margaret came closer. 'What are you in?' she said to Gareth.

'*The New Avengers*, Your Royal Highness,' he said, bowing smartly.

'We don't watch television,' said Princess Margaret and moved on.

We weren't even allowed to watch the film, but went home taking our gloves off and wishing that it had been . . . I don't know . . . better somehow. Wouldn't it have been nice if I had had the wit and courtesy to clear up the name, laugh and make light of it? But with royalty you have been told you must never speak first, so these colossal anxieties stalk us until the day we die.

The Queen is not, I think, a natural theatre lover. This is not disrespectful – just a fact. Some people love it and go to every play they can see; others give it a fairly wide berth. Princess Margaret loved show business, but even though the Queen is not hugely enamoured of the world of greasepaint she has always dutifully shown her support to the world of stage enter-tainment. This is a 1952 extract from Cecil Beaton's diary.

The Queen, it was said, wished to give her encouragement to the London theatre by paying one of her rare visits to a play.

Such is the effect of royalty that, although the play has been running for a hundred performances, the entire cast was nervous. Even the old professionals, like Ronnie Squire and Marie Löhr, were saying, 'Oh, we'll be too keyed up to give good performances,' and everyone was a bit too intent on putting their best foot forward. The women insisted that the wigmaker should re-dress their hair, their dresses were sent to the cleaners, and Marie Löhr told me she had walked for four hours to try, in vain, to get a champagne-coloured bow that I had suggested she should put at her stomach. Everyone behind the scenes was giving an extra spit and polish to their job. Paul Anstee hurried off with all the hydrangeas to have them given a certain dye-spraying as the blue had faded in the strong lights of the arcs.

The streets around the Haymarket were lined with people held back by a concourse of policemen. The audience had to be seated half an hour before 'the royals' arrived. It sat cheerfully talking. There was the usual air of expectation. The Royal Box was decorated with hideous small bronze and yellow chrysanthemums. The first thing to be seen was the approach of a bouquet. 'God Save The Queen'. Everyone stood to attention; the Queen quizzed the house out of the corner of her eye, not looking at all self-conscious at being stared at. The Queen Mother appeared, preceded by another bouquet and a bosom draped in white tulle. Then, without a tiara – perhaps with the wish to appear different – Princess Margaret. With precision the two Queens, having been politely cheered, sat down, the house lights were lowered, and the curtain went up . . .

The Queen sat relaxed and hunched, with head cocked backwards to listen concentratedly to the play. Princess Margaret had straight neck and back, and perhaps a more artificial interest in the stage performance. But the Queen Mother is an exceptionally bright woman, and tonight was in her most jovial mood, enjoying every nuance of the play's humour with a hearty relish, and alert to all the complicated twists of the mechanical plot. She was having a 'night out', and in such good spirits that she chuckled at many things that the audience would take for granted, and roared at the things that amused her most . . .

I wish that I could make a better impression on the Queen – not because she is the reigning monarch, but because I admire her character, her fairness and her judgement so much that I reproach myself for something inadequate within myself if she does not respond favourably. Yet I find her difficult to talk to. The timing always seems jerky and inopportune. I know I am at fault. As for her appearance, one would wish her to wear her hair less stiffly, or to choose dresses that would 'do' more for her, but one must admit that all these alterations would make no real difference. The purity of her expression, the unspoilt childishness of the smile, the pristine quality of her pink-and-white complexion, are all part of an appearance that is individual and gives the effect of a total entity.

How many Royal Performances and variety shows and extravaganzas have the Royal Family attended? In 1964 the Queen and Prince Philip visited Canada where Lester B. Pearson was the Prime Minister. His piece shows what a support and ally the Queen had in Prince Philip, always ready to lighten the mood and put people at their ease.

[Tuesday, 6 October] was devoted to celebrating the Charlottetown Conference's centennial, the opening of the building, parades, a lunch on the *Britannia* (very pleasant), and a very good Canadian variety show in the new theatre that night. I noted later: 'The Queen enjoyed it and Philip enjoyed it immensely. He really had been of great value on this trip. She is shy and not as forthcoming as her mother, for instance, though friendly and very charming when you are in touch with her. He is very outgoing, seems to seek out ways of establishing a close relationship with crowds and individuals and does not wait for others to take initiatives for him. At times his quips are a shade biting – especially when he is talking about the press – but he skates very skilfully over the thin ice of protocol and royal dignity and is of inestimable help to her, even though he always seems to keep her waiting while he has just another word with someone.' The Queen and Philip were at their best in meeting the performers backstage after the show. They were to be there for five minutes but stayed a full half hour. She seemed to be quite stage struck with Lorne Green, of TV *Bonanza* fame, the master of ceremonies. Apparently at that time the Royal Family watched his serial every Sunday. She was very warm and friendly with the *Feux Follets* dance troupe, chatting with them in French for some time. Later, however, she told me that her favourite had been Dave Broadfoot, the satirist, who had been very clever.

When I was at boarding school aged twelve, Cliff Richard smashed his way into the big time with 'Livin' Doll' (written by Lionel Bart, who later wrote *Oliver!*). I used to imitate Cliff using my tennis racquet as a guitar. When I met Cliff eventually, I told him this, and he signed his name beside the photograph in the first book I wrote about my life: 'To Joanna with lots of love and thanks for having me in your book, Cliff, the "Hero"'. I have been a lifelong fan, and always imagined that his super-smooth friendly and confident character could cope with anything. But look what Cliff writes about being knighted. I do love that man.

This was *such* a shock to me. Being awarded my OBE fifteen years earlier had been a big deal and a privilege, but people like me, who stick around the entertainment world for decades, do tend to get given them. But a knighthood? I had never even *imagined* that!

It's the ultimate honour and that was *exactly* what it felt like. The best thing was that I learned that, although they are awarded at the Queen's discretion, knighthoods are initially nominated by members of the public. It meant there were people out there rooting for me, and this made it even more special.

Having taken Mum when I got my OBE, this time my three sisters – Donna, Jacqui and Joan – accompanied me to Buck House. As ever, one thought was in my mind: *I wish Dad could have seen this*. My sisters waited excitedly in an anteroom as a courtier ran me through my paces.

The guy showed me a small kneeling stool with a handle, which was to be set in front of the tiny raised dais where HM The Queen would stand to knight me. 'I'd advise you to make use of the handle, sir,' he advised me. I was a little affronted. *How old did he think I was?*

'Oh, I don't think I'll need *that*!' I said briskly.

'I have seen people who are so nervous that they fall onto the stage, sir,' he said. 'I would use it.'

When Her Majesty came out, I put my right, slightly trembling, knee onto the cushioned stool and, yes, I found that I was gripping the handle. *Tightly.* The Queen was handed a ceremonial sword and tapped me lightly on both shoulders.

She didn't say, 'Arise, Sir Cliff!' but when I stood back up, she put the chain around my neck and said, '*This* has been a long time coming!' And I said . . . well, Lord knows what I said! My brain had frozen and I mumbled some utter gibberish. She just smiled, sympathetically – *I think!*

I felt so foolish. Back in the anteroom with my sisters, I

told them what had happened: 'The Queen must be wondering why she didn't give it to somebody who can speak English!' I said.

It doesn't matter if you have duetted with Liza Minnelli, or partied with Sir Mick Jagger, or sold out the Hollywood Bowl . . . an invitation to meet the Queen at Buckingham Palace thrills even the grooviest of cool people. I know heavy metal can't really be described as groovy, or cool, but I am reaching into my ancient lexicon to show how utterly over-excited we can get when confronted by an audience with the classiest superstar of them all. Here Rob Halford, lead vocalist of the heavy metal band Judas Priest, describes his visit to the Palace.

I can't think of many things in my life that have been as important to me as Judas Priest's triumphant comeback after I returned to the band. But meeting the Queen comes close.

Ever since Her Majesty gave me a special wave in Walsall Arboretum in 1957, I have always been an arch royalist. I have no idea why, but I am. So, I couldn't believe it when Jayne Andrews [his manager] phoned me with big news early in 2005.

The Queen was to host a reception in honour of British music and to recognise its contribution to Britain's culture and economy. And she had requested the pleasure of the company of . . . one of Judas Priest.

The rest of the band never even stood a chance. *Go to Buckingham Palace? Are you fucking kidding me? Yes, yes, yes!* So, Jayne accepted on my behalf and I started mentally ticking off the days and working on my bowing and curtseying.

On the day of the reception Priest were right up in the extreme Arctic region of Finland, but that wasn't about to stop me. We had a day off on the tour, so Jim Silvia [his tour manager] fixed me up a flight from the frozen North Pole to Heathrow.

As my taxi pulled through the gates of Buckingham Palace and into the inner perimeter, I couldn't believe I was there. *Wow!* Inside, I went up a huge, ornate staircase to be greeted at the top: 'Welcome, Mr Halford!' They gave me a name badge, so Her Maj would know who I was.

Once I got into the lavish party room, I knew a couple of people. I said hello to Roger Daltrey and had a bit of chit-chat with Brian May. One of the lads from Status Quo was there. But, after that, I found myself sitting on my own.

The royal invitation had been strictly for one person – no plus-ones – and so I was all on my tod. I looked around me at a room full of jazz musicians, classical musicians, impresarios and . . . Cilla Black?

Cilla was looking as lost and lonely as I was. *Cilla Black! What a legend!* I was drinking a glass of water, Cilla was sipping champagne, and I thought, *I should leave the woman alone. Give her some peace!*

Then I had another thought: *Bollocks to that! I've been a Cilla Black fan all of my life! If I don't go and say hello now, I'll always regret it!* I made my way over to her.

'I'm sorry to intrude . . .' I began.

'That's all right, chuck,' said Cilla, looking me up and down.

'I just want to say it's a thrill to meet you, and I love your music.'

'Oh, thank you!' she said.

'Are you with anyone?' I asked, although she obviously wasn't.

'No,' she replied. 'I wasn't allowed to bring anyone. I suppose you wanted to bring your wife, or your girlfriend?'

'I don't have a wife or girlfriend, Cilla,' I said. 'I'm gay . . .'

Cilla Black was clearly one of life's natural fag hags. The second I said that, she got up and gripped my arm. For the next two hours, we paraded around the room, arm in arm, and learned all there was to know about each other. We were inseparable!

We were having a whale of a time when, suddenly, the Queen appeared at the far end of the room. She is a tiny figure, hardly more than five feet tall, but she has such presence. How can I put it, exactly? She just . . . *radiates royalty.*

I'm a bit of a historian and, as I looked at her, being guided around the room by an equerry, the whole royal lineage passed through my mind, from the Tudors to the modern day. Cilla had met the Queen a bunch of times before, but I felt quite overcome.

So, I was standing with Cilla, drinking my water and trying to sneak a closer look at our monarch, when an equerry glided over. 'Would you care to meet Her Majesty?' he murmured.

'Oh, that would be great!' I blurted out, before Cilla had a chance to say that she wasn't bothered as she'd already met her. 'Thank you so much!'

A minute later, the Queen was standing in front of me. Receptions are one of the few times that she doesn't wear gloves, but she *was* holding a glass. Apparently, it's to stop people trying to shake her hand.

Well, it didn't stop *me*. Instinctively, without thinking, I stuck my hand out to her. Cilla gave me a poke in the ribs, as if to say, 'No!'

The Queen regarded me, and gave my hand the slightest

brush with the tips of her fingers. I didn't attempt a full-on bow, but I gave a very respectful nod.

'Thank you so much for coming,' said the Queen. 'Isn't it strange that we have no music playing, when it's a music event?'

'Yeah, that would've been nice!' I said, trying not to sound too yam-yam.

'I should have had a string quartet in the background,' mused Her Majesty. 'And what do you do?'

Before I could answer, Cilla chimed in: 'He's in this band called Judas Priest! He's come all the way from Finland to be here!'

'Oh,' said the Queen. 'And what kind of music do you play?'

'Heavy metal, Your Majesty,' I said.

The Queen gave me a slightly pained look. 'Oh, heavy metal,' she said. 'Why does it have to be so *loud*?'

Woah! The Queen just said the words 'heavy metal'! Possibly for the first time in her life! But . . . how do I answer THAT question?

'It's so we can bang our heads, Your Majesty!' I told her. Cilla gave me another dig in the ribs.

The Queen smiled, *regally*. 'It's been very nice to meet you,' she pronounced. As she turned to leave, I instinctively stuck my hand out towards her again. And got yet another jab in the ribs from Cilla.

'You don't shake the Queen's hand!' she scolded me, as our monarch walked slowly away.

'Nobody told me!' I said. 'I dunno anything about etiquette!'

'Oh, I can't take you *anywhere*!' sighed Cilla Black.

On my flight back to the Arctic Circle, I replayed the scene, and the encounter, in my head a million times. *Had it really just happened?* It was a day I will never forget. *The day I met the Queen.* And it had been even better than Walsall Arboretum.

Did Francis Rossi mishear the Queen? Possibly not. It doesn't matter: in his autobiography, *I Talk Too Much*, the co-founder of Status Quo tells a marvellous story, imbuing Her Majesty with yet another layer of fab-ness, about when he was visiting the Palace to be awarded his OBE.

> They stand you in circles while you wait for the Queen to arrive. Rick [Parfitt] and I are standing there at Buckingham Palace. It's kind of an audition before you get your gongs. I was talking to Sophie, Countess of Wessex, the one who married Prince Edward. She was very nice. Then up comes the Queen. I'm not a royalist by any stretch. But what their gig entails, they outwork any of us. They are really good for the country and that whole thing. I said, 'Nice to meet you again, ma'am.'
>
> She said, 'Do what?'
>
> Suddenly I could just imagine her and her sister Margaret, in the fifties, when 'Do what?' was a very hip saying. These days it doesn't sound right. But that's what the Queen said. 'Do what?' We made her smile.

Honours are given out to all branches of the arts: much is made of the well-known faces who are given 'gongs', with newspaper headlines, and photographs of the medal held up near the face: rather like the Wimbledon winner having to kiss the trophy, even though it's the last thing they would do in real life. But creative people of every kind are invited to events at the Palace. Rock bands and actors, dancers, artists and writers are all made welcome.

One of the finest writers we shall ever read is Hilary Mantel. She cannot write a duff sentence: these descriptions, scalpel-sharp, detached, will be recognised by many who have attended any large and grand event, or gone backstage after a play. Is it make-believe? Is there more to the monarchy than that?

A few years ago I saw the Prince of Wales at a public award ceremony. I had never seen him before, and at once I thought, What a beautiful suit! What sublime tailoring! It's for Shakespeare to penetrate the heart of a prince, and for me to study his cuff buttons. I found it hard to see the man inside the clothes; and like Thomas Cromwell in my novels, I couldn't help winding the fabric back onto the bolt and pricing him by the yard. At this ceremony, which was formal and carefully orchestrated, the Prince gave an award to a young author who came up on stage in shirtsleeves to receive his cheque. He no doubt wished to show that he was a free spirit, despite taking money from the establishment. For a moment I was ashamed of my trade. I thought, This is what the royals have to contend with today: not real, principled opposition, but self-congratulatory chippiness.

And then as we drifted away from the stage I saw something else. I glanced sideways into a room off the main hall, and saw that it was full of stacking chairs. It was a depressing, institutional, impersonal sight. I thought, Charles must see this all the time. Glance sideways, into the wings, and you see the tacky preparations for the triumphant public event. You see your beautiful suit deconstructed, the tailor's chalk lines, the unsecured seams. You see that your life is a charade, that the scenery is cardboard, that the paint is peeling, the red carpet fraying, and if you linger you will notice the oily devotion fade from the faces of your subjects, and you will see their retreating backs as they turn up their collars and button their coats and walk away into real life.

Then a little later I went to Buckingham Palace for a book trade event, a large evening party. I had expected to see people pushing themselves into the Queen's path, but the opposite was true. The Queen walked through the reception areas at an even pace, hoping to meet someone, and you would see a set of guests, as if swept by the tide, parting before her or welling ahead of her into the next room. They acted as if they feared excruciating embarrassment should they be caught and obliged to converse. The self-possessed became gauche and the eloquent were struck dumb. The guests studied the walls, the floor, they looked everywhere except at Her Majesty. They studied exhibits in glass cases and the paintings on the walls, which were of course worth looking at, but they studied them with great intentness, as if their eyes had been glued. Vermeer was just then 'having a moment', as they say, and the guests congregated around a small example, huddled with their backs to the room. I pushed through to see the painting along with the others but I can't remember now which Vermeer it was. It's safe to say there would have been a luminous face, round or oval, there would have been a woman gazing entranced at some household object, or perhaps reading a letter with a half-smile; there may have been a curtain, suggestive of veiled meaning; there would have been an enigma. We concentrated on it at the expense of the enigma moving among us, smiling with gallant determination.

And then the Queen passed close to me and I stared at her. I am ashamed now to say it but I passed my eyes over her as a cannibal views his dinner, my gaze sharp enough to pick the meat off her bones. I felt that such was the force of my devouring curiosity that the party had dematerialised and the walls melted and there were only two of us in the vast room, and such was the hard power of my stare that Her Majesty turned and looked back at me, as if she had been jabbed in the shoulder; and for a split second her face expressed not anger but hurt bewilderment. She looked young: for a moment she had turned back from a figurehead into the young woman she was, before monarchy froze her and made her a thing, a thing which only had meaning when it was exposed, a thing that existed only to be looked at.

And I felt sorry then. I wanted to apologise. I wanted to say: it's nothing personal, it's monarchy I'm staring at. I re-joined, mentally, the rest of the guests. Now flunkeys were moving among us with trays and on them were canapés, and these snacks were the Queen's revenge. They were pieces of gristly meat on skewers. Let's not put too fine a point on it: they were kebabs. It took some time to chew through one of them, and then the guests were left with the little sticks in their hands. They tried to give them back to the flunkeys, but the flunkeys smiled and sadly shook their heads, and moved away, so the guests had to carry on the evening holding them out, like children with sparklers on Guy Fawkes night.

At this point the evening became all too much for me. It was violently interesting. I went behind a sofa and sat on the floor and enjoyed the rest of the party that way, seeking privacy as my sympathies shifted. And as the guests ebbed away and the rooms emptied, I joined them, and on the threshold I looked back, and what I saw, placed precisely

248

at the base of every pillar, was a forest of little sticks: gnawed and abandoned. So if the Queen's glance had swept the room, that is what she would have seen: what we had left in our wake. It was the stacking chairs all over again; the scaffolding of reality too nakedly displayed, the daylight let in on magic.

We can be sure the Queen was not traumatised by my staring, as when next we met she gave me a medal. As I prepared to go to the Palace, people would say: 'Will it be the actual Queen, the Queen herself?' Did they think contact with the anointed hand would change you? Was that what the guests at the Palace feared: to be changed by powerful royal magic, without knowing how?

Do you believe in magic? Something happens when someone immensely famous suddenly appears beside you, an almost physical shock to the system. It is a kind of unintended super-power, interfering with actual time and weaving a kind of spell on the subject, in this case Mike Read, the radio DJ. This short encounter between him and the Queen on Birdcage Walk in 2004 has an almost dreamlike intensity about it.

Early one morning just after *I'm a Celebrity, Get Me Out of Here!* had finished, I was heading down to the South Bank to appear on a breakfast television programme.

Driving west along Birdcage Walk, the traffic was halted and a number of motorcycle outriders appeared and stopped just in front of me. They were obviously waiting for a car to catch up with them. I assumed, as you would, that it was a member of the Royal Family or a visiting royal, and I wasn't disappointed. The said car appeared and temporarily pulled up right next to me. It had to wait momentarily for more outriders from the escort to catch up. The window was down on that car and I was in a convertible with my roof off and my window down.

I looked across and it was the Queen. There was no time for formalities.

I simply smiled and said, 'Morning.'

'Morning,' replied the monarch, a second before her limousine moved off.

There wasn't even time to add, 'Your Majesty.'

It was rather a surreal moment. We were only a yard away from each other. My mother was thrilled when I told her this story and she pleaded, 'Tell me more. Tell me more.' I told her there was no more. That was it!

The smoothest-talking, least flappable and most charming man you could ever meet was Terry Wogan. He perfected the art of chuntering on the radio (the Queen would call it 'the wireless') and I never saw him nervous. Once when we were about to go on air on television, hosting together a huge charity event, I whispered, 'I'm shaking! Aren't you nervous?' He yawned and said, 'It's only television.' Although I sometimes wonder if the Queen and Prince Philip can actually recognise any performers without being prompted, as they meet so many, I am pretty sure they knew who Terry Wogan was.

A year or so ago, the Queen and Prince Philip hosted a grand levee at the Palace to celebrate the music industry's contribution to the public purse, and British life in general. I got there early and was given a special badge, then ushered through one great room after another, hung with magnificent paintings and impossible chandeliers. Gilt was everywhere, on the walls, the ceilings, the chairs. It was overwhelming, and there I was, the boy from Limerick, alone in this grand room, awaiting the arrival of the Queen of England. What would Michael and Rose Wogan have said? Or Auntie May, Muds or Great Aunt Maggie? Or all those teachers who thought I was OK, but would never amount to much? All those years in short trousers, on the crossbar of my father's bike, playing table football with myself on the floor of the front room in Elm Park – were they leading up to this?

Then the other rooms started to fill up, but only one or two joined me in what I was beginning to think was my own personal salon. Shirley Bassey, Vera Lynn, Tim Rice, Tessa Jowell, Phil Collins. In another room, Brian May from Queen and Eric Clapton were just a couple of the great names of British music who hadn't made the final cut. We lined up, Shirley Bassey knocking over an occasional table in her nervousness, and Her Majesty and Prince Philip entered, all welcoming smiles. They moved slowly down the line, exchanging pleasantries. When the Queen came to me, she told me what a wonderful musical afternoon she'd enjoyed, listening to the music of, among others, Katie Melua. She complimented me on my discovery of such a bright talent. I blushed modestly but didn't have time to tell Her Majesty that the discovery was my producer Paul Walters's, not mine, because with that charming smile of hers she had moved on to exchange airy badinage with the next in line, Phil Collins. Prince Philip asked me how I kept up my incessant babble every morning on the radio, and I said I was just babbling to myself, which seemed to satisfy him, and he followed the Queen, who by now was making her way to the door and the next bunch of hobbledehoys and ne'er-do-wells.

As she did so, Phil Collins whistled the five notes from *Close Encounters of the Third Kind*.

The Queen turned, still smiling, but puzzled. 'What was that?' she enquired.

Collins was speechless.

'He was calling ET, ma'am,' I said, even as I said it wishing I'd kept my mouth shut.

'Ah,' said the Queen, nodding understandably. They'd obviously warned her about the kinds of idiots she'd be meeting that evening.

As the door closed, Phil Collins turned to me, whining piteously, 'Why did I do that? What came over me?'

'The Royal Effect,' I answered sagely. 'You say the first thing that comes into your head, and you carry the memory of your foolishness with you to the grave.'

I love Shirley Bassey knocking over a table.

Even though most of us would be starry-eyed about an evening at Buckingham Palace, and talking to members of the Royal Family, there are always those who will be studiously blasé about it all. The architect Sir Denys Lasdun had constructed a massive grey Brutalist theatre complex on the South Bank, loved and loathed in equal measure. It would be the home of the National Theatre, and opinions about it were at boiling point at the time of this reception for the media in February 1975. Peter Hall, visionary creator of the Royal Shakespeare Company, was the chosen one to lead the National Theatre from its temporary lodgings at the Old Vic Theatre to its new concrete home. He was a brilliant diarist and his writing always contained a swish of acid.

To Buckingham Palace for the Queen's reception for the media, at least I suppose that's what we were. Newspaper editors; television controllers; journalists and commentators; Heath looking like a tanned waxwork; Wilson; Macmillan [Heath and Macmillan were former prime ministers; Wilson was prime minister at the time] a revered side show, an undoubted star; a few actors (Guinness, Ustinov, Finney); and all the chaps like me – John Tooley, George Christie, Trevor Nunn. And Morecambe and Wise.

It was two and a half hours of tramping round the great reception rooms, eating bits of Lyons pâté, drinking over-sweet warm white wine, everyone looking at everyone else, and that atmosphere of jocular ruthlessness which character-ises the Establishment on its nights out. Wonderful paintings, of course, and I was shown the bullet that killed Nelson.

As we were presented, the Queen asked me when the National Theatre would open. I said I didn't know. The Queen Mother asked me when the National Theatre would open. I said I didn't know. The Prince of Wales asked me when the National Theatre would open. I said I didn't know. At least they all knew I was running the National Theatre.

Home by 2 a.m. with very aching feet. Who'd be a courtier?

12. Queen of the Air

From the very beginning, from the first worldwide broadcast of the speech made on her twenty-first birthday, the Queen has known that every speech she makes will be preserved in amber, quoted, referred to, criticised and admired. The Queen's Christmas Broadcast was a part of Christmas Day. At three o'clock, presumably during or after the family lunch, before the crackers but probably after the Christmas pudding, the radiogram or wireless would be warmed up in the corner of the room, the beeps would tell the hour, and there was the Queen's voice. The first Christmas broadcast she made was when she was Queen but had not yet been crowned in 1952. We could only hear her voice, could only guess what she was wearing, and where she was: was she at a desk or sitting on a sofa? Did the Royal Family ever wear paper hats, and would she have taken hers off to make the speech? It never occurred to us that the broadcast had been recorded before it was aired. The Queen was obviously speaking to me.

We belong, you and I, to a far larger family. We belong, all of us, to the British Commonwealth and Empire, that immense union of nations, with their homes set in all the four corners of the earth. Like our own families, it can be a great power for good – a force which I believe can be of immeasurable benefit to all humanity.

My father, and my grandfather before him, worked all their lives to unite our peoples ever more closely, and to maintain its ideals which were so near to their hearts. I shall strive to carry on their work.

Already you have given me strength to do so. For, since my accession ten months ago, your loyalty and affection have been an immense support and encouragement. I want to take this Christmas Day, my first opportunity, to thank you with all my heart.

Many grave problems and difficulties confront us all, but with a new faith in the old and splendid beliefs given us by our forefathers, and the strength to venture beyond the safeties of the past, I know we shall be worthy of our duty.

Above all, we must keep alive that courageous spirit of adventure that is the finest quality of youth; and by youth I do not just mean those who are young in years: I mean too all those who are young in heart, no matter how old they may be. That spirit still flourishes in this old country and in all the younger countries of our Commonwealth.

On this broad foundation let us set out to build a truer knowledge of ourselves and our fellow men, to work for tolerance and understanding among the nations and to use the tremendous forces of science and learning for the betterment of man's lot upon this earth.

At my Coronation next June, I shall dedicate myself anew to your service. I shall do so in the presence of a great congregation, drawn from every part of the Commonwealth and Empire, while millions outside Westminster Abbey will hear the promises and the prayers being offered up within its walls, and see much of the ancient ceremony in which kings and queens before me have taken part through century upon century.

You will be keeping it as a holiday; but I want to ask you all, whatever your religion may be, to pray for me on that day – to pray that God may give me wisdom and strength to carry out the solemn promises I shall be making, and that I may faithfully serve Him and you, all the days of my life.

There is a skill in projecting a message which will be heard by millions but should sound as though you are talking to a small group of people whom you don't know but care about deeply. The essence of these speeches always moves me. There is always an emphasis on the brotherhood of nations and the gentle prompting to go on doing our best, being kind and thinking of others. The Queen is Patron of the Girl Guides. I think that those youthful ambitions to make the world a happier, fairer place have persisted.

Does she write all her own Christmas Broadcasts? I like to think she does: she delivers the speeches so comfortably, unlike some of the political timber she has to drag across the stage at the Opening of Parliament. Her messages are kind and inspiring and thoughtful, never preachy or dull. Sometimes she mentions a member of her family and we shuffle closer to glean every last syllable. When Prince Charles started that speech 'Your Majesty . . . Mummy' there was a roar of delight . . . He calls her Mummy! How fabulously normal! How . . . like us!

This, of course, is the crux of the whole matter: we like to believe that the Royal Family is just like us. In so far as they are human and mortal, they are, but everything about their lives has made them completely unlike us. The constant scrutiny of their appearance and behaviour, their jobs ('Never done a day's work,' when most of us would totter after even a week of what their workload demands), their choice of spouses, their frailties and how they speak . . . a strange mix of envy and adoration with scorn and fascination colours every report on their lives, presenting them as a race apart. We never know what they think as they can never answer back, and so the conundrum spins on: do we deserve to know everything about them or is it better to keep the monarchy shrouded in mysterious secrecy?

The word 'queen' carries supreme weight: queen for a day, homecoming queen, beauty queen, Queen of Heaven, queen bee, the all-powerful queen on the chessboard, who can travel in any direction . . . to be called queen is to be recognised as the very best. When the Queen addresses the nation, the National Anthem is played in full, and there is a sense of occasion unmatched by political broadcasts.

By 1957 the Christmas Broadcasts had started to be televised. The royal residence chosen for the setting for the Queen was Sandringham, quite probably because royal Christmases are often spent there. We were touched: we didn't have a Long Library but we were looking at the Queen at home and, what was more, the members of the Royal Family were crowded around a television set, just as we were, to watch and listen. It was ground-breaking.

Twenty-five years ago, my grandfather broadcast the first of these Christmas messages. Today is another landmark because television has made it possible for many of you to see me in your homes on Christmas Day. My own family often gather round to watch television as they are this moment, and that is how I imagine you now.

I very much hope this new medium will make my

257

Christmas message more personal and direct.

It is inevitable that I should seem a rather remote figure to many of you. A successor to the kings and queens of history; someone whose face may be familiar in newspapers and in films but who never really touches your personal lives. But now at least for a few minutes I welcome you to the peace of my own home.

In the old days the monarch led his soldiers on the battlefield and his leadership at all times was close and personal.

Today things are very different. I cannot lead you into battle, I do not give you laws or administer justice but I can do something else: I can give you my heart and my devotion to these old islands and to all the peoples of our brotherhood of nations.

I believe in our qualities and in our strength. I believe that together we can set an example to the world, which will encourage upright people everywhere.

In David Walliams's screen adaptation of his popular children's story *Gangsta Granny* in 2013, where a feisty granny plots with her grandson to steal the Crown Jewels, I was cast to play the Queen. Not the real Queen: a fictional representation, but easily recognisable as the Queen reimagined in a make-believe world. She was discovered in the Tower of London by the would-be thieves, wearing a dressing-gown and the State Crown, planning her Christmas speech, as she said she found it easier to think about her broadcast with a crown on her head. I don't look like the Queen or sound like her: there was no attempt to mimic her, no make-up to copy her appearance. At the end of the film she made her Christmas Broadcast, beside a huge Christmas tree, dressed smartly in a suit with pearls, and she broke into a sort of dance sequence, demonstrating some decent 'Gangnam' moves. This was warmly received by the public. The true Queen is a good dancer, mainly in ballroom and Scottish reels, and this 'throwing of shapes' seemed completely appropriate.

It is rather a relief to know that the Queen has a terrific sense of humour. She must have to take a thousand strange requests in her stride. Although she said so long ago in that 1957 speech 'In the old days the monarch led his soldiers on the battlefield and his leadership at all times was close and personal . . . I cannot lead you into battle . . . but I can do something else', she surely could not have envisaged the extraordinary request that was to put her in the forefront of a worldwide audience at the opening of the Olympic Games in 2012.

After the thrill of winning the coveted position of hosting the Games, preparations started in earnest. Sebastian Coe, chairman of the London Organising Committee for the Olympic Games, describes the Queen visiting the Olympic site in its development.

Once we had won the bid, the Queen expressed an interest in what was happening, and a visit was arranged for the following October. One of the first things we had done was to organise a viewing gallery – an upmarket version of a Nissen hut – to be craned on to the roof of a residential tower block to the east of the site. From the point of view of international sponsors, it was crucial to correct the allegation that we had stuck it out in the wilds of Essex. At twenty-one-storeys high, the building was one of the tallest in the area and provided a panoramic view, not only of the site itself but of the Thames, the NatWest Tower – all the way across London to the Wembley arch. It clearly demonstrated that we were the same distance east of Tower Bridge as Trafalgar Square was to the west.

Holden Point was actually sheltered accommodation for old people, and the lift was operated by the caretaker. Its interior was some kind of polished stainless steel and as it rumbled its way up to the top, the Queen commented favourably on its shine.

'Johnson's Baby Oil, ma'am,' the caretaker explained. He then itemised a variety of other uses to which it could be put, and equally the uses to which it should never be put, as the lady-in-waiting and the protection officer looked increasingly uncomfortable.

Looking down on the maze of railway lines and sidings, the first thing the Queen said was, 'That one over there. That's the line we take to Sandringham.' And indeed it was.

With very little to see at this point, barrage balloons of different colours had been tethered to key sites to show both the scope of the park and to enable me to point out where the different venues were going to be built. Unfortunately, I am mildly colour blind and, while I knew which balloon represented which site, differentiating the different colours was another matter. 'I must apologise, ma'am, but I am really struggling here.'

By the time of her next visit, in November 2009, the floor of the stadium was well on its way to resembling a running track, and I walked her down what would eventually be the finishing straight.

'So where am I now?' she asked.

'Well, ma'am, if you put in a surge over the next twenty metres, you would be the new hundred-metres Olympic champion.'

It seems to me to be the last time that this country was truly at ease with itself was the year 2012. It saw the Queen's Diamond Jubilee, and the sun shone and wildflower meadows were planted, and the massive Olympic Park, far from being completed late, was on time and ready. Smiling soldiers were on hand to guide visitors, and medals were to be won in profusion. Teams from around the world were to be welcomed and hosted with diligence, friendliness and professionalism.

There was a certain amount of tooth-sucking and chin-rubbing about how the opening ceremony would be handled. Would it all be bobbies on bicycles two by two and morris dancers? What was the identity of the United Kingdom as far as costumes went? Would it all be a bit . . . embarrassing? Step forward Danny Boyle, whose ambitious plan made listeners pale: would it work? Would SHE agree? He had only to ask, but what would be the answer from Her Majesty?

His idea for a show-stopping arrival at the stadium was bold beyond belief: The Queen was to be escorted from Buckingham Palace by James Bond in a helicopter to escape some unknown threat. She would be flown over famous London landmarks, over the Houses of Parliament and under Tower Bridge, and eventually she would leap out in a skydive into the area just behind the Olympic Stadium. Obviously, the Queen would have a stunt double dressed exactly as she was, in a peach-coloured cocktail dress, but Daniel Craig as James Bond would be real, the Palace meeting would be real – even the corgis would be real.

Word came back that the Queen was happy to shoot the film with Daniel Craig. We thought it was April Fool's Day. It was weird, but amazing. So we went to meet her. Edward Young, who is deputy private secretary to the Queen, was hugely helpful; it was his responsibility to make sure the film wasn't naff. It was easy for us because the Queen has the instincts of a performer – she is, after all, 'on stage' all the time – and therefore knows that she has to change with the times.

The Queen knew that the Diamond Jubilee celebrations earlier that year would be quite formal, so here was a chance to be the opposite. It was a great instinct. She showed great instincts again when she decided that no one in her family should know about the film so that it was as much a surprise and delight for them as for the nation.

It was a lovely afternoon. The Queen was very sweet. We filmed it in her private sitting room, where she usually meets with the Prime Minister. We set up in there and then went into another room, which was a much more human space. It was messy: there were papers and tea trays everywhere. She said she'd been to the dentist that morning and so wasn't in a very good mood.

She wanted to know what I wanted, so I told her certain specific things about pausing that were important. I didn't have to tell her a second time. You often have to remind actors, but she was as sharp as anything. I think she had a lovely time. It became clear that one of the reasons she agreed to take part was so that her immediate staff, who have been part of her life for so long, could also be in the film. It was a buzz for them. It was nothing to do with cameras, which they face virtually every day, but the presence of Daniel. Of Bond. A proper movie star.

There's a wonderful moment in the film where the Queen walks past Daniel, and you can see him thinking, I'm a fictional character, she's the real Queen. How is this even possible?

Apparently, the only stipulation the Queen made was that she would say, 'Good evening, Mr Bond.'

The plot was to be kept top secret, and not even the Royal Family knew what was in store. The dressmakers, who prepared an identical peach-coloured cocktail dress for Gary Connery, the stuntman who would double the Queen, were sworn to secrecy.

Sebastian Coe, a slim and wiry man at the best of times, must have lost a stone in waiting for the jump. The woman Prince Charles thought must be standing in for his mother was Jeannette Charles, whose similarity to Her Majesty is remarkable. The crammed stadium and the world watching on television could hardly believe their eyes when the sequence began. Sebastian Coe was sitting with the Royal Family and remembers every moment.

> During the opening ceremony itself I was sitting next to the Prince of Wales, with Prince Harry and Prince William directly behind us. None of them knew about the Queen's involvement, or that the film even existed. So when the sequence began, with the corgis racing up what were obviously very familiar stairs, Prince Charles looked at me and began laughing rather nervously, wondering where on earth this was going. And when the film cut to the shot of the royal back, he had exactly the same reaction as everyone else, which was to assume it was the lady who does the impersonations. But the moment she turned around, and everyone realised, 'My God! It really is the Queen!' he began roaring with laughter. As for his sons, they were beside themselves. As she started her descent two voices shouted out in unison behind me, 'Go, Granny!'

13. Private Passions

The Queen is well known to be an animal lover. One of Her Majesty's most endearing qualities is her compassion for and knowledge of country life, and her chosen non-human companions, dogs and horses, endear her to the public. It makes us all proud to see her riding, advancing age never diminishing her love of the outdoors. We grieve for her when a favourite dog has died: we cheer with her when one of her horses wins a race. Somehow knowing that she can muck out a stable or wade through a bog makes her nearer to us. For a moment there is no crown or pomp or protocol for her, just animals, the clink of the bridle, the breeze blowing and birds singing in the trees.

When you see a photograph of the Queen riding out in Windsor Park she is always accompanied by a man on a horse. The man will be Terry Pendry, who served twenty-one years in the Household Cavalry and has been the Queen's stud groom and manager of the Royal Mews at Windsor Castle for more than twenty-seven years. He is the only groom who takes the Queen riding. When she goes to Balmoral or Sandringham he goes too, with whatever ponies she asks for if they are not there already. His respect for the Queen is immense.

In April 2021 I visited Terry at Windsor. As we walked round the Royal Mews, we talked horses all the way: rather, Terry talked and I drank it all in. Like many small girls I got the pony bug when I was about four. By eight I was drawing horses all over my rough books at school. At eleven I dreamed that if I held onto a pillow tightly it would turn into my own little pony, and when I was eighteen I knew my chance to ride would appear only once in a blue moon, and then it would be on someone else's horse. But now I was talking to Terry about someone he considers to be the most remarkable and knowledgeable horsewoman he has ever met. He calls her his Equine Queen.

The Royal Mews are, of course, immaculate, even though they were built in Victorian times. The horses have their names on the stable doors; stars in themselves, they swung their great gleaming heads out to watch us as we walked by. The Queen often comes down to give them carrots when she is not riding. The facts tumble out: she names every horse and pony herself, and can remember the parentage of every single one. She breeds racehorses, carriage horses, hunters, riding horses. She breeds polo ponies, and rare breeds such as Cleveland Bays. She breeds Highland and Fell ponies. She has had favourite horses. As he spoke their names I scribbled then down: Betsy, Burmese, Doublet, Columbus, Sanction, Balmoral Curlew, Balmoral Jingle, and her present favourite, Emma. I met Emma, who gave me a cursory glance before turning to Terry Pendry. She is well over twenty years old.

The Queen had read about Monty Roberts, the horse whisperer, and sent a Crown Equerry, John Miller, to California to meet him. His revolutionary method of training horses impressed her so much that it is now used on all hers. It involves no force, no 'breaking in'. At the end of quite a short session the horse will do what you want it to do, which is, amazingly, what suits the animal as well. Terry is highly skilled in the method he learned from Monty Roberts, and was training up a young horse at the time: Diplomat was his name, but Terry said he could be a bit naughty at times. He was very pleased with Diplomat that day, as the horse had placidly followed him up a flight of stone stairs. Diplomat pushed his head over the stable door to greet me. 'He likes you,' said Terry, and I felt as happy as a bee. More facts came tumbling: some of the Queen's favourite horses are buried in the park with their own headstones. Her racehorse trainers call her in the morning and afternoon of a race. She likes to know what happens to her racehorses when they retire, especially the geldings: she likes them retrained for other jobs, and she has had many show champions produced by retraining some of her racehorses.

'If she were a horse,' said Terry, 'she would be matriarch of the herd. She is fearless. Her Majesty is so wise and knowledgeable about all things equine. She has passed this on through her genes to her daughter, the Princess Royal, and her granddaughter, Zara Tindall. Both are former European champions, Olympics competitors [Zara won a silver medal in 2012] and BBC Sports Personalities of the Year.' We walked past the stable lads and girls mucking out, grinning and chatting quietly as they forked clean bedding over the old stone floors.

'Her Majesty's attention to detail is legendary,' mused Terry. 'She can analyse the footfall of a horse and its action, and predict what ground it would be best suited to run on. She even looks to see which way the grass has been cut and rolled on a racecourse, away or against the way the horses are to race. That's detail.'

Would it be rude to ask why the Queen never wears a hard hat when riding? I wondered.

Terry Pendry gave a twinkly glance, and made primping

gestures with his hands around his head. ' You know what you ladies are like with your hair,' he said. 'But write down that the scarf she always wears is Hermès.'

In his book *Making the Running*, Ian Balding (father of Clare) describes his professional dealings with the Queen as a trainer of her racehorses.

The royal colours had hung in the trainer's tack room at Kingsclere as far back as the 1880s, when Prince Edward, later King Edward VII, had had horses with John Porter; but it was in October 1963 that the yard welcomed the first yearlings sent by the present Queen.

Her own first visit to the place, as far as I can recall, was in the spring of 1965, when she came to see the young horses out on the gallops. I could tell at once that she was very knowledgeable not only about horses' pedigrees (much more so than I was) but also about racing in general. I was to learn over the years what a superb natural horsewoman she was as well.

Things had gone well for us in my first season with ten winners in the royal colours, one of them, a sweet little filly called Garter Lady, at the Ascot autumn meeting. During the early summer of 1965 we learned that the Queen would like to go around evening stables, and that on this occasion Prince Philip would be coming with her. We looked at her ten horses plus a selection of ten others belonging to different owners. Almost at once Prince Philip was asking me questions in his usual inquisitive manner about any little defect he noticed. 'What is that spot on its neck?' he would say, and I would reply that the horse had had ringworm a few weeks before and this had left a bare spot on its coat. More than once he commented that the

Queen's horses seemed to look rather smaller than those of our other owners. Because I was patiently answering all his questions as best I could, we seemed to be taking a shade longer than usual to get round. Finally, towards the end of the tour, we came to Garter Lady, now a three-year-old. She was ready to run and I must admit she looked a shade on the light side. This time Prince Philip said to the Queen, who was just ahead of him, 'Why are your animals all so *thin*?'

The Queen turned to him and, with a touch of impatience, said, 'If you did but know it, that is how a fit racehorse should look!' She then moved fairly quickly on to the next horse. Prince Philip did not ask any more questions that evening and sadly has never been to Kingsclere since then!

Until Lord Porchester took on the role in 1970 the Queen had no official racing manager. Richard Shelley was her stud manager, and occasionally we would phone him, but generally Priscilla [Hastings, Balding's mother-in-law] or I would ring Buckingham Palace and speak directly to the Queen to give her all the necessary information on her horses.

At that early stage of my career her yearlings were being divided fairly evenly between Sir Cecil Boyd-Rochfort, who had trained very successfully for the Royal Family for years at Newmarket, and us at Kingsclere. She also leased some horses belonging to the National Stud, and these were trained by Noel Murless, also at Newmarket. On one visit to us she told the story, with some amusement, of how 'the old Captain' – as Cecil Boyd-Rochfort was known – had asked her rather directly, 'Ma'am, *who* decides which yearlings go where?' The Queen, somewhat taken aback at this rather abrupt approach, said that she replied after some thought, 'God!'

She meant, of course, that she herself made the decision –
but perhaps looked for some divine guidance in reaching it.
The old Captain, totally perplexed by this answer, just said,
'Who? Who?' . . .

Every year without fail, one morning in the spring the
Queen would come with Lord Porchester to see all the horses
out on the gallops. This evidently gave her great pleasure,
and I imagine it was fascinating for her to go to her various
trainers over the years and to see the different training
grounds and systems used.

She would always come on a separate occasion for a tour
around evening stables, when she liked to see as many horses
as possible rather than just her own. On these occasions
she would come into the box itself to see each particular
horse more clearly, and if it was one of her own I would
pass her a carrot or a handful of clover to give the horse
as a treat. She would give the horse its titbit and a pat, chat
to its groom, and spend a couple of minutes at least with
each one. Every once in a while we had the odd horse who
might be likely to bite or kick. With most owners I would
warn them not to come into that particular box, but in the
Queen's case this wasn't necessary: she seemed to have an
uncanny sixth sense about horses' temperaments and would
be staying outside the door before I turned to warn her not
to come in.

One year the Queen paid her visit when our stable had
been going through a rough time, with most of the string
suffering from respiratory problems and a distinct shortage
of winners. It was autumn, and we had kept all the outside
doors closed to try to keep the horses warm. We had returned
to the house for a drink, having been round stables, and
after a while she said thoughtfully, 'Ian, I noticed while we

were going round how stuffy and dusty it seemed to be. I really think you might have a problem with the ventilation in those old boxes.'

Almost at once I organised for a specialist firm to come in and test the ventilation. The Queen had been absolutely right: the number of air changes per hour was totally inadequate, and straight away we took all sorts of steps to improve the conditions.

There was one other occasion when I was made particularly aware of the Queen's natural horsemanship. During one of her many visits to our area, when she always stayed with the Porchesters at Milford Lake House, Emma and I were invited to go up with her and Lord Porchester to her stud called Polhampton, which is only a mile from us, to look at the yearlings. All the fillies – about eight of them – were in one field, and the five of us, including her stud groom Sean Norris, wandered across and looked at each one individually. Then we went across the lane to another paddock where the six colts were. Again all five of us walked towards the middle of the field, where the colts were milling around, and tried to have a look at them individually. It was just before these young horses were due to come in to be broken in, and they were in a very cheeky and playful mood. They had no wish to be inspected and suddenly they all took off at a gallop, went round in a small circle and came back at us and started rearing up just as they got near. They then began what might be described as 'dive-bombing' us and it became a little frightening. Three of our party took off and ran for the safety of the gate. The other two stood quite still where they were, realising that was in fact the safer thing to do and that the colts would not actually attack them. One of those two was, of course, the Queen.

Clare Balding, Ian's daughter, now well known to many of us as a broadcaster, was very young when the following incident occurred at her home. She wrote about it in her book *My Animals and Other Family*. She was eight years old when it happened.

My father rang his owners each Sunday to discuss the likely running plans for their horses. If he had shown any interest in current affairs or life outside Park House Stables, he would have had interesting conversations, as his owners had influence over a broad range of businesses and countries. Occasionally, if something so big had happened that even he couldn't miss it, he might stray off the topic of racing. There was betting on the general election, with prices offered on who would be prime minister, what the majority would be and which individual seats would be won. It was therefore covered in the *Sporting Life*.

When he rang Buckingham Palace, he was put through to the Queen immediately.

In May 1979, he started their conversation thus: 'Your Majesty.'

'Ian, how are you?'

'Fine. All well here. The horses are in good shape and I think we'll have runners at Royal Ascot.'

He went into more detail about which horses were being aimed at which races and told the Queen about the one or two who had had slight setbacks and would need time to recover. She took it all in, made the odd comment and, as he reached the end of his update, the Queen said, 'By the way, what do you think of the election result?'

The Conservatives had won and Margaret Thatcher had become the country's first female prime minister. Dad was vaguely aware that this event had occurred, but as it did not affect his daily life, he had not given it an awful lot of thought. My father is not a stupid man, but he does sometimes lack intelligence and that is the only way I can explain his reply.

'Well, it's going to take a while to get used to a woman running the country.'

Honestly, that's what he said. *To the Queen.*

I have always thought it is entirely to her credit that the Queen did not remove her horses straight away. Maybe she thought my father was a 'card', an oddity, a bit of a loose cannon. Maybe he amused her. Or maybe she just concentrated on his ability to train racehorses and ignored the rest.

The Queen liked to track the behaviour of her horses from birth onwards – which ones were being difficult, which were showing promise, who liked to lead on the gallops, who might pull and who might show reluctance. Whenever she came to see her horses, my father would make sure Andrew and I were prepped well in advance:

- 'Your Majesty' on first greeting. 'Ma'am' (as in 'Spam' or 'jam', not as in 'farm' or 'palm') from then on.

- Don't grip the hand, touch it lightly, and curtsey or bow. Left leg behind right, or right behind left, Dad wasn't clear. Consequently, I have never been sure.

- Don't speak unless you're spoken to, and look the Queen in the eye.

- Don't swear – you might think this was obvious, but I had been developing an impressive array of profanities and anything could happen.

272

On this April day in the early 1980s, my father had neglected to tell us that the Queen was coming to Kingsclere. So it was that I came charging in from riding Hattie to find two men wearing suits sitting at the kitchen table. I thought perhaps someone had been murdered and these two charlies were in charge of the investigation. I had been watching *Bergerac* and that was just the sort of thing that was always happening in Jersey.

'Wotcha,' I shouted through the door, as I tugged off my jodhpur boots in the dogs' room. 'Where's everyone else?'

'Next door in the dining room,' said the one who looked like the chief inspector.

Skidding along the cork floor in my socks into the kitchen, I saw Mrs Jessop carefully placing bacon and sausages on to one of the smart china serving dishes.

'Oh, great, cooked breakfast!' I said excitedly. As I ran out of the kitchen I thought I heard Mrs Jessop saying something about someone feeling queasy or queer – it started with a Q.

I flung open the dining-room door and, in my haste, fell into the room. I was wearing my green-cord riding jodhpurs, with stains from two weeks of wear, one red sock, and one blue, my favourite rugby shirt and a spotted handkerchief around my neck.

The Queen, who was sitting at the head of our dining-room table, was dressed rather more soberly in a navy-blue dress coat. My entrance had caused a break in the conversation, one of those uncomfortable silences you always hope will not happen because of you. And then it does, and there's not a lot you can do except say, 'Sausages. Yummy!'

My father made the growling noise that I thought must make his throat feel a bit sore as I headed for the table in the corner where there was a hotplate with my mother's best china dishes, laden with scrambled eggs, bacon, sausages and mushrooms.

I had rather missed any moment to curtsey and say, 'Your Majesty,' so I just carried on with breakfast, as if nothing was any different. Keep your line and kick on – that's what Dad always said about riding. I figured it was the same in life.

The Queen drank tea, not coffee. She liked it weak and without milk. Only one slice of toast, and none of the eggs, sausages, bacon, hash browns, mushrooms or tomatoes that were on offer. Her gloves were to the side of her plate, and on her feet were black court shoes. She seemed very small and rather quiet – not at all as she was on the television when my father made us watch her Christmas speech.

My father glared at me, but it was too late to say anything now. So I concentrated on buttering my toast, smothering it with marmalade and cutting my sausage long-ways. It was an American delicacy – sausage on toast with marmalade – and I had decided that this would be part of what made me 'interesting' and 'different'. Sausages on toast with marmalade would form part of my statement to the world.

The trouble with concentrating hard on cutting a sausage long-ways is that, if you press too hard, it's a bit like squeezing a bar of soap. The sausage can shoot out of your grasp. I know this; I know this only too well. I can still recall in slow motion the way my sausage shot across the table towards the Queen as she sipped her tea.

Quick as a flash, I tried to grab it. I knocked over the milk jug. My mother yelped. My father growled again. The Queen glanced at me and raised an eyebrow.

I froze, wishing I could crawl under the table and pretend I was a dog. My brother seized the sausage and shoved it back on my plate. My mother mopped up the milk with the look in her eye that said, 'I am not even going to count to ten. You are in so much trouble.'

I knew my parents couldn't actually say or do anything until the Queen had left. That gave me time. Time to escape. My father escorted the Queen out of the front door and took her to the stables to watch Second Lot 'pulling out' of the yard. The horses walked around the huge flowerpot as my father identified each one and told Her Majesty about their breeding and their achievements.

The Queen's knowledge of racing is extraordinarily detailed. She remembers all sorts of facts and behavioural quirks of horses from previous generations and can spot inherited traits in her own horses and those of other people. As the horses left the yard to begin their trek up to the Downs, my father jumped in his Subaru truck and told the Queen's chauffeur to follow him in the royal Range Rover.

The Queen's racing manager and great friend, Lord Carnarvon, was with her as they headed up to the gallops. The Queen never said very much when watching her horses. She asked questions and absorbed the answers, fascinated by the detail and diversity of equine behaviour.

I was not on hand to witness any of this, as I had disappeared to the stud to sit in the corner of a field and talk to the foals. It was something my mother liked me to do, as it familiarised the foals with human contact. I would just read a book and wait for them to come up and nudge me.

The timid ones would take a while but, as they realised I wasn't a threat and that I was more a curiosity, they came closer and started to take an interest. It was a game of patience but, in moments like this, it was a useful one to play. I did not want to go back to the house and, at least if I was here with the foals, I was doing something useful.

In my absence, the Queen watched through binoculars as her horses galloped, she talked to the lads riding them and discussed options with my father and Lord Carnarvon. An hour or so later, with the detectives in tow, she was driven back through the village and headed off to Newbury Races.

If you want to do a shorthand sketch of the Queen you would always include a dog, usually a corgi. Pictures of Her Majesty boarding trains, descending from aircraft, sitting on sofas often show a cohort of little dogs at her heel or, occasionally, on her lap. That dogs and horses are adored by the Royal Family is commonly known; the Queen and her family have always kept dogs, sometimes Labradors, a Sealyham, a Tibetan lion-dog, sometimes a cross between a corgi and a dachshund called a dorgi, but always Welsh corgis. Books have been written about the lineage of the royal corgis; it has been noted that the Queen would have liked to show her corgis in competition, she prized them so highly and their pedigrees were so impressive. But it is her special affinity with animals that is so valuable and so charming. She seems, like Dr Dolittle, to be able to talk to the animals, and they to her.

Tom Beaumont, whose parents had known the Royal Family for a long time, reveals more of the Queen's thoughtfulness, and also her sixth sense, which the dogs seem to pick up at once. Tom's father was Clerk of the Court at Ascot, and his family had the most cordial relationship with Her Majesty. Tom wrote down his memories especially for this book.

Watney was a dorgi who was bred by The Queen and generously given to my mother. He was a wonderful dog. Perhaps even a dog of a lifetime. Kind, loving, sensitive, fiercely independent, an enthusiast, loyal to the core with an amazing sense of humour. He was, incredibly, the second such gift from The Queen who had been kind enough to give my mother another dog called Mossy. My mother named her after an equally doggy friend Mossy Morrison [Mary Morrison] who was lady-in-waiting to The Queen.

I myself had been the recipient of a kind act and was given a one-year-old Labrador who was at the time called Streamer, but I changed her name to Katrina. I was given her because I had another black Lab called Hector, who ran out on to Ascot High Street one night during Royal Ascot Week and was killed. Hector managed to hold on, mortally wounded until I arrived, and he died in my arms acknowledging me before giving one last breath. It was one of life's tragic moments which you never forget.

I went to collect Katrina from The Queen's dog trainer, famous breeder and head keeper at Sandringham Bill Meldrum (now retired). He took me into a paddock and taught me the rudiments of Katrina including a trick (which he taught all the Labradors), where he got her to sit facing him and when he clapped his hands she jumped up into his outstretched arms. In fact, it was said that The Queen had once come to visit her dogs and there were four Labradors sitting looking at her, but no one had mentioned to her about this trick, so when she clapped her hands in appreciation, all four dogs leaped at once and The Queen nearly ended up flat on her back.

My mother, when she was told of the amazing gift of a dorgi, went to visit Mrs Fenwick, the wife of Bill Fenwick the retired head keeper of Windsor Great Park who looked after The Queen's dogs and was asked to choose a puppy. She chose Watney out of a litter of four puppies – the others were called Cider, Guinness and Berry – 'Very drinkable names,' Mrs Fenwick said. Watney was the smallest of them all and had a certain character, which was apparent from the start. Mrs Fenwick adored him and The Queen was also very fond of him and kept tabs on him all through his life.

My father had spent some time in his childhood close to the Royal Family as his father, my grandfather, Viscount Allendale, was lord-in-waiting to both King George V and King George VI. He lived at Breton Hall in Yorkshire but when in London resided at 144 Piccadilly. Next door at No.145 lived the Duke and Duchess of York (later to become King George VI and Queen Elizabeth) with their daughters, Princess Elizabeth and Princess Margaret. He was Clerk of the Course at Ascot Racecourse for twenty-five years and came into contact with The Queen with her terrific support and enthusiasm for the course. Mother also had met various members of the Royal Family in her childhood in Aberdeenshire.

When Father retired from Ascot they moved to Northumberland and Watney arrived after they had gone north.

So when The Queen came on an official visit to Vindolanda [a Roman fort south of Hadrian's Wall], it was common knowledge that they lived only thirty minutes away and a request was sent that The Queen would very much like to see Watney. Poor Robin Birley, the late famous archaeologist and one of the prime movers of making Vindolanda the success it is today, was suddenly faced with the problem of adding two people and a dog to the official guest list – who had absolutely no connection with the place or the work being done there. The day had been planned around a colourful pageant of banners, people dressed as Roman soldiers and serious discussions about the Roman world in Northumberland. There was also the exceptional fact that The Queen was the first monarch to visit Vindolanda since Emperor Hadrian.

Mother, Father and Watney crept into the enclosure, through the gate with the sign on it which stated 'No Dogs Allowed' and joined the line of the leading dignitaries of the north-east. People were scratching their heads, wondering who they were.

The Queen arrived and walked down the line shaking hands at the bowing and curtseying individuals. When she got down to Mother and Father she stopped, chatted briefly before turning her attention to Watney. To prove that dogs have long memories and remember their friends and people they trust, Watney looked up, wagged his tail and licked or tried to lick The Queen's nose. At that very moment Helen Smith released the button on her camera and that was the end of Vindolanda getting the correct publicity it was rightly due. Watney took front stage and was headline news on many TV channels and newspapers.

Fifteen years later Watney met The Queen again, but at a less formal occasion. My father was killed in a car crash weeks before the Ascot Racecourse Tercentenary Dinner at Windsor Castle he had been due to go to. Ascot generously asked my brother, me and our wives to stand in. Watney stayed the night with his brothers at Mrs Fenwick's house. He got out of the car, wagged his tail at Mrs Fenwick, walked straight past her into the house and sat next to his brother Cider. It was humanlike behaviour. He knew he was home.

The next morning The Queen came to visit him. Again he instantly recognised her and gave his customary greeting.

It was a second remarkable meeting.

Tom wrote to me: 'It is difficult to know what to say about the Queen and dogs: there seems to be a sort of feeling of mutual understanding. In this, as with nearly everything else about her, she is remarkable. There also seems to be respect from all the top dog trainers and breeders, and many others in the dog world speak of the Queen's knowledge and professionalism in all aspects. She is simply a brilliant dog handler. The meetings with Watney were a little bit of magic: how lucky we were as a family to witness it.'

14. The One and Only

A few days after King George VI died in 1952, when the young Queen was stepping into the limelight that would illuminate her for the rest of her life, the Queen Mother, as she had now become, made a speech to the nation. In it she said: 'I commend to you our dear daughter. Give to her your loyalty and devotion: in the great and lonely station to which she has been called she will need your protection and your love.'

By 2002 there were very few people who could remember a world without Queen Elizabeth, the Queen Mother. Everything about her was admired and adored, her sweetness and occasional steeliness, her sense of fun and love of glamour, the Queen who stayed beside her husband and daughters as the bombs dropped in wartime, and who stole the scene wherever she went with her charm and compassion. Even though she was old when she died, the country dreaded the news: how much more painful it was for her immediate family is recorded here by Margaret Rhodes, her beloved niece.

As I arrived at Royal Lodge, I saw that the Queen's car was there. I went straight to my aunt's bedroom and found her sitting in her armchair. The Queen was beside her, wearing riding clothes. She had been alerted while riding in the Park, her groom always carrying a radio link to the Castle. The nurse from the local surgery and my aunt's dresser – or Royal Household speak for ladies' maid – were also there. My aunt's eyes were shut and thereafter she did not open them or speak another word. The doctors came and went, but the nurse, the dresser and I stayed throughout. John Ovenden, the parish priest of the Royal Chapel, Windsor Great Park, arrived and went straight into Queen Elizabeth's bedroom. He knelt by my aunt's chair, holding her hand and praying quietly. He also recited a Highland lament: 'I am going now into the sleep . . .' He later told me that he was sure she knew what was happening, because she squeezed his hand. She was 101 – such a very great age. She had arrived in the time of horse-drawn carriages and was leaving it having seen men walking on the moon.

After a while I was persuaded to take a break and went for a walk in the garden. When I came back she had been put to bed. She looked so peaceful. At her bedside was the Queen, accompanied by Princess Margaret's children, David Linley and Sarah Chatto. John Ovenden also came back, and we all stood round the bed when he said the prayer: 'Now lettest thou thy servant depart in peace.' We all had tears in our eyes and to this day I cannot hear that being said without wanting to cry. Queen Elizabeth died at 3.15 in the afternoon on 30 March 2002.

'Time like an ever-rolling stream / Bears all its sons away; / They fly forgotten, as a dream / Dies at the opening day.'

That verse comes from a hymn, 'O God Our Help in Ages Past', which I once read was a favourite of the Queen, along with 'All People That on Earth Do Dwell'. Even if it's just a rumour, I learned to love them both, too; but I think people take a while to be forgotten. If even one person remembers them, they are not forgotten, and history books keep characters alive long after centuries have passed. On the other hand, the idea of the ever-rolling stream gathering us up as it moves inexorably to an unknown sea is rather comforting.

In 1986 Princess Margaret came to see *Blithe Spirit* at the Vaudeville Theatre in the Strand: some of the cast were asked to stay in their stage costumes as the Princess wanted to meet us backstage before going to the reception laid out in the Circle Bar. Playing the ghost Elvira, I was white and grey from head to foot, palest blonde hair and a light grey chiffon backless dress, and on my body 'wet white', a kind of old-fashioned stage make-up that dries completely leaving you pale and interesting but non-greasy. I wore red lipstick, the only splash of colour in what must have looked like Ectoplasm Woman. Princess Margaret came into my dressing room, followed by Jane Stevens, her lady-in-waiting that night; I knew Janie quite well.

Princess Margaret said at once: 'Why did you wear red lipstick?'

'I thought it would help people to see who was speaking, Your Royal Highness. Without it I looked a bit like mashed potato.'

'If she was a ghost, she would have had a pale mouth,' said Princess Margaret. 'Let's go to this reception,' and off she went.

At that time the theatre had been sent a caveat: we were to see that Princess Margaret didn't have anything alcoholic to drink. This ruling was to be strictly enforced, which was both rude and impossible. Suddenly I found myself with Princess Margaret leading the way from the reception to one of the boxes in the dress circle, Janie Stevens and I making frantic eyes at each other as we followed her. In the darkness of the box, Princess Margaret lit a cigarette and produced a small flask of whisky. We sat there drinking and smoking and laughing our heads off: it was the nearest thing I can remember to a midnight feast at school.

Anne Glenconner, who had been a maid-of-honour at the Queen's Coronation as Lady Anne Coke, became one of Princess Margaret's ladies-in-waiting. She was obviously used to dealing with small differences that arose from time to time between the Queen and her younger sister.

One day, the Queen came to tea with Princess Margaret. I stayed in the drawing-room so they could have some time together and she went off to the bedroom to find Princess Margaret. Quite soon after she had gone in, she reappeared.

'Oh, ma'am, is everything all right?' I asked.

'No, it isn't,' the Queen replied. 'Margaret is listening to *The Archers* and every time I try to say something she just says, "Ssh!"'

I wasn't surprised. Princess Margaret's defiant streak extended to her sister, despite her being the Queen. I had always noticed that she had a very subtle strategy for one-up-manship, which contributed to the bickering that went on between her and the Queen Mother.

I said, 'Let's go back up together.'

When we got to the bedroom, I said to Princess Margaret, 'Ma'am, the Queen is here, and she can't stay all that long. Would you like me to help pour the tea?' I switched off the wireless, made sure they both had a cup and left the room.

Princess Margaret, a shining star in her own right, died in February 2002, the year of the Golden Jubilee. Her whole life had been followed voraciously by the media, and the nation felt that it had lost someone very familiar, bold and beloved. As ever, the Queen had to grieve her terrible loss and simply carry on with her public duties. There is no compassionate leave now for the Royal Family, unlike in the days of Queen Victoria, who virtually withdrew for forty years after Prince Albert died.

Even at the darkest moments of her life the Queen is being watched and recorded. Sometimes this might seem intrusive, but the royal correspondents mostly take their duties very seriously, and I am grateful to Jennie Bond for this sympathetic snapshot of the Queen at the tremendously sad and soul-destroying event, the fire at her home, Windsor Castle. This is the day after the fire had been put out, 21 November 1992.

Back at the Castle the next day, the drizzle had turned to driving rain, making the blackened mess look even more miserable. We spent another long, cold day there as firemen struggled to deal with dozens of hot spots inside, and smoke continued to drift up into the grey sky. Matters were made worse when the Heritage Secretary, Peter Brooke, declared that the government would foot the bill for the restoration of the Castle. His words provoked an almost immediate public outcry. To my eye, the whole gloomy scene was encapsulated in one small, involuntary action by the Queen as, in wellington boots and headscarf, she surveyed the damage to her home. As she picked her way carefully across the courtyard, which was littered with debris, she sneezed violently, her head jerking forward to rest, briefly, on her chest. For a moment she looked like any other vulnerable elderly woman, weighed down by the woes of a personal tragedy.

This is, I think, the hardest thing to remember: that the Queen is an ordinary woman, a mother and sister, a daughter, grandmother and now a widow. She feels the same sorrow and happiness as we do and must face the same dilemmas and anxieties. She is a vulnerable human being, with this one great distinction: she must also feel for the wider family she has, a really colossal family made up of many nations, millions of people whose faces and names she does not know but who know her, and look to her for leadership, guidance and comfort. Until this year, she has always had as her rock of support and counsel the Duke of Edinburgh. His death, even though it may have been expected, must have changed her life immeasurably. His lifelong service to the country and his steadfast bravery made him irreplaceable, for her and for us. From now on, she is alone as Queen, whereas before it was always the two of them; and the sight of her on her own in St George's Chapel on the day of his funeral pulled at the heartstrings of even the toughest critics of the monarchy.

I hope she knows how strong the compassion and admiration was for her then, and is now, as she simply carries on with her duties, smiling and friendly, beautifully turned out, her head held high, still apparently unfazed by anything Fate can throw at her. So, although she is an ordinary woman, she is extraordinary too, because she has to be; and because she promised she would be.

All through her reign, the Queen has been a healer of wounds, a supporter of the weak, a mender and maker, a figurehead on the great ship of state. She has dedicated her energies into protecting and expanding the Commonwealth, uniting countries that otherwise would have no obvious link: she has been a peacemaker. Margaret Rhodes, who was at the bedside of the Queen Mother as she passed from this world to the next, sums up the Queen's commitment to service, which runs in tandem with her love for her family.

And for us. The Queen loves us, not individually, obviously, but she does. We are her people, and she loves us.

Here is a passage from Margaret's book *The Final Curtsey.*

I have been fortunate to have had the Queen as my cousin and to have seen first-hand what she has achieved. She did not expect to become the monarch, which happened as her Uncle David abdicated the throne, which passed to the Queen's father, George VI, as the second brother. He was a very successful monarch, with my aunt, Queen Elizabeth, at his side. But his life was cruelly cut short at fifty-six, and the Queen became monarch at the tender age of twenty-five.

I knew the Queen from a young age when I shared family holidays in Scotland with Princess Elizabeth and Princess Margaret. I had the chance to realise what a special person Princess Elizabeth was. When she was not even a teenager, she knew that she would one day succeed her father, who had become King in 1936. This was something that she accepted with seriousness and a strong sense of duty, as she knew that it was very unlikely that there would be a brother who would become the monarch instead of her.

Throughout her life, my cousin has had this strong sense of service. Since she became Queen, she has always had deep concern for her subjects. Throughout her reign, she has served twelve prime ministers, and has always assiduously carried out her constitutional duties. She has kept herself informed of the important affairs of state. In her lifetime, the country and the monarchy have markedly changed, but the one constant has been the role of the Queen.

Reference points for certainty are rare, but Her Majesty

is without doubt one of them. In 1952 she found herself young, bereaved, and yet head of state at a time when her country urgently needed to reshape its identity and its world role. That she rose to the occasion is, in my view, a remarkable achievement. Loyalty and service have been her priorities throughout her reign. She has upheld the constitution and, above all, she has kept a sense of perspective and a level head when others have been losing theirs.

The Queen has made it absolutely clear that 'My job is for life. It has been a question of maturing into something that one has got used to doing and accepting the fact that it is your fate.' The Queen, to my intense pleasure, has emerged as the consummate master of her role. The nation has cause to be grateful. I certainly am.

When the pandemic turned the whole world upside down, the Queen was there to comfort us in a broadcast she made to the United Kingdom and the Commonwealth on 5 April 2020. She has always been a strong guiding spirit when things turn to chaos. By choosing the words 'We will meet again' she scrolled back the years to when the world was in the middle of its last terrible crisis, the Second World War: Vera Lynn's song had comforted us then; the Queen comforts us now. She is the mother ship, and a beacon in the darkest hours: she is the one and only. Here is her speech.

I am speaking to you at what I know is an increasingly challenging time. A time of disruption in the life of our country: a disruption that has brought grief to some, financial difficulties to many, and enormous changes to the daily lives of us all.

I want to thank everyone on the NHS front line, as well as care workers and those carrying out essential roles, who selflessly continue their day-to-day duties outside the home in support of us all. I am sure the nation will join me in assuring you that what you do is appreciated and every hour of your hard work brings us closer to a return to more normal times.

I also want to thank those of you who are staying at home, thereby helping to protect the vulnerable and sparing many families the pain already felt by those who have lost loved ones. Together we are tackling this disease, and I want to reassure you that if we remain united and resolute, then we will overcome it.

I hope in the years to come everyone will be able to take pride in how they responded to this challenge. And those who come after us will say that the Britons of this generation were as strong as any. That the attributes of self-discipline, of quiet good-humoured resolve and of fellow-feeling still characterise this country. The pride in who we are is not a part of our past: it defines our present and our future.

The moments when the United Kingdom has come together to applaud its care and essential workers will be remembered as an expression of our national spirit; and its symbol will be the rainbows drawn by children.

Across the Commonwealth and around the world, we have seen heart-warming stories of people coming together to help others, be it through delivering food parcels and medicines, checking on neighbours, or converting businesses to help the relief effort.

And though self-isolating may at times be hard, many people of all faiths, and of none, are discovering that it presents an opportunity to slow down, pause and reflect, in prayer or meditation.

It reminds me of the very first broadcast I made, in 1940, helped by my sister. We, as children, spoke from here at Windsor to children who had been evacuated from their homes and sent away for their own safety. Today, once again, many will feel a painful sense of separation from their loved ones. But now, as then, we know, deep down, that it is the right thing to do.

While we have faced challenges before, this one is different. This time we join with all nations across the globe in a common endeavour, using the great advances of science and our instinctive compassion to heal. We will succeed – and that success will belong to every one of us.

We should take comfort that while we may have more still to endure, better days will return: we will be with our friends again; we will be with our families again; we will meet again.

But for now, I send my thanks and warmest good wishes to you all.

We are so lucky to have lived in the reign of Queen Elizabeth II. When our great-grandchildren have grown up, the world will have spun on its axis a thousand times and life on earth will be vastly different. But we have lived in an age in which the monarch was one of a kind: the longest ever to reign over us, the one who has represented us at all times with dignity, kindliness and humour. She has never given an interview; but in these pages, and through the eyes of these contributors, we might begin to understand a little more of her character, which is as platinum-gleaming and diamond-bright as it can be. She has visited more countries and met more leaders, attended more ceremonies and inspected more factories, made more speeches and accepted more tributes, than we can even start to comprehend. More small posies and huge bouquets have been received with a smile, more curtseys dropped, and more photographs taken than anyone we can think of. She knows more than most politicians about the workings of state, both here and abroad: her intuition, her sixth sense, has brought her shrewd judgements, which she keeps to herself.

She has worn the most precious jewels in the world but still prefers her own old clothes, which she wears for ages longer than many women. The wartime awareness of waste has made her careful with resources: but her passions, like her horses, she has indulged: and to that we say, 'Hurrah! She is just like us!' Her commitment to service and her duty to the crowned position she holds have been unwavering. By continually aiming to do her very best, all the time, for ever, she has somehow turned into another kind of being, who never sulks, or pulls out because she is tired and can't be bothered or doesn't care. We have taken her so completely to our hearts that we are in danger of suffocating her with affection and admiration and love. Seventy years on the throne: ninety-five years alive, and still here, for her family, for us and for the Crown. 'My whole life, whether it be long or short . . .' she promised; and she has never let us down.

And now there she stands, centre stage, the spotlight trained on her alone. The gauze curtain begins to fall but the audience rises to its feet with a roar of applause; the ovation goes on and on, and down the road, in bars, cafés and other theatres, the thunder of approval and affection catches fire, the drumming of feet, and yells of 'Brava! Brava!' fill the air. From the side of the stage, the cast and chorus are clapping and shouting, the stage hands yell, and far above someone releases a cloud of confetti, which swirls and glitters as it twists and turns over that small figure, who stands and smiles, and waves back at us.

The Crown

Carol Ann Duffy

The crown translates a woman to a Queen –
endless gold, circling itself, an O like a well,
fathomless, for the years to drown in – history's bride,
anointed, blessed, for a crowning. One head alone
can know its weight, on throne, in pageantry,
and feel it still, in private space, when it's lifted:
not a hollow thing, but a measuring; no halo,
treasure, but a valuing; decades and duty. Time-gifted,
the crown is old light, journeying from skulls of kings
to living Queen.
                              Its jewels glow, virtues; loyalty's ruby,
blood-deep; sapphire's ice resilience; emerald evergreen;
the shy pearl, humility. *My whole life, whether it be long
or short, devoted to your service.* Not lightly worn.

Acknowledgements

If Tom Perrin had not been there guiding, prodding and encouraging me, this book would never have been written.

Without the contributions from all these generous people, from long ago right up to the present day, these pages would be blank.

For this tremendous team effort, a thousand thanks to you all.

Picture Acknowledgements

Photo Section 1

Page 1: Top © Alamy/Shawshots,
Page 1: Below © Alamy/Keystone Press,

Page 2: Top left © Getty Images/Terence Spencer/Popperfoto,
Page 2: Top right © Alamy/ The Print Collector,
Page 2: Below left © Alamy/Keystone Press,
Page 2: Below right © Getty Images/Fox Photos,

Page 3: Top right © Getty Images/Central Press,
Page 3: Below left © Alamy/PA Images,

Page 4: Top © Shutterstock/Sipa,
Page 4: Middle right © Getty Images/Picture Post/Haywood
        Magee,
Page 4: Middle left © Alamy/World History Archive
Page 4: Below © Getty Images/Universal History Archive/
        Universal Images Group

Page 5: Top left © Shutterstock/AP
Page 5: Top right © Shutterstock/Eddie Worth/AP
Page 5: Below © Getty Images/Paul Popper/Popperfoto

Page 6: Top © Alamy/Keystone Press
Page 6: Below © Alamy/Keystone Press

Page 7: Top © Alamy/Trinity Mirror/Mirrorpix
Page 7: Below © Getty Images/Bettmann

Page 8: Top right © Alamy/PA Images
Page 8: Top left © Getty Images/Ray Green/Bob Thomas Sports
        Photography
Page 8: Below right © Getty Images/Mirrorpix /NCJ Archive
Page 8: Below left © Alamy/Trinity Mirror/Mirrorpix

Photo Section 2

Page 1: Top © Alamy/PA Images
Page 1: Middle left © Getty Images/Max Mumby/Indigo
Page 1: Middle right © Alamy/PA Images
Page 1: Below right © Alamy/PA Images

Page 2: Top right © Getty Images/Anwar Hussein
Page 2: Top left © Shutterstock/Jeremy Selwyn/Evening Standard
Page 2: Below © Alamy/REUTERS/Andrew Milligan/Pool

Page 3: Top © Alamy/Reuters
Page 3: Middle © Alamy/ Reuters/Maxwell's/ Pool
Page 3: Below © Alamy/Chris Jackson/PA Wire

Page 4: Top © Getty Images/Frank Barratt/Keystone
Page 4: Middle © Camera Press/ROTA
Page 4: Below © Getty Images/Julian Parker/UK Press

Page 5: Top © Getty Images/Cameron Spencer
Page 5: Middle right © Alamy/Allstar Picture Library Ltd
Page 5: Middle left © Getty Images/Keystone
Page 5: Below © Getty Images/ Pool/Fiona Hanson/Tim Graham
        Picture Library

Page 6: Top left © Alamy/GL Archive
Page 6: Top right © Getty Images/Tim Graham Photo Library
Page 6: Below © Alamy/PA Images

Page 7: Top left © Shutterstock
Page 7: Below right © Alamy/PA Images

Page 8: Top © Getty Images/Georges De Keerle
Page 8: Below © Getty Images/Anwar Hussein

Text Permissions

Eric Sherbrooke Walker, *Treetops Hotel*, Robert Hale Limited, 1964, pp.102-108.

Pamela Hicks, *Daughter of Empire: My Life as a Mountbatten*, Weidenfeld & Nicolson, 2012, pp.199-205.
Copyright © 2012 Pamela Hicks. Reprinted with the permission of Simon & Schuster, Inc and The Orion Publishing Group, London. All rights reserved.

Winston Churchill, Speech on the Death of the King, 7th February 1952: "For Valour:" King George VI, Finest Hour 114, Spring 2002, p.18.
https://winstonchurchill.org/publications/finest-hour/finest-hour-114/for-valour-king-george-vi-in-remembrance-of-his-late-majesty/
Reproduced with permission of Curtis Brown, London on behalf of The Estate of Winston S. Churchill. © The Estate of Winston S. Churchill.

Counting One's Blessings: The Selected Letters of Queen Elizabeth the Queen Mother, William Shawcross (ed.), Macmillan Publishers, 2012, p.444.
The Royal Archives © Her Majesty Queen Elizabeth II. Reproduced with permission from Macmillan Publishers through PLS Clear.

James Pope-Hennessy, *The Quest for Queen Mary*, Hugo Vickers (ed.), Hodder & Stoughton, 2018, p.619.
© 2018 James Pope-Hennessy and Hugo Vickers. Reproduced by permission of Hodder and Stoughton Limited.

'Grief And Pageantry At Funeral Of King George VI. Two Millions See Solemn Procession In London', *The Canberra Times*, 16 February 1952, p.1. https://trove.nla.gov.au/newspaper/page/699250
Reproduced with permission.

Audrey Russell, *A Certain Voice*, Ross Anderson Publications, 1984, pp.111-112, 117, pp.86, 88 and pp.102-103.

Normal Hartnell, *Silver and Gold: The autobiography of Norman Hartnell*, V&A Fashion Perspectives, 2019.
Extracts from Silver and Gold by Norman Hartnell. © Hardy Amies London Ltd. First published by Evan Brothers Limited, 1955. New edition published by V&A Publishing, 2019. Reproduced by permission.

Cecil Beaton, *The Strenuous Years: 1948-55*, Sapere Books, 2018. Reproduced with permission from the Literary Estate of Cecil Beaton.

Anne Glenconner, *Lady in Waiting*, Hodder & Stoughton, 2019. © 2019 Anne Glenconner.
Reproduced by permission of Hodder and Stoughton Limited.

Her Majesty The Queen, The Queen's Coronation Oath, 2 June 1953. https://www.royal.uk/coronation-oath-2-june-1953
The Royal Household © Crown Copyright.

Long to Reign Over Us: Memories of the Coronation and Life in the 1950s, Kenneth and Valerie McLeish (eds), Bloomsbury, 1992.

Mary McLay, Mass Observation on Twitter, B15. https://twitter.com/massobsarchive/status/876703576533454848
Reproduced with permission of Curtis Brown Group Ltd, London on behalf of The Trustees of the Mass Observation Archive. © The Trustees of the Mass Observation Archive.

R.J. Prickett, *Treetops: Story of a World Famous Hotel*, David & Charles, 1987, pp.75-80, 149-50, 156 and 160-165.
Reproduced from the title Treetops - Story of a World Famous Hotel, copyright © R. J. Prickett, David and Charles Ltd, 1988. With permission.

The Royal Gazette (Bermuda), 26 November 1953, p.1. https://bnl.contentdm.oclc.org/digital/collection/BermudaNP02/id/160101/rec/2
Reproduced with permission from the editor, *The Royal Gazette*.

Cherill Suckling, Judith Foy, Lindsay Watson, The New Zealand Ministry for Culture and Heritage, Royal Visit of 1953-54, 'Remembering the royals'. https://nzhistory.govt.nz/culture/royal-visit-of-1953-54/remembering-the-royals

'Queen Begins Long Journey Home, Moving Farewells as Gothic Sails Into Setting Sun', The Age, April 2, 1954. https://www.theage.com.au/national/from-the-archives-1954-queen-elizabeth-s-historic-australian-tour-ends-20210326-p57eff.html

Pietro Annigoni, An Artist's Life, W. H. Allen, 1977, pp.80-86 and pp.171-187. Reproduced with permission from Annigoni / Camera Press.

Jack Straw, Hansard, Commons: 7 March 2012, Commons Chamber, Diamond Jubilee, Volume 541: debated on Wednesday 7 March 2012.
https://hansard.parliament.uk/Commons/2012-03-07/debates/12030753000001/DiamondJubilee
© UK Parliament 2021. Licensed under the Open Parliament Licence v3.0. https://www.parliament.uk/site-information/copyright-parliament/open-parliament-licence/

Andrew Duncan, The Reality of Monarchy, William Heinemann Ltd, 1971, pp.240-246.
Reproduced with permission from Andrew Duncan.

Nikita Krushchev, Memoirs of Nikita Krushchev: Volume 2, Pennsylvania State University Press, 2004, pp.433-434.
Reproduced with permission from Pennsylvania University Press.

'Inclusion of Virginia Indians in Jamestown Anniversary Makes History', Indian Country Today, 26 May 2007.
https://indiancountrytoday.com/archive/inclusion-of-virginia-indians-in-jamestown-anniversary-makes-history-2
Reproduced with permission from Indian Country Today, LLC.

United Nations Press Release, 6 July 2010.
https://www.un.org/press/en/2010/sgsm13000.doc.htm

From: United Nations, Press Release Deeming Queen Elizabeth II 'Anchor for Our Age', Secretary-General Pledges to Heed Her Call to Devote Full Strength to Charter Ideals, Realize Better World for All, by Secretary-General, © 2010 United Nations. Reprinted with the permission of the United Nations.

Sarah-Jane Dumbrille, *Royal visit to Prescott, September 27, 1984: its preparation and staging*, St. Lawrence Printing Company, Prescott, Ontario, 1984.
Reproduced with permission from Sarah Jane Dumbrille.

Dermot Morrah, et al., *The Queen's visit: Elizabeth II in India and Pakistan*, Asia Publishing House, 1961, p.122.

A speech by The Queen at the Irish State Banquet, 2011, 6 January 2016.
https://www.royal.uk/queens-speech-irish-state-dinner-18-may-2011
The Royal Household © Crown Copyright.

Frank Roberts, *Dealing with Dictators*, Weidenfeld & Nicolson, 1976, pp.241-245.
Reproduced with permission from The Orion Publishing Group, London.

Antonio Polito, 'Ode to the Queen's Handbag', *La Repubblica*, 17 October 2000.
https://ricerca.repubblica.it/repubblica/archivio/
repubblica/2000/10/17/la-regina-che-piace-agli-italiani.
html?ref=search
Found translated in: Carola Long, 'The Maggie-Thatcher-meets-Her-Majesty look is one of this season's multiple bag trends', The Independent, 22 January 2011 © The Independent. https://
www.independent.co.uk/life-style/fashion/features/carola-long-
maggie-thatcher-meets-her-majesty-look-one-season-rsquo-s-
multiple-bag-trends-2188797.html
Translation reproduced with permission.

'Paris crowd turns out for glimpse of Queen Elizabeth II', France24, 7 June 2014.

https://www.france24.com/en/20140607-paris-queen-elizabeth-ii-flower-market
Reproduced with permission from France 24.

Richard Crossman, *The Diaries of a Cabinet Minister: Volume One Minister of Housing 1964-1966*, Hamish Hamilton & Jonathan Cape, 1976, p.20, October 1964.
Reproduced with permission from Virginia Crossman.

Richard Crossman, T*he Diaries of a Cabinet Minister. Volume Two. Lord President of the Council and Leader of the House of Commons 1966-68*, Hamish Hamilton and Jonathan Cape, 1976, p.44, September 1966.
Reproduced with permission from Virginia Crossman.

Margaret Thatcher, *The Autobiography*, Harper Perennial, 2013, pp.255-256.
Reprinted by permission of HarperCollins Publishers Ltd. © 2013, Margaret Thatcher.

Tony Blair, *Tony Blair: A Journey*, Random House, 2010, pp.13-14 and pp.148-149.
Excerpts from A Journey: My Political Life by Tony Blair, copyright © 2010 by Tony Blair. Used by permission of Alfred A. Knopf, an imprint of the Knopf Doubleday Publishing Group, a division of Penguin Random House LLC. All rights reserved. Reproduced with permission from Penguin Random House Ltd.

Noel Coward, *The Noel Coward Diaries*, Graham Payn and Sheridan Morley (eds), PaperMac, 1983, p.678.
The Noel Coward Diaries edited by Graham Payn and Sheridan Morley, Phoenix, Orion Books Ltd 1998. © Graham Payn 1982. Copyright Agent Alan Brodie Representation Ltd. Reproduced in the United Kingdom with permission from Orion Books.

Dirk Bogarde, *A Particular Friendship*, Viking, 1989, pp.117-118 and pp.121-124.
Reproduced with permission from the Literary Estate of Dirk Bogarde.

George Carey, *Know The Truth: A Memoir*, HarperCollins, 2004, pp.400-401.
Reprinted by permission of HarperCollins Publishers Ltd.
© 2004 George Carey. Reproduced with permission from Lord Carey.

Alan Titchmarsh, *The Queen's Houses*, BBC Books, 2014, pp.130-138.
The Queen's Houses by Alan Titchmarsh published by BBC Books.
Copyright © Alan Titchmarsh 2014. Reprinted by permission of The Random House Group Limited.

Margaret Whitlam, *My Day*, William Collins Australia, 1973, pp.40-43. Reproduced with permission from the Estate of Margaret Whitlam.

Sir Roy Strong, *The Roy Strong Diaries 1967-1987*, Weidenfeld & Nicolson, 1997. Reproduced with permission from The Orion Publishing Group, London.

Adrienne Clarkson, *Heart Matters*, Viking Canada, 2006, pp.227-229.
Excerpt(s) from *Heart Matters* by Adrienne Clarkson, copyright © 2006 Winding Stair Productions Inc. Reprinted by permission of Penguin Canada, a division of Penguin Random House Canada Limited. All rights reserved.
With permission of the author.

David Nott, *War Doctor*, Picador, 2020, pp.306-308.
Extract © David Nott, originally published in War Doctor (Picador), reprinted by permission of David Higham Associates.

'Three guinea prize letter' in the *Sunday Express*, 22 September 1968.
Reproduced with permission from Mirrorpix/Reach Licensing.

Dreams about HM The Queen, Brian Masters (ed.), Blond & Briggs Ltd, 1972, pp.24-25.
Reproduced with permission from Brian Masters.

Michael and Vivien Noakes, *The Daily Life of the Queen: An Artist's Diary*, Ebury Press, 2000, p.219 and pp.14-15.
Reproduced with permission from The Estate of Vivien Noakes.

Precious McKenzie, recollections of the Queen, courtesy of the author.
Reproduced with permission from Precious McKenzie.

Michael Parker, *It's All Going Terribly Wrong*, Bene Factum, 2012, pp.xi-xiii.
Reproduced with permission from Sir Michael Parker.

Sir Roy Strong, *The Roy Strong Diaries 1967-1987*, Weidenfeld & Nicolson, 1997. Reproduced with permission from The Orion Publishing Group, London.

Pamela Street, '1952-1977', courtesy of the author.
Reproduced with permission from Rupert Davies.

Excerpt from the unpublished Diary of Hugo Vickers, Monday 6 June 1977 at Windsor Castle, courtesy of the author.
Reproduced with permission from Hugo Vickers.

A speech given by The Queen at Guildhall, 4 June 2002.
https://www.royal.uk/golden-jubilee-speech
The Royal Household © Crown Copyright.

Stephen Bates, 'One million join party at Palace', the guardian.com, 4 June 2002.
https://www.theguardian.com/uk/2002/jun/04/jubilee.monarchy5
Copyright © Guardian News & Media Ltd 2021. Reproduced with permission.

'A Weekend to Remember', editorial comment, London Evening Standard, 6 June 2002.
© The Evening Standard. Reproduced with permission.

Dan Jarvis, David Cameron, Hansard, Commons: 7 March 2012, Commons Chamber, Diamond Jubilee, Volume 541: debated on Wednesday 7 March 2012.

https://hansard.parliament.uk/Commons/2012-03-07/
debates/12030753000001/DiamondJubilee
© UK Parliament 2021. Licensed under the Open Parliament
Licence v3.0. https://www.parliament.uk/site-information/
copyright-parliament/open-parliament-licence/

'A monarch of true majesty: As the Queen breaks remarkable
record, John Major - one of her 12 PMs - pays tribute', Sir
John Major Former Prime Minister, *The Mail on Sunday*, 6
September 2015.
https://www.dailymail.co.uk/debate/
article-3223858/A-monarch-true-majesty-Queen-breaks-
remarkable-record-John-Major-one-12-PMs-pays-tribute.html
Reproduced with permission.

First Minister Nicola Sturgeon, Tweedbank, 9 September, 2015.
https://web.archive.org/web/20170401025236/https:/news.gov.
scot/speeches-and-briefings/opening-of-borders-railway
© Crown Copyright.

Lester B. Pearson, Mike: *The Memoirs of Lester B. Pearson,
Volume Three*, John A. Munro and Alex I. Inglis (eds),
University of Toronto Press, 2015, pp.294-295.
© University of Toronto Press 1975; reprinted 2015. Reprinted
with permission of the publisher.

Cliff Richard, *The Dreamer*, Ebury Publishing, 2020, pp.276-
277.
Copyright © Vox Rock Ltd 2020. Reprinted by permission of
The Random House Group Limited.

Rob Halford, *Confess*, Headline, 2020, pp.307-310.
© 2020 Rob Halford. Reproduced by permission of Hodder
and Stoughton Limited.

Francis Rossi, *I Talk Too Much*, Constable, 2019, p.278.
Reproduced with permission from Little, Brown Book Group
Ltd.

Hilary Mantel, *Royal Bodies*, London Review of Books, Vol. 35, No. 4, 21 February 2013.
https://www.lrb.co.uk/the-paper/v35/n04/hilary-mantel/royal-bodies
Reproduced with permission.

Mike Read, 2004, *What the Queen Said to Me*, Chilli Brener (ed.), Unicorn Publishing Group, 2017, pp.38-39.
Reproduced with permission.

Terry Wogan, *Mustn't Grumble*, Orion, 2006, pp.26-28.
Reproduced with permission from The Orion Publishing Group, London.

Peter Hall, *Peter Hall's Diaries: The Story of a Dramatic Battle*, John Goodwin (ed.), Hamish Hamilton, 1983, p.148.
Reproduced with permission.

Her Majesty The Queen, Christmas Broadcast, 25 December 1952.
https://www.royal.uk/queens-first-christmas-broadcast-1952
The Royal Household © Crown Copyright.

Her Majesty The Queen, Christmas Broadcast, 25 December 1957.
https://www.royal.uk/christmas-broadcast-1957
The Royal Household © Crown Copyright.

Sebastian Coe, *Running My Life: The Autobiography*, Hodder, 2013, pp.367-368 and pp.438-440.
© 2013 Sebastian Coe. Reproduced by permission of Hodder and Stoughton Limited.

Danny Boyle, in conversation with Amy Raphael, *Creating Wonder*, Faber, pp.400-403.
Reproduced with permission from Faber and Faber Ltd.

Ian Balding, *Making the Running: A Racing Life*, Headline, 2014, eBook Locs: 2280-2349.
© 2014 Ian Balding. Reproduced by permission of Headline Publishing Group.